BATHSHEBA SPOONER

A Revolutionary Murder Conspiracy

Andrew Noone

Table of Contents

Preface

Green Hill Park in Worcester includes, among its several hundred acres, a skateboard rink, Barnyard Zoo, golf course, two ponds, vernal pools, miles of trails, soccer and baseball fields, and the Massachusetts Vietnam Memorial. It would surprise virtually every park visitor to know that somewhere in that vast expanse, a hole was dug two-hundred and forty-two years ago to hold the bodies of the most notorious eighteenth-century murderer and that of her not yet born five-month-old son.

Shortly after moving into our first house many years ago, a dinner guest reminded me that somewhere across the street lay the resting place of Bathsheba Spooner and her son. As a local history buff, I paused to consider that I had never run across any serious work devoted to the topic. A preliminary look into available resources convinced me very soon afterwards that the tragedy needed a closer, more thorough study—its importance as a singular reflection of the political/cultural milieu of the time needed attention. In the middle of my research, with the book about half written, that study did appear, but by a different author. I decided to continue my own book, its style and context being rather different.

Centuries later, it is difficult for us to appreciate the magnitude of the event which rocked New England at the midpoint of the American Revolution. Though only a village at the time, Worcester's size was disproportionate to the significance of its contribution to the rebellion; according to recent scholarship, the town might properly be regarded as the true birthplace of the conflict, many months before any shots were fired at Lexington and Concord.

Twenty-first century media assaults us from all sides, saturating us with tales of real or inflated scandal whose oceans of details bore us as often as they entertain. To place ourselves in the mindset of an eighteenth-century New Englander whose knowledge of wider events was limited to gossip or the newspaper is perhaps impossible. As impossible, perhaps, as it was for contemporaries to grasp news of the murder of Joshua Spooner, bludgeoned to death by his wife's three apparent lovers (two British POW's, the third a seventeen-year-old veteran) nearly three years into the war. And his widow, the mastermind of the affair, daughter of the colony's most notorious Loyalist, now in exile!

A marker, Joshua's grave, several documents and two or three buildings are all that remain. History's role is not to simulate, but rather to stimulate us to consider how it might have been, to portray however incompletely a particularly lurid moment during a time of tremendous upheaval. Eighteenth century legal practice, women's role in that society, the radically shifting political realm—this book can only touch upon the many facets of so rich a topic. It's my humble ambition that this narrative will stimulate the reader's curiosity to investigate even further.

Acknowledgments

My thanks to the friends, family and institutions who helped in this book's creation. For technical support, I am grateful to Tom and Sue Noone, Mary and Steve Lacaire, Amanda Elinoff, Steve Wage and my multi-talented daughter, Julia. Thank you, Beth Young, for helping me in my search for agents. Jim Sullivan offered me his medical expertise, as did Emil Smith for all things pharmacological. Bill Grohe was helpful as editor. Thanks to Lee Bartlett for providing material on early Worcester. My appreciation also for the kind encouragement offered by two late, legendary professors, Pauline Maier (MIT) and Jay Fliegelman of Stanford University. Special thanks to Aleksandar Novovic, the book's cover designer.

I am indebted also to the following: the Massachusetts Historical Society, the New England Genealogical Society, Clark University, the Worcester Historical Museum, Worcester Art Museum, Worcester County Registry of Deeds, Nancy Gaudette in the Worcester Room of the Worcester Public Library, the library at Old Sturbridge Village, West Boylston Historical Society, the Massachusetts State Archives, the Massachusetts Teachers Association, Preservation Worcester, and the Massachusetts libraries of Brookfield, North Brookfield, West Brookfield, Cambridge, Hardwick and Ipswich--and the Annapolis Heritage Society (Nova Scotia). Above all, my special appreciation to the staff of Worcester's archival gem, the American Antiquarian Society, without whom this book could never have happened.

My wife, Becky, to whom this work is dedicated, has been my most patient supporter, and my most demanding critic; she deserves my greatest thanks.

CHAPTER ONE

The Baron of Hardwick

On April 20, 1776, in the mid-Atlantic, a British fleet comprised of more than one hundred ships sailed toward Halifax, Nova Scotia, en route to British-controlled New York. The warships moved at a relaxed pace of just under five knots, their thousands of infantrymen destined for the battlefields of Long Island, Brandywine and Trenton.

It was late afternoon. Aboard one ship, the captain and officer had just sat down to dinner. None of the men above deck had paid much attention to the soldier on the forecastle, a distraught, brutal-looking man, his eyes set upon the rolling sea. In an instant, he leaped from the bow into the frigid water, the ship making her way over him. Suddenly, he arose at the stern. In desperation, to distance himself from the ship, he swam against the current with all his strength. Several men raced below deck to alert the captain and officer, who ordered the ship's direction changed. A boat was manned and hoisted out, and he was soon overtaken, despite struggling mightily to escape his rescuers. Once forced into the boat, William Brooks, not yet twenty-five years of age, was returned to the ship, and ordered between decks, where a sentinel was placed over him. A day earlier, Brooks had stolen a shirt from the knapsack of one of his messmates.[1]

Like many of His Majesty's troops in America, Brooks was an ex-convict. Within two years, his self-destructive character helped to make him a central player in the most notorious crime of eighteenth-century New England.

The central Massachusetts town of Worcester would play the key role as the site of the murderers' trial and execution. John Adams began his work life there as a school teacher and law apprentice; when a young attorney years later, he admired Timothy Ruggles, whose charisma, he wrote

> Consists in the quickness of his apprehension, the steadiness of his attention, the boldness and strength of his thoughts and expressions, his strict honor, conscious superiority and contempt of meanness. People approached him with dread and terror.[2]

Whether or not Bathsheba ever approached him in the same manner, it seems that his influence over her was unlike that of any other.

The Ruggles clan claimed a lofty ancestry. Its earliest forebear, born in 1220, was William de Ruggele (from the Latin, "of the rugged land", a town in Staffordshire), like General Ruggles a military man, who in Flanders served in the army of Edward I.[3] Later, the Ruggles became allied with the Bolleyne line, who, through Sir Thomas Nollye led to Mary, sister of Anne Boleyn. As Henry VIII's queen, beheaded after a conviction based upon dubious charges of incest and adultery, Boleyn emerges from the family's past as an ill omen. The Ruggles coat-of-arms, foreboding in its majesty, features as its crest a tower aflame, pierced by four arrows.

Bathsheba's more prosperous forebears, representing a different line of the family, included George Ruggle of Lavenham,

England, one of the founders of the Virginia Company of London. A stock company formed in 1606, its purpose was to found settlements along North America's eastern seacoast, all of which was then called Virginia. Plymouth was one site, and the other Jamestown, established in 1607. Ruggle, a playwright of some distinction, counted among his closest colleagues the Earl of Southampton, Shakespeare's friend.[4]

Bathsheba's branch of the family tree, making voyage for New England about three decades later, came from more humble roots. In 1637, Thomas Ruggles of Nazig, Essex County, disembarked from the Hopewell anchored in Boston Harbor, and settled in nearby Roxbury along with his wife Mary and children, Samuel and Sarah. Although genealogical records are conflicting, it appears that the Ruggles' first son had died in England, and that the next eldest, John, arrived in Boston two years previously in the company of Philip Eliot, a relative of the famous Indian preacher, John Eliot, now pastor of the First Church in Roxbury. The Ruggles, through marriage, further strengthened their ties to the Eliots, one of Massachusetts Bay Colony's most influential families.[5]

In Roxbury, John's son Samuel, Bathsheba Spooner's great-great-grandfather, kept the Flower de Luce Tavern, assisted by his wife, Hannah, and their brood of eight children.[6] As owner of a public house, Samuel played a key role in the community, and avidly pursued politics, a family tradition destined to endure for a century-and-a-half. Like that of other colonies, the charter of Massachusetts Bay included the right to call an assembly of representatives. Each colony's charter guaranteed through its constitution some measure of autonomy, reinforcing the colonists' rights as Englishmen.

In the late seventeenth century, the colonists grew increasingly fearful of Britain's threats to reclaim authority by revoking the charters. Virginia, only a few years after its settlement, found itself governed as a Royal Colony, whereby the royal governor, serving as the king's representative, exercised veto power over all legislation. Fears of a similar government being foisted upon the people of Massachusetts intensified. In October of 1664, Samuel Ruggles signed a resolution asking that the General Court "stand fast in our personal liberty's",[7] recommending that the Court ask the Lord "to assist them to stere right in these shaking times."[8]

Less than three weeks later, Ruggles experienced shaking times of a more immediate nature, an event which, had its outcome been otherwise, would have put an end to our story. In May of 1667, under threatening skies, Samuel ascended Meeting House Hill in Roxbury, leading a pair of oxen pulling a cart to which his horse had been tied. Lightning struck, instantly killing all three animals. A contemporary diarist recorded that "...a chest in the cart, with goods in it, burnt in sundry places, himself coming off the cart, carried twenty feet from it, yet no abiding hurt."[9] Samuel served many years as both selectman and representative, positions likely earned through his influence as tavern keeper, his public house a hotbed of political debate. Establishing another Ruggles tradition, Samuel served as captain of the Roxbury militia.

In 1686, England's James II, a Roman Catholic, instituted the Dominion of New England as a means both to unite the colonies against the French to the north, and increase his power over the colonies as well. A royal charter replaced the charters of the region's colonies (Massachusetts Bay, Rhode Island, New Hampshire and Connecticut) which had guaranteed the right to representative assemblies. The former governor of New York, Edmund Andros, was appointed Dominion governor. Prior to his appointment, few had expressed dissatisfaction with the new government. As soon as Andros arrived in 1686, however, he quickly made enemies. The Puritan propaganda machine set to work. One tall tale making the rounds told of a book given to the Wampanoag tribe by Andros, a book vile in its popish excesses, including as it did illustrations of the Lord, his mother, and the twelve apostles.[10] It was even claimed that he had asked the Indians to call on the Virgin as their intercessor. One justice whom Andros had appointed rightly concluded that "a parsell of fellows had devised a Parsell of lys and had fathered them on a pore Indian."[11]

Ultimately, Andros and a cohort were rumored to be about to set fire to Boston, an accusation consistent with those being leveled against Catholics in London. Likely at the behest of Cotton Mather and others close to the champion of Puritanism, the north end of Boston was rife with rumors that citizens to the south of town were preparing to revolt; those in the south end heard the opposite. About a thousand Bostonians responded with arms. Soon, the settlements around Boston were sending hundreds into the capital, among them the militiamen of Roxbury headed by Samuel Ruggles. Active in the revolt, he was likely one of the guard who helped to imprison Andros and his staff.[12] The colonists' victory was Pyrrhic. In 1691, the new Massachusetts charter was signed which, while assuring the people the same rights and liberties as enjoyed by Englishmen overseas (including religious freedom for all Christians but Roman Catholics), gave final authority to the royal governor, hand-picked by the king. It is ironic that this Ruggles of an earlier generation sought to limit the king's power, which his great grandson during even more contentious times would do more than any other to fight for the continuance of that power.

Also in 1686, Samuel Ruggles joined the interests of several Roxbury citizens, an association which proved fateful to our story. At a cost of twenty pounds, several Indians conveyed to Ruggles and a half dozen other men "a tract of land eight miles square near The English town of Wooster, named Wombemesscook."[13] Within two generations, the town of Hardwick was incorporated, the second home of Bathsheba Spooner's childhood.

Little is known of Samuel Jr., who succeeded his father as selectman, representative, and militia captain. Later generations of the family referred to themselves as the royal Ruggles, a characterization based less upon the Anne Boleyn connection that that of Samuel's wife, nee Martha Woodbridge, a direct descendant of France's Henry I. Samuel fathered ten children, three of whom became clergymen, most notably his second son, Timothy, who, like John Adams, taught as a Latin master (in Roxbury) following his graduation from Harvard. Now a minister, Timothy served his church for nearly six decades, and continuing his father's work, actively promoted the continued settlement of Hardwick.

By 1710, the Ruggles had moved south from Roxbury to Rochester, near Cape Cod. A year later, Mary gave birth to the first of twelve children whose extraordinary career would make him at once Rochester's most revered and most notorious son, Timothy Ruggles.

A Harvard graduate like his father, in 1732 Timothy returned to Rochester, and by 1735 had begun his law practice. His reputation as an able attorney spread rapidly, helping him to secure a seat as Rochester's representative to the General Court, the colonial legislature. His travels included frequent visits to the southeastern Massachusetts counties of Taunton, Plymouth and Barnstable. When called to Barnstable, Ruggles lodged at the Newcomb Tavern in Sandwich, which Peter Newcomb had built in 1702 on Grove Street, its white clapboards and black-shuttered windows still gracing the town center today.

Peter's son, William, attended Harvard College a decade before Timothy Ruggles, thanks to the sponsorship of the Rev. Rowland Mather, first cousin of the alternately venerated or scorned Puritan apologist, Cotton Mather. The year of William's enrollment is unclear, but he may have entered as early as 1718, following his sixteenth birthday. Whatever lofty professional ambitions Peter may have envisioned for his son, they were not to be. Another father from a previous generation advised his own son at Harvard to "Abhor...one hour idleness as you would be ashamed of one hour of drunkenness." If young William heard similar advice, it went unheeded; while at Harvard, the young Newcomb went on a glass-smashing rampage. The colonies would not manufacture their own glass until late in the century; imported glass was costly. Rev. Mather reimbursed the college for William's vandalism. Drunkenness notwithstanding, William seems to have conquered idleness, receiving his degree in 1722, the first American Newcomb to complete college.[14]

William returned to Sandwich not to pursue law, medicine or the ministry but rather, as the only son, to inherit the family business upon his father's death a year later. Peter was thrilled with his son's choice of a bride, Bathsheba Bourne, daughter of the Hon. Melatiah Bourne, scion of a family even more heralded than the Ruggles. Bourne, an astute politician, like Ruggles, had served as representative in the General Court, as well as Justice of the Common Pleas, which handled general trial matters. Few men in Barnstable County were as connected (or as wealthy) as he; also involved in shipping, he extended his influence through marriage ties with eighteen families boasting large landholdings.[15]

More than a decade and eight children later, William died at the age of thirty-four, leaving a considerable estate valued at over twenty-seven hundred pounds, including the tavern and shops. There is no evidence of any serious disharmony in their marriage, unlike that which plagued his widow's second marriage to Timothy Ruggles, Bathsheba Spooner's father. Timothy, occupied by the filing of deeds and writs, still found time to foster his acquaintance with Bathsheba Newcomb. Within five months of William's death, Ruggles became her second husband—and stepfather to her eight children, the eldest barely out of grammar school.

Bathsheba's descendants on her maternal side were instrumental in shaping the character of Cape Cod. In 1637, a group of settlers from Lynn, north of Boston, formed the Cape's first community, at Sandwich. One of its founders, Richard Bourne, whose home stood on the eventual site of the world-famous Boston and Sandwich Glass Company, had been trained in England as a solicitor, but established his fame as a missionary among the Wampanoag tribe. He was described as "thickset with iron grey hair [known] to the...Indians as the White Sachem or Little Father, energetic, gentle, with square shoulders thick from wrestling with Lucifer." Missionaries constantly vied for the Indians' loyalty, an ongoing competition which gave birth to the most famous legend attributed to a Ruggles ancestor. During one dispute, a medicine man lost his temper, and began chanting an old rhyme, which caused Bourne to become mired in quicksand. The men agreed to a contest to determine who would best survive a two-week-old fast. While the Indian's strength waned, Bourne enjoyed the decided advantage of a dove who visited from time to time, dropping a juicy "cherry" in his mouth. Days into the contest, unable to cast a spell upon Bourne's providential pet and swooning from thirst and hunger, the medicine man collapsed, and Bourne was a free man. During one foray, the dove dropped the fruit into the bog, and it multiplied, endowing Cape Cod with its first crop of cranberries.[16]

In time, Bourne came to own the entire Cape Cod town of Mashpee. Richard and his wife, Bathsheba (the first of six so named in the family) gave birth to three sons. Shearjashub, the second, eventually inherited his father's lands in Mashpee and Falmouth. Like Richard, he worked among the Wampanoag natives, and like his son, as a justice. This son, Melatiah, married and settled in Falmouth, birthplace of Bathsheba Newcomb. In 1710, he headed north across the Cape to Sandwich.[17]

And so, Bathsheba Bourne, Bathsheba Spooner's mother, transplanted from Falmouth to Sandwich, within a few years married the innkeeper's son, William Newcomb, and then upon his death, his former guest, Timothy Ruggles, seven years' Bathsheba's junior. It was a union blessed in talent and resources. To her second marriage, Bathsheba brought a handful of businesses including a well-established tavern, not to mention considerable wealth and influence from her father. Her new husband, Timothy, "...being above six feet and magnificently proportioned with a noble head...dark, handsome, with a strong and commanding face" would one day shine not only as the brightest among attorneys in southeastern Massachusetts, but as one of the colony's most respected statesmen.[18] His star's quick ascent would be followed by an even more rapid plunge to destruction.

Ruggles, though married to Bathsheba and frequently called to court at Barnstable (which had jurisdiction over Sandwich), nevertheless maintained his legal address at Rochester, which enabled him to continue representing that town in the General Court at Boston. Ruggles' big break came in 1739 with the death of the man who had monopolized the legal business in Sandwich, Nathaniel Otis. Never one to gather moss, Ruggles almost immediately relocated to Sandwich, and went on to represent the community for six terms in Boston. At long last, Ruggles could hang his professional "shingle" alongside the tavern sign, proudly-paired symbols proclaiming Timothy's dual career. Ruggles poured his guest's rum with the same flair that he curried his horse, a role he savored, and one well-suited to his dynamic charisma.[19]

> He dressed carefully but not elegantly. He was social, witty, profane, wise about human nature, quick to drop ceremony and convention if they ceased to be of social value. He was a man of few words and never said anything silly. He drank nothing stronger than a small [weak] beer, and was almost a vegetarian in a society in which gluttony was one universal excess.[20]

Another historian described Ruggles as one who "seemed through life to realize the beau ideal of his ambition—the Magnus Apollo of his adherents."[21]

The success of Ruggles' practice enabled him to represent the Crown at a fixed fee. A frequent adversary was James Otis, father of the famed Revolutionary radical, and brother of Nathaniel, the lawyer whose death created a professional opening for Ruggles in Sandwich.

The high maternal mortality rate in the eighteenth century accounted for large numbers of men who, upon their first wife's death, remarried women usually younger themselves with whom to produce more children. It was much less common for a woman such as Bathsheba to outlive her first husband after delivering eight children, then remarry with a man several years her junior—and provide him with seven more children: Martha in 1737, Timothy, Jr. two years later, then Mary in 1741, the next year followed by John, then Richard in 1744, Bathsheba in 1745, and finally Elizabeth three years later. Psychologists continue to debate the relevance of birth order and its impact on personality; Bathsheba was the last of fifteen children but one, and the child destined to be her father's favorite.

From 1740 on, Ruggles indulged an occasional passion for military adventure, particularly if there was potential for financial gain. The Treaty of Utrecht of 1713 largely forbade British trade with the Spanish Empire, which gave rise to widespread smuggling, increasing tension between the maritime rivals in the West Indies. In 1731, Capt. Robert Jenkins claimed that Spanish coast guards had severed his ear during a brief engagement off Florida. Jenkins displayed his wound to a horrified House of Commons, setting in motion a propaganda machine (fueled by additional conflict) which eight years later resulted in a British declaration of war.

From 1740 on, the town of Sandwich received word that men were being assembled in Boston, and Ruggles, at his own expense, recruited one hundred men, mostly Indians, by now reduced to poverty.[22] A recent British proclamation declared that any captain whose ship proved victorious against the Spanish would be splendidly rewarded with three-eighths of the booty, the remainder to be shared by the officers and crew. The lack of any portion reserved for the Crown indicates how very generous George II could be—such grand incentives served the lustier goal of British domination in the Caribbean. Ruggles, a non-swimmer, was persuaded to pursue his captain's commission. To be fair, patriotic fervor likely played a part as well as greed, a fervor displayed often in the decades to follow. Ruggles' up-front reimbursement was four hundred pounds, a princely sum for his recruitment efforts, which likely cost far less.[23]

Ruggles was named excise collector for Barnstable County in 1743. Though now in a position which in its small way enhanced his image with the king, he probably incurred the wrath of at least a few Cape Codders during a decade which found the Massachusetts economy in shambles, its extreme indebtedness aggravated by runaway inflation. The War of Jenkins' Ear, by the mid-1740's, had widened to become the War of the Spanish Succession, with Austria and Britain allied against France and Spain. In the colonies, the conflict became known as King George's War, a struggle between France and England whose greatest prize was the Nova Scotian port of Louisbourg, in French hands since 1713. One of the strongest fortresses anywhere in North America, Louisbourg commanded the chief entrance to Canada, the Gulf of St. Lawrence. Gov. WIlliam Shirley, a British emigre, was preoccupied with a bankrupt Massachusetts treasury and declining fisheries. Nevertheless, believing there was little room for two world powers in the North Atlantic, he set his sights on French Nova Scotia, especially Cape Breton, its northernmost partition, a constant threat to the Bay Colony's fisheries. Aided by William Pepperell, a Maine merchant now turned commander,

Ruggles recruited over thirty-two-hundred men for the venture.[24] As plans for the siege of Louisbourg were finalized, Bathsheba (Bourne) Ruggles gave birth to her next-to-last child, Bathsheba, on February 13.

Did fate restrain the will of Timothy Ruggles and Bathsheba Bourne, who waited until their third daughter before sharing her mother's name, for the Biblical beauty whose story would offer parallels with that of Bathsheba Spooner?

The second Book of Samuel relates that one evening, King David

> ...arose from his bed, and walked upon the roof of the king's house: and from the roof he saw a woman bathing; and the woman was very beautiful to look upon. And David sent and inquired after the woman. And one said, Is not this Bathsheba, the daughter of Eliam, the wife of Uriah the Hittite? And David sent Messengers, and took her and she came unto him, and he lay with her... and she returned unto her house. And the woman conceived; and she sent and told David, I am with child. David sent to Joab saying, send me Uriah the Hittite...David wrote a letter to Joab...Set ye Uriah in the fore-front of the hottest battle, and retire ye from him, that he may be smitten, and die... When the wife of Uriah heard that Uriah was dead, she made lamentation for her husband. And when the mourning was past, David sent and took her home to his house, and she became his wife, and bore him a son. But the thing that David had done displeased Jehovah...And Jehovah struck the child ...and it came to pass on the seventh day, that the child died.

Little Bathsheba's father undoubtedly kept a close eye on the last-minute preparations for the assault upon Louisbourg. His recruitment skills likely came in handy. Over fifty transports set sail from Boston in late March, joined later by contingents from

New Hampshire and Connecticut, which besieged the fort in early May. The weeks-long battle of blockade and bombardment finally resulted in French capitulation on June 17. The British navy now ruled the seas. The French flag was kept flying over the town of Louisbourg to lure French ships into the harbor, their million-dollar cargo seized and divided up between the king, officers and crew. Boston received word of the victory two weeks later, and marked the occasion with bonfires, cannon, fireworks, and candles in every window. The French needn't have felt too disheartened. Only three years later, per terms of the Treaty of Aix-la-Chapelle, the region was returned to them.

By then, Ruggles had been named to a key committee appointed to site several forts in upper New York, on the western frontier against the French. The area was claimed by both world powers, its indigenous Iroquois courted by each side. Not long after, the region became yet another battleground between the subjects of George II and Louis XV.

In Sandwich, in 1748, the Ruggles celebrated the arrival of their last child, Elizabeth. The children of this marriage, Bathsheba Bourne's second, now ranged in age from infancy to eleven years.

Little is known regarding Ruggles and his family over the next five years, although given subsequent events, the erstwhile captain seems to have done nothing to jeopardize his political or financial ascent. The family's story picks up again in 1753, a fateful year for the family.

Nearly seven decades earlier, Timothy Ruggles' great grandfather joined several other citizens of Roxbury in purchasing an eight-mile square tract of land twenty-five miles northwest of Worcester.[25] In 1732, the men's heirs obtained a grant of the township, naming it Lambstown after the original deed holder, Joshua Lamb.[26] The town was formally incorporated by the General Court in 1738, and its name changed to Hardwick, comprising most of the original tract. A town of gently rolling hills, its situation was ideally suited for dairy farming, which flourished almost immediately, the town supplying the county with large quantities of cheese, butter and beef, as well as fruit.

Timothy and Bathsheba's decision to move their huge family to Hardwick in 1753 had not come easily, requiring as it did a good deal of coordination from many parties. The town of New Braintree had only recently broken off from Hardwick, a move engineered by Timothy's uncle, the Rev. Benjamin Ruggles of Middleboro, who settled there with his eight children. Benjamin's move proved to be the key catalyst. Another aunt, Patience, transferred to Hardwick, as did four couples from Roxbury or Dartmouth (in southeastern Massachusetts) sharing the name Ruggles—or Spooner. Three of Timothy Ruggles' brothers and one sister joined him in Hardwick, another brother, Samuel, settling in nearby Barre. All told, perhaps two dozen Ruggles and related families moved to northern Worcester County, none more illustrious (or richer) than Timothy and Bathsheba.[27]

The convivial host of the Newcomb Tavern, once let loose in the rural interior of Massachusetts, proved himself a man of continuing undaunted ambition and grand design. His estate would be matched by few others in the county. He designed and stocked a deer park, and brought together thirty excellent horses of imported and domestic breeds (his stud farm enjoyed an unparalleled reputation), and developed a dairy herd with his purchase of prize bulls. His resplendent orchard featured a wide variety of trees. In both horticulture and animal husbandry, Ruggles' renown was second to none. Of course, no estate (his lands in Hardwick alone included seven farms totaling one thousand acres) could be complete without a pack of hounds at the ready to indulge his favorite pastime, fox hunting. An invitation to the Ruggles estate was much envied, where the lord and lady of the manor entertained lavishly. Even the family's worship was done in great style, owning as they did three of the choicest pews in the meeting house.[28]

The Worcester Art Museum includes in its collection a fine primitive depicting the Ruggles estate, painted by a daughter's brother-in-law. The charmingly provincial portrait of the farm in Hardwick shows two homes facing each other at an angle, each at the end of a row of trees forming a grand allee. Two riders on horseback trot between the homes, the home on the right featuring four family members, one of whom appears to be an elegantly arrayed Timothy in the doorway (or perhaps an Anglican bishop, representing the faith of most of his future fellow Loyalists, Timothy being a rare Congregationalist among them). Timothy's wife stands below, while above a child, who might be the young Bathsheba Spooner, peeks out of a second story window. In the left foreground, a pair of the captain's hounds flush a hare from the undergrowth.

While many of the Ruggles clan settled north of Worcester, not so a single Bourne (his wife's family), nor any of her in-laws, the Newcombs, all of whom remained at the Cape or thereabouts. The separation is noteworthy. Did his wife's isolation increase marital stress? Writers have suggested that Timothy and Bathsheba's marriage was strained, a supposition which might too handily (presumptuously?) explain daughter Bathsheba's criminal propensity, not to mention her own conjugal misery. As one writer mused during the heyday of psychoanalysis

> Today, analysts would seek the roots of Bathsheba's emotional instability in her family background and would doubtless stress the fact that she was the child of an inharmonious but wealthy household.[29]

Were the Ruggles unhappy? It is reasonable to assume that Mrs. Ruggles was displeased about leaving the town which her ancestors had civilized with great distinction over the course of nearly a century-and-a-half. Further, in the mid-eighteenth century, moving well over one hundred miles into the interior, practically speaking, was little different than if the Ruggles had instead chosen the Ohio Valley.

Timothy's wife may also have found her domestic world turned upside down. Though her hands had undoubtedly been full sixteen hours daily running the Newcomb Tavern in Sandwich, it was a schedule she had grown accustomed to over a thirty year period. Suddenly, she found herself managing a large farm, a role for which she had likely little if any experience. Now in her 50's, an age which many women could never hope to reach, the new demands must have seemed overwhelming.

An ugly anecdote (apocryphal?) related that one evening, Timothy Ruggles sat down to dinner, only to learn from his wife that she had prepared one of his favorite hounds as the main course. If true, the incident may suggest mental instability, a possibility discussed later at length. If untrue, might Timothy's defenders have created the tale to blame Mrs. Ruggles for the downward spiral into which their marriage would descend, or even as a means to cast her, again, as the chief negative influence upon her wayward daughter? It has also been suggested that Timothy had strayed from his marital vows. A century following his death, one of his descendants rejected the idea outright.

> ...The stories of the results of domestic infelicity in her [Bathsheba Spooner's father's] family have been very much exaggerated. There is not the slightest foundation for the statement that has sometimes been made that General Ruggles set his daughter an example of domestic infidelity. He was an exceedingly hospitable man, but himself, certainly during portions of his life, very abstemious. He was also pure...[30]

Writing about the same time, Lucius Paige, a descendant of one of Hardwick's founders, concurred, finding insinuations of Ruggles' moral turpitude "utterly incredible" while conceding

> ...as to his domestic relations, although an unhappy compatibility of temper was notorious, and was the subject of free conversation among those who personally knew the parties, I do not remember to have heard the slightest suspicion of "conjugal infidelity" on the part of either husband or wife.."[31]

Young Bathsheba was eight years old when the family moved from Sandwich to Hardwick. Her education had likely been typical for a child of her family's standing. On a day-to-day basis, she would have witnessed the comings and goings of some of Massachusetts' most illustrious citizens—judges, attorneys, pastors, professors, perhaps even a governor or two, and would have been exposed to the most sophisticated ideas of a genteel culture removed only thirteen decades from utter wilderness.

More formally, she likely studied at a dame school. Such a school, run usually by a widowed or unmarried woman, offered instruction in the teacher's home. More rarely, the dame traveled from town to town; one such school in Maine operated out of a neighbor's barn. For very young boys, dame schools served as preparatory training for the town schools, many not established until the late eighteenth century. For most girls of all ages (and of sufficient means), dame schools were the only option. When allowed to study in town schools, girls were often taught when boys were absent, or during the summer months. The curriculum of course varied, but generally included the alphabet, spelling, reading, writing, knitting and sewing, skills evidenced through the large number of embroidered samplers still extant.[32] Such opportunities were more readily available in an old, established town such as Sandwich, and less probable in a newer, rural settlement like Hardwick, although as a regional center nearby Brookfield may have had its own school. In her early teens, Bathsheba was likely sent to attend one of Boston's leading schools for ladies. Music, dancing and needlework were the favored pastimes, as well as japanning (the application of black varnishes) and eglomise, painting on glass.[33]

A humorous dialogue, published in the Boston Evening Post in 1744, pits husband against wife as they debate the type of education best suited for a young girl. The wife has asked her husband if their daughter might attend dancing school. He replies

> Prithee, good madam, let her first be able
> To read a chapter truly in the Bible,
> That she mayn't mispronounce God's people, popel,
> Not read Cunstable for Constantinople;
> Make her expert and ready at her prayers
> That God may keep her from the devil's snares;
> Teach her what's useful, how to shun deluding,
> To roast, to toast, to sew, to make or mend
> To scrub, to rub, to earn and not to spend,

I tell thee wife, once more, I'll have her bred
To book'ry, cook'ry, thimble, needle, thread
First teach her these, and then the pritty fool
Shall jig her crupper at the dancing school.

His wife countered

You see my neighbor grub, that sorry fool
Can keep his daughter at a boarding school
Nay Amus the Smith gives all his children breeding
And sends them out to writing and reading;
I'm sure we live as well, and save as much
Why then should you so small a matter grudge?
Prithee consent, you'l never the sooner break
"Tis hard we cannot scrape for one poor
An only daught, and a hopeful girl
Who if she'd breeding might deserve an Earl.[34]

However reasonable the wishes of these imaginary parents, evidence suggests that Bathsheba rejected their every recommendation.

CHAPTER TWO

Who Can Find a Virtuous Woman

Though frustrated earlier as a captain without a vessel, Ruggles in 1755 seized the opportunity for some genuine heroics, and became a key player in North America's most far-reaching conflict before the Revolution, the French and Indian War. In the late 1740's, the Ohio Company of Virginia had been organized by aristocratic Virginians seeking new land and opportunities in the fur trade. The French disfavored any such plans, and responded by fortifying the upper Ohio River. In 1754 Major George Washington, then twenty-one years of age, was sent by the Virginia governor to express disapproval. A French officer graciously invited Washington to dinner, a welcome respite following his five-week long trek. Full of liquor, one Frenchman loosened his tongue to inform the young Virginian that his country had every intention of making Ohio their own, and that the English would be too slow in responding. Relations between Virginia and the French steadily deteriorated until at last, five months later, Washington and his men were overcome by the French and Indians at Fort Necessity, and surrendered, at least temporarily making good the Frenchman's promise. Upon receiving word of Washington's capitulation, London sent regiments under the command of General Braddock. One of their objectives was to capture Crown Point, near the south end of Lake Champlain, wedged between what is now Vermont and New York, an outpost which could serve handily as a French base of attack against New England and New York.

Enter Timothy Ruggles, now given command of the Massachusetts troops who joined William Johnson and his three thousand Englishmen from both sides of the Atlantic to meet French regiments from Quebec and Montreal under the command of Baron de Dieskau.[1] Ruggles' gifts were not limited to strategy; time and time again he proved invaluable in communicating with the natives.[2]

Unlike many of his compatriots, Ruggles dealt respectfully with the Iroquois, as equals. Johnson, never one to enter an engagement without adequate defenses, ordered the construction of Ft. Edward, about halfway between the southern end of Lake George (the tail of Lake Champlain) and Saratoga, the town which a generation later would find itself the pivot upon which fortune turned favorably toward the Americans—and a battle site fateful to our story. The ensuing battle at Lake George (one New England soldier declared that "the Hailstones from Heaven have not been much thicker than their Bullets came") resulted in the wounding of both Johnson and Dieskau. Although the British succeeded in holding on to their smaller forts, they neglected to capture Crown Point. Their numbers greatly reduced, both by inter-colonial bickering and Indian desertion, in the face of heavy casualties the British were forced to abandon the effort. Dieskau was captured by Ruggles, and was denied any future role in the conflict. The Prince of Hardwick, newly promoted to the rank of brigadier-general, returned to the hills of Worcester County in a trail of glory.[3] Almost immediately, Ruggles was named an associate justice of the Court of Common Pleas, the venue handling most civil cases.

If the general's marriage was its own battleground, it was likely due to sins of omission as well as those of commission on Timothy's part—it is hard to imagine when he found time to linger at Hardwick. Recent events may have also aggravated another probable source of marital discord which had been worsening since the family's move from Sandwich. As a young man, Ruggles had moved from Rochester to Sandwich, joining the household of a woman who for over a dozen years enjoyed a reputation as Sandwich's favorite tavern keeper. Ruggles' fame was on the rise, but the public house was still known as the Newcomb Tavern, a testament to Bathsheba's first husband's family. Then, it was his wife's turn to be uprooted—and transported to a rural county which regarded her husband as blameless—and now deified as a returning war hero. Indeed, in such a climate, Timothy's absences may not have been a source of disagreement, but rather a necessity encouraged by both partners.

Ruggles' respite would be brief. General James Abercromby, a Massachusetts lawyer and politician whose talents as a military leader would remain appropriately unsung, assembled fifteen thousand troops for an attack upon Ft. Carillon at the base of Lake Champlain, a fort remembered more famously as Ticonderoga. Brigadier General Ruggles was appointed commander of the third division under Abercromby. Ft. Carillon, situated upon a hill overlooking the lake, was located at the end of the portage route between Lake Champlain, and Lake George to the south. During the French and Indian War, the strategic outpost was engaged in a tug-of-war, first between the French and British, and then, during the Revolution, between the British and colonists. This first assault proved disastrous for Abercromby and his men.[4]

British fortunes changed dramatically during the conflict's final two years. In a stunning string of victories, His Majesty's troops captured Niagara, then quickly re-trook Louisbourg. Aided by Worcester's Captain Goulding (apocryphally, famous as the Capt. Gooding of Yankee Doodle), the troops next overwhelmed the French at Frontenac, Duquesne and Quebec (the commander for both sides were mortally wounded at the Plains of Abraham). A year later, somewhat anticlimactically, Montreal fell. All of Canada and the eastern Mississippi River Valley were now in British hands, her thirteen colonies freed from an enemy which had blocked western expansion.

Ruggles continued in his role as commander-in-chief of the Massachusetts forces, and following this last tour, returned to Hardwick one last time.[5] It was during this year that John Adams wrote glowingly of Ruggles' grandeur. Adams, the young upstart attorney and still very much the British patriot, was surely intimidated by this giant of a man whose dynamism and hubris seemed destined for the governor's office. Ruggles could not have foreseen how fickle his fellow colonists could be, nor how, five brief years later, one misstep would alter his family's fortunes in ways no contemporary could have predicted, least of all the general himself.

As he had in Rochester then Sandwich, Ruggles served as representative to the General Court for Hardwick. In 1762, he attained his political apex as Speaker of the House, the same year he was appointed Chief Justice for the Court of Common Pleas at Worcester; an associate justice, Artemas Ward, would later command the American troops prior to Washington. One last dog anecdote, happier than the first, dates from this time. Sitting as Chief Justice, and piqued over the tenor of the court during one session, Ruggles "reprimanded a dog who had taken his seat beside his master, for appearing on the bench before he had been qualified as a Justice of the Peace, and directed him to go and be sworn before he came to vote there."[6] Accomplished, brilliant, urbane, yet down-to-earth—Ruggles' charm was inescapable.

As Ruggles neared the completion of his two-year term as Speaker, the king, through the General Court of Massachusetts, honored Ruggles' military service with something more tangible than words. In late January of 1764, the court granted

> ...to the Hon. Timothy Ruggles, Esq. his heirs and assigns, for Ever in Testimony of the greatfull sence this Court has of the Important services the grantee Rendered his County Dureing the late War for the reduction of Canada...[7]

fifteen hundred acres of the colony's lands less than twenty miles north of Worcester, which bordered the newly incorporated town of Princeton, to which the land would soon be annexed. The property played a continuing role in the lives of the Ruggles and Spooners over the next fourteen years—even, though never realized, as the planned site of his future son-in-law's murder.

Timothy's daughter, now a woman, realized that her days on the family estate were numbered, a realization she likely embraced. Bathsheba's father, whose favorite she was, rarely appeared. All but one older sibling had married. Her closest sister, Mary, had wed a member of the prominent Greens of Worcester, while Martha, the eldest, would soon be engaged to a wealthy suitor from nearby Brookfield. Bathsheba remained alone with her younger sister,

Elizabeth, and her mother, a woman who does not appear to have figured prominently in Bathsheba's childhood, and as the evidence will show, even less so in her adult years. As one of the younger daughters, Bathsheba did not enjoy such pecuniary advantage in courtship as had Martha and Mary. But her beauty, as well as the fact that next-to-youngest daughter or not, she was still the child of Gen. Ruggles—these combined to guarantee that in short order, she too would find a worthy mate.

Much regarding Bathsheba's betrothal remains a mystery. Joshua Spooner was the second son of John Spooner who, if related to the ancient William Spooner family of Plymouth (and no evidence survives), was a more recent American arrival. Born in Sheffield, England in 1696, Spooner (a name originally given not only to spoon makers, but to bell makers and ringers) immigrated to Boston sometime in the early eighteenth century. It is not clear whether he married his wife, the former Elizabeth Wells (born 1699) here or in England. John established himself as a Boston merchant, like his first son, also John, who was born in 1732. Joshua followed nine years later.[8] We know that Mrs. Spooner died before 1744. Did she die in childbirth along with what would have been her third child—or following the birth of Joshua?

By the late eighteenth century, New Englanders had adopted a liberal attitude toward courtship; rarely would a parent, especially one from the upper class, withhold his or her blessing from a child's choice of mate. As land grew scarcer, and families lived apart at ever increasing distances as businesses and commerce developed, parents continued to lose authority over their adult children. The concept of romantic love was taking hold. One Massachusetts mother advised her daughter that "...she should not wish any friend of hers to give their hand where they could not give their heart."[9] A year before Bathsheba's wedding, a lady wrote to her gentleman "...All I desire...is a companion who would make it his endeavor to be both a friend and lover to me when he chose for life," and still another reminded her husband that "Every joy in anticipation depends on you...and from you I must derive every pleasure."[10]

Although England had tightened its marriage laws with the Marriage Act of 1753, In America a more casual attitude lingered. Formalities were often dispensed with—mutual consent and open cohabitation were viewed in some communities as evidence enough of an existing marriage.

Bathsheba, in her twenty-first year, was more than ripe for marriage; the majority of her peers had wed by the age of nineteen. Women were not alone in experiencing marital pressure. In some towns, bachelors were fined or otherwise penalized—even registered as "suspected criminals". Unattached men unlucky enough to reside in Hartford were taxed twenty shillings a week as "lonemen...for the selfish luxury of solitary living."[11]

Laurel Thatcher Ulrich, in her enlightening study of women's roles in colonial society, Good Wives—Images and Reality in the Lives of Women in Northern New England 1650-1750, refers to the contemporary idealization of the biblical Bathsheba, sermonized as the virtuous housewife and godly woman, if forgotten as the beauty whose unintended seduction of David brought the king much sorrow. Ulrich lists as the wife's virtuous roles those of willing servant, skilled manufacturer, hardworking agriculturalist, and resourceful trader, a paradigm of godliness as eulogized in Proverbs 31:10-12.5

> Who can find a virtuous woman? For her price is far above rubies. The heart of her husband doth safely trust in her, so that he shall have No need of spoil. She will do him good and not evil all the days of her life.[12]

Finding her was not always easy. Though the Revolution would de-populate young men throughout the colonies, the decades prior instead witnessed a shortage of marriageable women which caused men to find a mate by whatever means possible—even if she had to be bought. As testament to the great scarcity of qualified women, the Boston Evening Post in 1736 advertised a women sale—prospects were imported from Europe.[13]

In keeping with a recently established British custom, a "wife sale" occurred following a couple's agreement to separate, when the wife was symbolically offered for sale, usually to a pre-arranged buyer who might be the woman's cousin or lover.[14]

In modern minds, Puritan morality of the seventeenth century is often extended to cover the eighteenth as well, a generalization not justified by statistics. One historian noted that in Hingham, Massachusetts, there was a far greater likelihood that the fiancee would be pregnant at marriage than would her counterpart a century earlier.[15] Between 1741 and 1760, more than thirty-eight percent of Hingham brides delivered within nine months of their nuptials; between 1641 and 1660, not one case is recorded.[16] It appears, however, that these less inhibited couples were predominantly from the lower class, presumably because fathers with no ready cash lacked the necessary leverage to negotiate, or rather to threaten wayward children.[17] There is also evidence of a newfound sexual conservatism among the upper class toward the end of the eighteenth century.[18]

Among many such couples, if premarital intercourse was frowned upon, then bundling, that quirky New England substitute, could suffice. Traveling to America in the early 1780's, the Marquis de Castellux described the Yankee custom with fascination.

> ...the young couple lie down together upon a featherbed and pull its warm cover-let over them. It matters not whether the bed be in the same room as that of her parents. Indeed, her mother may oblige by tucking them in, bidding them good night as she retires to her own apartment. Unheeded, lad and lass whisper the night through. No harm need come of it. They have lain down fully-clothed, save for their shoes and mayhap some of their outer garments. Sometimes, 'tis said, a special bundling dress is worn by the maid—a garment with legs, like breeches, drawn at the waist and back with strings tied with a very strong knot, and over it ordinary apparel...A maiden may bundle virtuous and innocently. A sofa in summer, say the Yankees, is more dangerous for young lovers than a bundling bed in winter. Bear in mind that a girl does not admit any passing gallant to her bed but only a favored suitor, and he only after long and continued urging. Where there Are no bad intentions, there can be no evil consequences...[19]

During the early months of his own courtship with Abigail, John Adams advised his nieces

> ...You must therefore associate yourselves in some good Degree, and under certain Guards and Restraints, even privately with young fellows...And, tho Discretion must be used, and Caution, yet on...the whole of the Arguments On each side...I cannot wholly disapprove of Bundling...[20]

It is likely that Joshua and Bathsheba indulged in the practice themselves, although given Bathsheba's later history, bundling may have been merely among other preliminary amusements. Despite the acceptance of bundling, sexual misconduct was frequently punished, especially in the early eighteenth century. In Brookfield, the Widow Killon of Enfield was charged with "breaking the Sabbath and for lascivious carriage in that she was found upon the bed, under the bed clothes, with a man who was a stranger, upon a Sabbath morning."[21]

In 1763, probably as at no other time, the colonists were delighted to call themselves British citizens, members of an empire upon which, as they boasted, the sun never set. To which their chief rivals, the French, would one day respond, "That's because God would never trust the bastards in the dark." Verbal jousting notwithstanding, British prestige and power was becoming an international phenomenon, the country's reputation enhanced by a government viewed as among the most progressive. Late that year, a proclamation was issued which prohibited settlement in any territory west of the original thirteen colonies, the very land for which the colonists had so recently fought at dear expense. George III's intentions seemed pure, wishing to prevent any disagreements with tribes occupying the lands of the Ohio Valley, even beyond to the Mississippi. The proclamation served a further purpose in keeping the colonists within easier reach of London, a circumstance likely pleasing to His Majesty.

It was a small misstep—Rule Britannia remained the motto for virtually every rationally-minded subject on both sides of the Atlantic—but it represented the first drop in a growing tide of resentment destined to overwhelm a nearly one-hundred-and-sixty-year-old bond. In 1764, Lord George Grenville, First Lord of the Treasury and Chancellor of the Exchequer, pushed through Parliament a modified version of the earlier Molasses Act, which sought to enforce existing trade laws that had been largely ignored by the colonists. The cost of collecting customs revenues in America far outweighed the amount ever received. Molasses, used to sweeten everything from beans to meat and beer, and distilled to make rum, was to be taxed sixpence per gallon.

A still more reviled piece of legislation, the Sugar Act, actually reduced the tax, which at face value might have pleased the colonists, but in fact was a source of contention; very little revenue had ever been collected under the earlier Molasses Act, and now the king's men were determined to strictly enforce the taxation. From London's vantage point, it was high time that the debt be repaid. Hadn't the empire safeguarded America's interests? Tensions increased with the Currency Act, first passed against New England over a dozen years before, the earlier version now extended to all of the colonies, which forbade the issuance of any new currency. The law delighted many British merchants stung by the rapid depreciation of colonial tender while angering the colonists who wanted control over their own money.

Prior to Grenville's appointment, Parliament ruled that an army of at least ten thousand regulars was required to maintain the colonies' security, their unstated secondary role that of an intelligence network. Grenville and Parliament found it only reasonable that the colonists should fund the venture through the Stamp Act, a byzantine piece of legislation drawing more wrath from America than any of its predecessors. An impression would be embossed on virtually every document, including diplomas, licenses, pamphlets, dice, playing cards, wills, deeds, subpoenas, bills of sale, affidavits—even newspapers and every advertisement they carried. The court could not have engineered a more thorough public relations disaster, and most incomprehensibly, one so encumbering the legal and journalistic professions.

The colonists' reaction was immediate and direct. Mobs filled the streets of Boston and New York, laying to waste the property of tax collectors while intimidating vocal supporters of the king. More formally, the Nonimportation Agreements, a boycott of British goods organized on a colony-by-colony basis, served as a prelude to the Stamp Act Congress. The congress, an intercolonial body assembled to present a unified response to the crisis, may have been first proposed by Ruggles' old arch rival, James Otis, Sr. Whatever its origin, Massachusetts was first to approve the idea, sending three delegates to New York: Oliver Partridge from western Massachusetts, a justice of the Court of Common Pleas who came slowly to the American cause; James Otis, Jr., son of Ruggles' sometime-nemesis, who though now solidly neutral eventually gained fame as one of the colony's most prominent Patriots, and Timothy Ruggles. Bathsheba Spooner's father, not actually one of the first three chosen, had been selected as an alternate to Colonel John Worthington who had excused himself. The delegates traveled to the New York convention like royalty, each granted the extraordinary sum of over one hundred pounds sterling to defray expenses, a sum which would have sustained the average family for months.

On October 7, twenty-seven delegates from nine colonies assembled in New York's old city hall. As Massachusetts had initiated the convention, Otis and Ruggles were nominated for its chairmanship which Ruggles (carelessly transcribed as "Buggles") won by a single vote to the dismay of several progressively-minded colleagues. The body, after weeks of spirited debate focused mostly upon legal technicalities, finally presented its "Draft of the Resolves", which cautiously endorsed obeisance to the king, but remained unclear in its position regarding Parliament's authority. Most importantly, as British citizens, the delegates agreed that the colonists could not legally be taxed by an assembly in which they were not represented.

Ruggles accepted his post, hoping to convince fellow members to submit to the Stamp Act while petitioning Parliament to repeal it, a position initially supported by the less conservative Otis. When the moment for signing the draft at last arrived, delegates from three colonies balked, explaining the need for their legislatures back home to vote on the accord before affixing their signatures. The remaining six voted to make do with their own votes. Ruggles made the show-stopping suggestion that none of the delegates sign before receiving approval from their colonial assemblies, a position which ran directly counter to the intentions of the Massachusetts General Court which had already granted the three delegates its authority to approve the congress's recommendations.

Thomas McKean, a delegate from the Low Counties (later Delaware), was enraged at Ruggles, and challenged the general to declare his colleagues' action as treasonable if he so dared. Ruggles was incensed to be harangued by a man twenty years his junior, and found no cause to explain himself. Refusing to sign, Ruggles challenged McKean to a duel.

McKean later told a friend that he had informed Ruggles of his plan to stay in New York for ten more days to accommodate Ruggles, if need be. The duel never took place, and Ruggles never signed. He left the next day for Boston. Less than half of the original delegates approved the draft.

No longer the conquering hero, Ruggles instead found himself reviled as the wayward Loyalist called upon to justify his insolence. He declared that

> ...the Petition agreed on by the Congress to be presented to His Majesty, not being conceived in Terms clearly enough expressive of that Duty and Loyalty which are due to the best of Sovereigns, and consequently not agreeable to my above Instructions from this House, left as a mere Matter of Judgment and Discretion, if I had signed it, I must have acted in direct opposition to those instructions, and thereby have exposed myself not only to the Censures of this House but to the Reproaches of my own Conscience, a Tribunal more awful to me than this (however great) by which I have been condemned.[22]

Ruggles went on to challenge the very legal authority of the Stamp Act Congress, a challenge which struck his colleagues as disingenuous—if such were his feelings, why had he presided over the body for weeks without protest? Could he not have resigned in disapproval? The new Speaker of the House formally reprimanded Ruggles, and refused him permission to publish his defense in the House's journal. Despite the furor, Ruggles retained his seat as Hardwick's representative. John Adams, dazzled by the general a decade earlier, reappraised his idol, who now exhibited "...an inflexible oddity...which has gained him a character for courage and probity."[23] Over the eight years, his opinion of Ruggles deteriorated further, in 1774 hyperbolically claiming that Ruggles was "held in utter contempt and derision by the whole continent."[24]

The Crown, of course, rejoiced at the obstinacy of its now greatest defender, and in reward appointed Ruggles inspector of unclaimed lands in New Hampshire, a sinecure.

How best to understand Ruggles—as loyal subject, or devil's advocate? However we may judge him at this decisive juncture, two facts are certain: he was fully cognizant of the step he had taken, and given that his political powers of acumen were second to none, and in light of the determined course which his future actions would take, he had at least a strong inkling of the ramifications. Had he been a delegate from a less influential colony, his dissent would have made few waves. As a representative from the colony leading the charge, and more to the point, as the congress president, his dissension was viewed by the progressively-minded as nothing short of startling. Overnight, Ruggles had catapulted himself to the status of pre-eminent Tory in a colony soon to be recognized as the most radical. Had Ruggles tried to regain favor with his increasingly dissatisfied fellow colonists (which he never attempted), it would not have mattered. His stance at the Stamp Act Congress became the albatross of his career.

Ruggles had crossed a threshold, but, more significantly, had closed the door behind him, preventing any hope of his return to that happier world, meanwhile barring the entry of most of his family into the new one.

CHAPTER THREE

And Lady Which I Much Admired

In the eighteenth century, Thanksgiving was celebrated as one of the year's highlights, a holiday honoring the virtues of home and family. New Englanders had long shunned Christmas festivities.[1] The celebrations of the fall harvest and winter solstice were joined in the Pilgrim holiday, observed quietly as a people not long descended from the first Puritans. Children received new clothing, either homespun, or for the wealthy, sewn by a seamstress, to be worn not only for the holiday weekend, but for district school which resumed the following Monday.[2]

Bathsheba and Joshua's nuptials took place either during the last week of 1765, or a week later, when they were recorded. Marriages in early New England were modest affairs. Plans were initiated only shortly before the big day, and barely a week lapsed between the granting of invitations (handwritten or word-of-mouth) and the ceremony. A guest's absence was hardly a faux pas—members of the groom's own immediate family were often not present. (As late as 1842, Nathaniel Hawthorne's family absented themselves from his wedding in Boston). There were no bridal attendants.[3] Bathsheba's wedding gown, of a delicate shade (white was rare) was likely fashioned of brocade, velvet and plush.

A bonnet completed the ensemble, veils being the exception until late in the century.[4]

Like most contemporary ceremonies, that of Bathsheba and Joshua likely occurred in the bride's home. Although ministers were increasingly called upon (necessitating midweek weddings, the ministers' weekend schedules devoted to worship), couples generally preferred to be wed by a magistrate or Justice of the Peace.[5] In this instance, General Ruggles probably not only gave Bathsheba away to Joshua, but likely united them as well.

Wedding memories of one Mary Guion from the turn of the next century provides details of the typical early American wedding. On a Tuesday afternoon in February, the wedding guests assembled, comprising the groom's parents, siblings, "and eight others."[6] The ceremony was performed an hour later, followed by dinner, with tea in the evening. The next day, a party and dance were held in the Guion home. Families visited the newlyweds in the weeks afterward. Honeymoons, viewed as extravagant, were rare.[7] Besides, there were chores to be done and deals to be struck. In contrast, funerals, as we shall see, were much more elaborate affairs.

Joshua Spooner brought his bride to Brookfield, already familiar to Bathsheba as the home of her sister Martha Tufts, only a few miles from the newly established Ruggles estate in Hardwick. Like many ambitious men of his class and time, Joshua, seeking his fortune during one of the most unstable decades since the colony's founding, turned chiefly to land speculation. For a century-and-a-half, land had been regarded as the most precious, most reliable asset, easily attained by men like John Hancock who amassed huge holdings, or on a smaller scale, by the local pewtersmith or cooper.

Borrowing and lending were rife among all classes. The turbulent economy drove many to pursue land as a hedge against rampant inflation; when investing, they usually turned to their neighbors, continuing the tradition of mutual dependence. Any financial gain so won usually encouraged further speculation.

As evidenced by records at the Worcester County Registry of Deeds, Joshua Spooner's name appears on no fewer than twenty transactions. Between 1765 when he purchased one-hundred-and-seven-acres from John and Thankfull White through 1777, Joshua acquired, in Brookfield alone, over fifteen hundred acres, acreage nearly twice that of New York's Central Park.[8] Since hard labor (at great cost) was needed to clear such vast properties, much of it remained untended—only a few acres were cultivated. Most of Brookfield's unimproved woodlots were used for little more than firewood.

For over three years, Spooner restricted his transactions to purchases. What was the source of his funding? The answer may relate to a second question: Why did Joshua marry a woman so distant from his native Boston? It is likely that General Ruggles offered Spooner generous cash inducements to convince him to settle in Brookfield where father and favorite daughter would never be far apart, at least when he was not attending business in Boston. Evidence suggests that Joshua and Bathsheba began married life as innkeepers. The 1765 purchase from the White family included a building later known as the Colonel John M. Fisk House, which contained sixteen rooms.[9] It was natural that Joshua and Bathsheba should operate a tavern as her parents had with such success a dozen years earlier—might Timothy and his wife have arranged and funded the purchase?

Whether desperate for ready cash, or as a means to indulge further speculation, Spooner began selling property in 1769, and continued buying and selling for the next nine years.[10]

The Spooners may have owned a tavern which was located in the heart of Brookfield (now West Brookfield) by the town common, near the Old Post Road, linking Boston and New York. Its location was ideal. By the 1760's, Brookfield, the third oldest and one of the largest towns in the county, boasted a population of about twenty-five-hundred (compared with eighteen thousand in Boston), making it substantially larger than Worcester. Like Worcester, its beginnings were tenuous. In 1660, a group of men from Ipswich (north of Boston) requested and received from the General Court a tract of land six miles square.[11] One speaker on the occasion of Brookfield's bicentennial celebration on July 4, 1860, reminded his audience that the landlust of men

> ...from all the seaside settlements [whose] impulse for a westward and inland migration carried nearly all of the second generation from the half-furnished and half-protected homes of their fathers, into the deep wilderness... House lots, in the maritime settlements, were not broad enough for youth with the blood and birth of Puritan Pilgrim stirring in them...[12]

The town of Brookfield, established in 1673, was deep within hostile Indian territory, thirty-five miles from Marlborough to the east, barely closer to Springfield to the west. In 1675, during one of the first attacks of King Philip's War, the Nipmucks had slaughtered settlers at Mendon, forcing a meeting between Capt. Edward Hutchinson of Boston, the governor's representative, and several Sachems (tribal chiefs) at Brookfield, many miles west.

Hutchinson traveled with a troop of about twenty men to the rendezvous site, two miles from town.

The sound of birds and insects buzzing in the warm August sunlight greeted their arrival. Threading through a narrow passage between a steep hill and thick swamp, they were ambushed by several dozen Nipmucks who shot eight of their company, including Capt. Hutchinson, who died two weeks later. The remaining men fled back to Brookfield using a secondary path, and by the time the Nipmucks had gained ground, the alerted townspeople were gathered in a house above the village, a structure fortified by only a pile of logs in front and feather beds against the inside wall. In terror, they watched as their homes were torched—not even barns or outhouses were spared.[13]

Over the next forty-eight hours, the villagers' frustrated the raiders' continued attempts to burn them alive with a hail of fire arrows. Finally, as the third afternoon drew to a close, the Nipmucks filled a cart with hemp, and setting it ablaze, thrust it through the gates. Capt. Thomas Wheeler of Concord, second in command, bore witness later to the providential shower which doused the flames. Even more luckily, Major Willard arrived with nearly fifty men, having been alarmed by friendlier natives further east. The Nipmucks opened fire. Fleeing, they burned the remaining buildings and killed the livestock which had sought refuge on the hilltop. Despite Maj. Willard's heroism, the General Court censured him for marching the thirty miles to Brookfield, neglecting his other mission.[14] Brookfield lay abandoned for over a decade before being resettled.

Three generations later, Joshua and Bathsheba Spooner were welcomed into the town's highest social circle. The Spooner name was respected among merchants, but that of Ruggles—war hero, Speaker of the House, Chief Justice—one could not have ascended much higher in 1766. Of course, the general's name, honored by those who remained firmly loyal to the Crown, was now pronounced with venom by an increasingly bitter segment of the population for whom it represented appeasement, and later, betrayal.

In happier eras, the young couple might have seemed destined for a charmed life. How more cruelly indifferent could fate have been than to see the scion's favorite daughter married off the same year as his political condemnation? Bathsheba, despite her father's difficulties, never lost her love and respect for him, through these and still more painful trials to follow.

Bathsheba's great beauty was recorded by two contemporaries, one of whom visited Hardwick the year of her marriage. Hardwick boasts one of the nation's oldest country fairs, begun three years before the Spooners' wedding. Brigadier Ruggles appears to have been the guiding hand behind its formation, the fair serving as a showplace for his advances in horticulture and animal husbandry. A friend of Ruggles, John Rowe, whose diary of the years before and during the Revolution was published over a century after his death, entered under May 22, 1766

> ...Breakfasted with the Brigadier and went to Hardwick Fair where there were a large company of people. Dined at Brigadier Ruggles with a very large Company among them Mr. Joshua Spooner and lady which I much admired also Miss Betty Ruggles...[15]

Aside from singling out Bathsheba as object of his attention, the reference to Joshua may also indicate her husband's prominence as a man of bearing and distinction.

Along with the occasional fair, musters were popular celebrations, held each spring and fall. Mock skirmishes and real one-on-one battles vied for attention alongside booths and peddlers offering favorites such as gingerbread, or rare treats such as oysters, all washed down with a deluge of rum. Con artists made a flourishing trade before fleeing to the next town. The annual May sheep shearing offered further opportunity for revelry.[16]

As a lady with apparently considerable means at her disposal, Bathsheba, while not escaping entirely from the exhausting demands of a colonial housewife, was likely blessed with an ample supply of servants. The list of chores endured by less prosperous women of her time was prodigious—gardening, canning, cooking, cleaning, sewing, tending animals, butchering, dyeing, chopping wood, tending the fire, drawing the water, marketing, milking, baking, knitting, berry picking, wool spinning, quilting, churning, laundering, ironing, brewing—and all of this before the first child made its appearance.[17] The gentlewomen painted by Smibert and Copley in their resplendent silks and taffetas first strike the viewer as having little more to do than plan elegant dinner parties—and sit for portraits. Evidence suggests a different reality, one which placed upon the affluent some of the same burdens carried by their more humble peers. Despite assistance from housekeepers and stable hands, wealthier women found it necessary to pitch in due to the sheer number of labor-intensive duties.

Was Bathsheba so occupied? If in fact she and Joshua operated a tavern, she had little time for herself, running the business during her husband's frequent absences. We have no information with which to evaluate her role as housewife during these early years of marriage. Later, however, we know that the Spooners employed at least four servants, and evidence shows that they ran errands, maintained the horses, cooked, served food, cleaned, ironed, and watched the children. While it may have been typical of patrician women to share in the tasks, in this realm as in others, Bathsheba cannot be judged by typical standards. Further, it will be shown that she did not lack inventiveness in finding alternate ways to occupy her time. In the final analysis, one fact is clear: Bathsheba was glaringly atypical.

If she had been a tavern keeper, Bathsheba played a part as indispensable then as computers play today. Taverns served as social centers, mailrooms, sources of news and gossip, even as venues for entertainment and business—and of course as welcome oases from travel, an affliction endured only by the most hardy.[18] Even short journeys promised long hours in a bone-rattling coach as it jerked its way along thickly mired, deeply rutted roads alternately choked with dust in the summer. Winter travel, at least by coach, was something best avoided altogether.

At a public house, the traveler might witness a court session, muster, election—even wax works and freaks, ventriloquists, concerts, and lotteries. On Sundays in winter, they were especially popular sites. Following morning services, worshippers fled the frosty meetinghouse to warm themselves before the afternoon sermon and prayers which could last four more hours. Blazing fireplaces welcomed churchgoers eager for a mug or two of flip, a beer, egg and nutmeg concoction spiked further with rum, and sweetened with molasses or dried pumpkin, often scorched with a red-hot iron poker for an even more bitter, earthy flavor. Back in church, away from the fire, footstoves were popular with women, but considered too dainty an indulgence for the man of the household, who often brought the family dog along to lie at his feet. Should Rover become boisterous during the service, the appointed dog whipper or dog pelter appeared pewside to expel the offending mutt.[19]

In August of 1766, about eight months into her marriage, Bathsheba became pregnant, and typically would have relied upon other women in her family. Martha was close by, young Elizabeth lived next door in Hardwick, and her favorite sister, Mary, though eighteen miles distant in Worcester, may have assisted. If sweltering, low-ceilinged New England homes made pregnancy a trial during the summer, winter pregnancies must have been especially trying, a season even more cruel to children. The kitchen evolved as center of the home by its constant activity, as well as being the only comfortable room between November and March. Icy blasts shook both great chimneys and loose windows. A roaring fire's benefits were limited to a range of three feet from the hearth. Cotton Mather noted in his diary that the ink froze in his pen as he wrote near the chimney. Sap, forced from the blazing wood, sizzled briefly before freezing at the end of the log. Fluffy featherbeds and weighty bed curtains made sleep barely tolerable. Another diarist south of Boston observed that a tub of water placed on the bedroom hearth had frozen solid overnight—in front of a blazing fire.

Only relations between London and Boston were chillier in the late 1760's. Although Parliament had nullified the Stamp Act, in 1765-66 the Quartering Acts were instituted, which obligated each colony to transport, feed and quarter British soldiers in barns, taverns, and in a later stipulation which especially provoked the colonists, if unoccupied houses were unavailable, in private homes.

In early April of 1767, Bathsheba gave birth to Elizabeth, who shared the name of her youngest aunt. The delivery was likely attended by Bathsheba's three sisters, and by neighboring women as well, at least one of whom served as midwife. As mother-to-be, Bathsheba was expected to provide (aptly named) groaning cakes and groaning beer to her attendants, who in turn offered emotional and physical support.[21] Since colostrum was considered unhealthful for days following the birth, one of the ladies took on the role of wet nurse. Prior to delivering her child, the expectant mother was sometimes offered the same milk, regarded as an antidote against difficult birth.[22] Men, while providing some assistance during the onset of labor, were always out of sight. Childbirth was one arena over which women exercised complete control, although in the decades to follow, ministers and physicians played an increasingly central role.

In May of that year, the town of Worcester requested that its representatives to the General Court work to "obtain a law to put an end to that unchristian and impolitic practice of making slaves."[23] It was the first step on the path toward a Worcester court decision seventeen years later which would contribute to the abolition of slavery in Massachusetts, an institution incompatible with the Patriots' struggle for their rights, and eventually, liberty.

Charles Townshend followed Lord Grenville as Chancellor of the Exchequer in 1767, and pushed through Parliament the acts bearing his name. Their enforcement would never trouble him, as he died days before they took effect. The Board of Customs Commissioners was established in Boston to assist tax collection as required by a revenue act, which now levied duties on lead, oil colors, glass, paper, and tea. Customs officials could use Writs of

Assistance to inspect at will warehouses, even private homes for contraband. Vice admiralty courts were now authorized to try offenders without benefit of jury. As a final insult to the colonists, a portion of the revenues collected were reserved to pay the officials' salaries, circumventing the authority of the General Court, an especially grievous measure, considering how long the colonies had struggled to maintain control of officers' pay. In 1768, the royal governor dissolved the General Court.

In 1850, Worcester hosted the country's first national women's rights convention (the 1848 Seneca Falls convention cast a smaller net). That collective indignation, however, was not the town's first such expression. In 1768, several Patriotic ladies of Worcester held their own "women's rights meeting", and agreed to a tea boycott, substituting a native shrub to create "Labrador tea". Loyalist women reacted accordingly, refusing to swear off the beverage they enjoyed all hours of the day.[24]

As Bathsheba's role in the more narrow domestic sphere was transformed, that of her father's in the wider realm continued to worsen. That Ruggles closely sympathized with the Crown is not cause for remark—his ranks were legion. However, that he should have repeatedly sought opportunity to broadcast his sympathies, given his fame, put him in a unique situation. It may be that Ruggles was not aware just how deeply he could dig his own grave, or perhaps he did not care a whit for public opinion, an admirably heroic, if dangerous stance for any politician. Viewing him in the best light, Ruggles simply may have been convinced of his own rectitude.

Parliament had consistently sought to limit American manufacturing as a means to bolster British industry. In February of 1768, the General Court in Boston considered a measure to encourage local industry. The vote would have been unanimous, had it not been for the representative from Hardwick. A short while later, the assembly debated the subject of colonial representation in Parliament. Timothy's old comrade (now chief opponent), James Otis, argued the inseparability of representation and taxation.

Ruggles interrupted Otis. "When representatives are to be sent," he sneered, "I would like to be given the privilege of recommending a merchant who would transport them to England for half of what they would sell when they got there."[25] A year later, already showing signs of insanity, James Otis suffered a blow to the head during a brawl with a British customs officer which only aggravated his seriously erratic behavior. Ruggles was robbed of one of his favorite sparring partners, and the Patriots of Massachusetts lost one of their most eloquent spokesmen. In 1783, he died from a lightning strike.

Later in 1768, in Worcester, Ruggles was again the lone dissenter during a vote to encourage local industry. Sounding a bit like Thomas Jefferson, he wished that Worcester County remain an agricultural region.[26] It was not a sentiment to be fondly remembered by local posterity, for within seventy years Worcester would be well on its way to becoming a key industrial center. Neither would his more entrepreneurial contemporaries have been pleased. Joshua Upham, one of Ruggles' few legal colleagues in the county, had just joined several men in Brookfield to build one of the region's first textile mills.

Timothy Ruggles was not a man to catch his breath once gaining momentum. That spring, the General Court circulated a letter to the other colonies protesting yet another act of Parliament which imposed further duties on imported goods. London, through Governor Bernard, demanded that the assembly rescind the resolution which had inspired the letter. By a vote of ninety-two to seventeen, the representatives refused, with Ruggles leading the charge for the minority.

The Spooners celebrated the birth of their first son, Joshua, in late February of 1770. Barely two weeks later, on the evening of March 5, a group of young Bostonians taunted, then hurled snowballs at a lone British guard outside the customs house (other disturbances nearby contributed to the general tension). Reinforcements arrived to restore some order, who in turn were pummeled with snow, even clam shells. Someone (it was never determined who) shouted "Fire!"; the British shot into the crowd, killing five and wounding several others. The circumstances of the attack may have taken many by surprise, but such violence had been long predicted. Watching the victims' funeral procession, the Rev. Mather Byles commented, "They call me a brainless Tory, but tell me...which is better—to be ruled by one tyrant three thousand miles away, or by three thousand tyrants not a mile away?"[27]

For their role in the shooting already propagandized as the Boston Massacre, Captain Thomas Preston and eight of his soldiers were indicted for murder, and tried in October of 1770. John Adams, growing less sympathetic toward Britain, nonetheless offered to represent the soldiers, outraged as he was by the trumped-up charges against the men. Robert Treat Paine, who eight years later would lead the prosecution against Bathsheba Spooner and her accomplices, represented the colony. Two of the soldiers received manslaughter convictions, and were branded on the hand and released. Seven others were acquitted, including

Preston. The incident inspired Paul Revere's fanciful engraving which aided splendidly in demonizing the British as wanton criminals throughout the colonies.

In 1771, Timothy Ruggles marked the end of his final term as representative. He was by this time, among Patriots, widely regarded as the colony's most notorious Loyalist (and among Loyalists, as an indefatigable defender), sharing that distinction with Governor Hutchinson and the Oliver family. The more Ruggles' standing among radicals plummeted, the higher it rose in the eyes of the Crown. That same year, Ruggles was appointed Deputy Surveyor of Woods. As a titular position requiring little effort, Ruggles was lavished with an astonishing salary of three hundred pounds.[28] All things considered, the general was well on his way to becoming the richest man in Worcester County. One more political appointment, his most controversial ever, would come his way, but his career in politics was finished.

CHAPTER FOUR

Jarring Strifes Between the Parties

Months later, the colony's first Committee of Correspondence was established in Boston by Samuel Adams, John's irascible cousin. While coordinating local resistance to the king, the committee was also created to maintain contact with Patriots throughout the colonies. Within two months, Massachusetts would boast eighty such groups, including those in Brookfield and Worcester. One Loyalist later referred to the committees as "...the foulest, subtlest and most venomous serpents ever issued from the egg of sedition."[1] Continually frustrated by Parliament and itching for a fight, these serpents were moving at an ever quickening pace from guarded dissent to open rebellion.

In 1772, Timothy Ruggles sold off nearly two-thirds of his land in Princeton to four different parties, including Joshua Spooner, who bought the lion's share of five-hundred-and-fifty acres.[2] It was certainly one of the most cursed tracts of land in central Massachusetts. The land which Ruggles had received from the king only eight years earlier as a reward for his military service was as much a magnanimous gesture as it was an opportunity for the legislature to finally be rid of it. A Mr. Plaisted rented the land in the early 1760's, in an attempt to establish a potash manufacture.

Potash, or potassium carbonate, a white, granular, water soluble powder, was used chiefly in the production of soap, glass, and potassium salts. In Massachusetts, and especially Worcester County, it was an important product. By the end of the Revolution, the state boasted over two hundred such ventures. Wood ashes were treated with water until the potash was exhausted, and from the lye a salt was produced through evaporation. The method was simple, and for many, its product lucrative. Mr. Plaisted, who had erected several buildings at the site, was not so lucky, and soon abandoned the property.

Ruggles would be the next owner. Though a gift from the General Court, the land was nevertheless taxable, as Ruggles discovered when he and several other landholders were asked to not only recruit the town's first schoolmaster in 1765, but to foot the bill for his salary as well. It is likely that Ruggles himself attempted to make a go of the potash works, and failed.[3] Why would Joshua Spooner have been interested in the losing venture? Although such liberality of spirit seems to contradict Joshua's frugality, he may have paid his father-in-law at least partially out of kindness, likely at the insistence of Bathsheba.

Was Timothy Ruggles liquidating his holdings? He had lost his position as representative, and certainly by this point had started to lose clients—and may have seen still more ominous writing on the wall. It has been suggested that Ruggles was trying to provide for his daughter in the short time he had left.

Even today, two-and-a-half centuries later, the property remains heavily wooded.

On February 26, 1773, John Spooner was born, living barely three weeks. In an era rife with infantile and maternal mortality, it was the only birth tragedy the Spooners would experience.

As with the earlier Stamp Act, Parliament withdrew the hated Townshend Acts. It was all in vain. By now, each side had largely adopted an all-or-nothing, mercilessly uncompromising attitude. Lord North, the very day of the Boston Massacre, had suggested that Parliament preserve one lone remnant from the Townshend measures, the tea tax, if for no other reason than to remind the colonists who was still boss. In 1773, the Tea Act was passed to strengthen the East India Company's monopoly, and late that year, two-hundred-and-fifty tons of tea made their way to America. As historians have pointed out, the Tea Act actually called for a reduction in the tax on India tea, allowing it to compete more realistically with cheap Dutch tea, which the Americans had been smuggling. The Patriots acted to protect their lucrative black market.

Meanwhile, the Committees of Correspondence continually increased pressure upon not only the king's most vocal supporters, but upon his most public henchmen as well, especially his customs officers. One witness has recorded the prolonged horror to which Jonathan Malcolm, a tidesman (an inspector who boarded ships) was exposed.

> He was stript stark naked, one of the severest cold nights this Winter, his body covered all over with Tar, then with feathers, his arm dislocated in tearing off his Cloaths, he was dragged in a Cart with thousands attending, some beating him with clubs and knocking him out of the Cart then in again. They gave him several severe whippings, at different parts of Town. This Spectacle of horror and

> sportive cruelty was exhibited for about five hours...They brought him to the gallows and put a rope about his neck saying they would hand him; he said he wished they would, but that they could not for God was above the Devil. The doctors say that it is impossible that this poor creature can live. They say his flesh comes off his back in stakes...[4]

The victim's wife and children witnessed the attack.

The excesses of zealots such as these (to be fair, tar-and-featherings were extremely rare) were decried by the vast majority of more temperate Patriots, men like John Adams, who wrote to Abigail after witnessing a similar assault.

> ...a mob...broke into [a Loyalist's] house, and rifled his papers and terrified him, his wife, children and servants, in the night. The terror and distress, the distraction and horror of his family, cannot be described in words, or painted upon canvas. It is enough to move a statue, to melt a heart of stone, to read the story. A mind susceptible of the feelings of humanity, a heart which can be touched with sensibility... for human misery and wretchedness, must relent, must burn with resentment and indignation at such outrageous injuries. These private mobs I do and will detest.[5]

Brookfield town records from the early 1770's reveal an increasingly sympathetic attitude toward the difficult situation endured by Bostonians. In May of 1773, a Patriotic committee was formed, and presided over by Jedediah Foster, a local justice who would play a key role in the future murder scandal. The committee recommended that

> ...the town...be ever ready to assist, and in every legal and proper way maintain those rights and liberties for our children, which with so much labor, blood and treasure was purchased by our ancestors, whose memory is and ought to be esteemed by us; and we hope, notwithstanding the

> attempt of our constitution, to deprive us of those rights, yet by a steady, firm and constant exertion we shall not finally be deprived of them...[6]

Three months later, the name of Joshua Spooner appears as a Brookfield selectman on a petition sent to the General Court. Within two weeks, the selectmen took the opportunity "to thank the town of Boston for their great care and vigilance in the Common Cause and look upon ourselves embarked in the same battle...let us...stand fast in the liberty wherewith Christ has made us free."[7]

A much popularized detail of the Spooner tale has been Joshua's Patriotic leanings which were incompatible with Bathsheba's sympathies, a situation which gave rise to domestic tension. A contemporary noted in his memoirs of the Revolution that Bathsheba "was remarkable for attachment to the Royal cause, although Mr. Spooner was decidedly devoted to the opposite interests."[8] Joshua's signature as selectman during the stormy months of 1773 is the only bit of evidence we have of his political beliefs, which does seem to suggest that he was in fact a Patriot.

The relationship between Bathsheba's father and Joshua has never been addressed—Joshua's purchase of the largest share of Ruggles' land in Princeton is the only instance of their names being mentioned together, besides the earlier Hardwick dinner party. While it does not appear that Joshua ever faced any serious financial difficulties (although as a land speculator he was as susceptible to the erratic economy as anyone), his income in no way approximated that of his father-in-law. What would the up-and-coming entrepreneur have thought of one of the colony's premier Tories as he luxuriated at his Hardwick estate? Did Ruggles continue to provide for Bathsheba once married?

We should pause to consider the extraordinary blend of elements comprising the relationship between Timothy and his wife, Joshua and Bathsheba Spooner: a legendary, rich Tory mouthpiece now politically marginalized, a spouse with whom he fiercely quarreled, an ambitious Patriot/speculator, and, as will soon be demonstrated, a Tory woman of dangerously erratic character. It was a volatile mixture, needing only the flames of war and passion to ignite.

Meanwhile, tons of tea began arriving at colonial ports. New York and Philadelphia merchants refused to accept the cargo; in Charleston, tea made its way no further than the warehouses. In Boston, three shipfuls arrived. The captains agreed not to unload any, but Governor Hutchinson refused their departure before the levy was paid.

News of the governor's extraordinary move raced through the colony. At a December 3 meeting in Brookfield, Judge Foster and his aggrieved Patriots were spitting fire.

> ...We think it our indispensable duty in the most public manner, to let the world know our utter abhorrence with the last and most detestable scheme in the introduction of tea from Great Britain, to be peddled out among us by which we were made to swallow a poison more fatal in its effects to the national and political Rights and Privileges of the People of this country than ratsbane would be to the national body...we will not, by any ways or means, knowingly encourage or promote the sale or consumption of Tea, whatever, subject to a duty, payable in America, but all persons, whoever they may be, who shall be concerned in a transaction so dangerous, shall be held by us in the utmost contempt, and be deemed enemies to the country...[9]

On the evening of December 16, 1773, the Patriots of Boston acted.

Two weeks after the Boston Tea Party, about thirty of Worcester's leading Patriots met to form the American Political Society, which, in theory, was formed to counter Worcester's many prosperous Tories; it was, in reality, an elaborate spy network. The society was determined to maintain strict secrecy, as detailed in its by-laws.

> One...That no discourse or transaction in any of our meetings shall be communicated or divulged to any person or persons not belonging said society...[if dishonored] he or they shall be punished with expulsion ...Nine: [any man choosing to terminate his membership will promise the society] that he will inviolably keep all the secrets of said society as faithfully as if he still belonged to it...Ten: that each particular member binds Himself by the ties of honor, virtue, truth, sincerity and every appellation that is dear to him in this life...[10]

For nine years, the stakes had gotten higher and higher, and in the spring of 1774 the tug of war between Britain and the colonies lurched violently from the colonists as Parliament enacted a set of laws, the severity of which had never been witnessed in the new world. The port of Boston was sealed. Any person accused of murder while resisting arrest would be tried in England. The quartering of troops was given new authority. Quebec's boundaries were extended into the Ohio River Valley—and especially galling to Congregationalists, religious tolerance was granted to Canadian Catholics. Finally, in Massachusetts, the government was brought under tighter royal control—even town meetings could now be regulated.

And Timothy Ruggles would play his part for the last time in Massachusetts politics. To be labeled a Tory during the spring of 1774 was a charge borne freely by only the most adventurous.

To willingly accept from George III an appointment which symbolized above all others one's complete contempt for the Patriots' cause was outrightly foolhardy, even suicidal. As the colony's government realigned more firmly to the Crown, the royal governor's councillors would no longer be chosen by the General Court, but by the king himself—men known as Mandamus Councillors, among them Timothy Ruggles.

The rebels unofficially declared open hunting season upon such men, considered fair game in a colony reeling toward anarchy. Who, after all, was in control? For Timothy and his comrades, the situation had become untenable. Fight was no longer an option, flight the only choice for most obdurate Tories. In 1774, Boston was the only town still safe for Loyalists, fortified as it was by so many of His Majesty's troops. The capital provided sanctuary for most of the newly appointed Mandamus Councillors.

That May, at the bridge in Hardwick, Timothy Ruggles sat upon his horse, and for the last time, scanned the village whose land his family had purchased nearly a century ago. The townspeople surrounded horse and rider, most prominent among them Benjamin Ruggles, his younger brother by two years, "between whom he and [Timothy] had always existed the tenderest fraternal attachment."[11] Each now represented opposite poles of the political spectrum; enmity had fractured the familial bond.

Benjamin pleaded with Timothy not to take the oath for office in Boston. Upon Timothy's refusal, he swore his own oath, pledging that his brother would never return to Hardwick alive.[12] With one last glance toward Benjamin, Timothy pulled his horse's reins to the left, and leading the animal through the taunting, hateful crowd, headed east.

So did Timothy Ruggles bid Hardwick farewell. His wife remained behind.

By now, the Spooners had relocated three miles to the town's east side (now Brookfield), their tavern days behind them. Bathsheba had only recently determined that she was pregnant with her fourth child. It is easy to imagine her state of mind. A very attractive woman still in her twenties, Bathsheba spent much of her time at home with two children under the age of eight. Most of her neighbors were Patriots, and even if she could have kept her political beliefs to herself—which, apparently, she could not—whenever any of these neighbors met her, their recognition of her was less Bathsheba Spooner than Bathsheba, daughter of Timothy Ruggles. It was impossible to picture Bathsheba outside the sphere of her alternately celebrated/vilified father. Timothy had been, and would remain the only man she had known who had towered above her, a kindred spirit whose hubris had formed much of her own fiery character.

In late eighteenth-century America, more attention was paid to the recorded thoughts of men than to women. At the same time, journals and letters written by women are plentiful. How can we explain the fact that not a shred of communication survives between Bathsheba and her mother? No one has ever suggested the slightest affection between the two; the absence of such a suggestion seems to go beyond a mere attempt to portray her personality strictly within the confines of her father's, whose personality was everywhere. The wife of Timothy Ruggles was rich, high born, likely well-educated for a woman of her time, mother to fifteen children, wife to two prominent men, tavern keeper, and lady of the largest estate in northern Worcester

County. Not one letter? Even during the worst trials of Bathsheba Spooner's life, glaringly public trials unlike those endured by any other woman, not a word between mother and daughter has been preserved, despite the volume of news reports, letters, journal entries, etc. which remain. Bathsheba was very much her father's daughter, and his permanent departure from the county left her dangerously isolated, an isolation not lessened even by her three sisters' proximity. Joshua was rarely at home, and when he was, his presence likely made their estrangement all the more difficult. One contemporary noted that

> ...[Bathsheba's] hostility to her husband was fostered in hatred greater than could be owing to mere political difference of opinion. Her odium of him must be truly desperate, and a reflection arises of the mischief frequently produced by jealousies, and jarring strifes between the parties in the wedded state. The blessing of connubial unanimity is great indeed, but the misfortunes of discord in the married condition, cannot be described. As in the case of the Spooners, it generates vengeful distractions, and death itself in all its terrors! This discord by degrees begets deadly feuds.[13]

A Brookfield neighbor repeated often-heard gossip. "Very little Harmony and cordiality has subsisted between her and her husband for many years—She has long cherished a hatred in her bosom."[14] Writing in early 1778, what did "long" indicate? Two years? Ten? For how long were they pitted one against the other, spite adding to contention, bitterness to grief? Other externals poisoned relations further: rampant inflation, high taxation, scarcity of goods, etc.

The summer of 1774 generated far more heat than light in the political arena. Tensions in New England were climaxing. That

July, in the village of Worcester, the Rev. Thaddeus Maccarty, pastor of Old South, preached what would become his best-remembered sermon, one which railed against the king for so harshly punishing Boston. Aware also of the sufferings endured by Worcester Loyalists, he decried a growing spirit of intolerance.

> Civil liberty it is acknowledged is a most valuable enjoyment, and what all are earnestly desirous of...And as everyone is desirous of it himself, so everyone ought to be willing that his neighbor should enjoy it. But is it acting a consistent part to vilify and reproach others, because they take that liberty which God and nature has given them to think and speak differently?[15]

Few New Englanders, at least the vocal ones, would adopt such a conciliatory tone in the months to come. Maccarty proved himself as one who practiced what he preached. He could never have predicted that within a few years he would be, excepting her sister, Bathsheba Spooner's best confidante.

Virtually every Massachusetts town was divided against itself, Tory against Patriot. In few towns, however, were the lines of demarcation so sharply drawn as in Worcester. The spirit of acrimony between the two camps was made all the more intense by the town's relative isolation. Boston, Salem, Plymouth—these were population centers on the coast, well-infiltrated by British spies. In Worcester, the Patriots held free reign, as General Thomas Gage, the last royal governor of Massachusetts, described in a letter to the Earl of Dartmouth the year of Gage's appointment, 1774.

> In Worcester, they keep no terms, openly threatening resistance by arms; have been purchasing arms, preparing them; casting balls; and providing powder and threaten to attack any troops who oppose them. Mr. Ruggles, of the new council, is afraid to keep his seat as judge of the inferior

> court which sits at Worcester, on the sixth of the month, and I apprehend that I shall be obliged to march a body of troops into that country, and perhaps Into other townships, as occasion happens to preserve peace...[16]

More troublesome to Worcester's Patriots than Ruggles' inferior court was that of the superior court, with Peter Oliver as Chief Justice, a Loyalist whose notoriety was barely second to that of Ruggles. As the only superior court justice to openly defy the colonial legislature by accepting a bounty from the Crown, Oliver now faced impeachment. In Worcester, a grand jury was impaneled to sit with Oliver at the next session of the superior court, headed by blacksmiths Timothy and Joshua Bigelow. A year later, Timothy would lead the farmers of Worcester eastward following news of the Battle of Concord.

The grand jury sent a letter of protest to the justices

> We, the subscribed, being returned by our respective towns to serve as jurors of inquest for this court, beg leave humbly to inform your honors that it is agreeable to the senses of those we represent, that we should not empanel, or be sworn into this important office, provided Peter Oliver, Esq. sits as chief justice of this court...[17]

Oliver never showed.

Worcester's Tories were coming to the realization that they were a loyal minority surrounded by an ever-testier band of Patriots, enduring a siege many miles removed from His Majesty's troops who could or would do little to protect them. At a March town meeting, it was voted that "some action be taken" in response to yet another tea tax measure, and a committee recommended that all transactions involving tea be suspended, a suggestion decried by the town's Loyalists.[18] Forty-three of them gathered at the King's Arms Tavern, their favorite rendezvous.The site was undoubtedly familiar to Bathsheba, located but a half-mile from the estate of Mary Green, her sister. Led by James Putnam, John Adams' former mentor, the Tories here signed their names to a petition now known as the Tory Protest. While accusing the Patriots of mistreatment, they also demanded that all Committees of Correspondence be disbanded. Considering the dangerous times, their action was unquestionably courageous.[19]

Their petition was rejected. As town clerk and prominent Tory (related to Bathsheba by marriage), Clark Chandler would not be so easily deterred, officially entering the Protest in the town's records. The American Political Society got word of his effrontery, and petitioned the town fathers to take appropriate action. On the 24th of August, it was voted : "that the town clerk do, in the presence of the town, obliterate, erase or otherwise deface the said recorded protest and the names thereto subscribed, so that it may become utterly unintelligible."[20] Clark Chandler complied, bequeathing to New England its best known such document, inkblots and all.

Not since the destruction of the town's second settlement following King Philip's War a century earlier had Worcester experienced such tumult. The atmosphere continued to worsen. On August 22, as related years later by Judge Oliver, a mob of nearly three thousand from surrounding towns gathered not long after sunrise, and chose a committee to call upon Mandamus Councillor Timothy Paine, demanding his resignation. The judge's home, then only partly built, still stands on Lincoln Street, very near the estate of Mary Ruggles Green, Bathsheba's sister. The ad hoc committee forced Paine's resignation, then accompanied him to the town common, where they joined the mob,

> ...a thousand of whom were armed. It being at the Time when the Court of Common Pleas was [preparing to sit] the Mob made a lane, and compelled ye Judges, Sheriff, and Gentlemen of the Bar, to pass and repass them, Cap in Hand, in the most ignominious Manner, and read their Disavowal of holding Courts under the new Acts of Parliament no less than thirty times in the Procession.[21]

One member of the committee read Paine's resignation on his behalf. Some protested that the judge should read it himself. Paine, panicking, insisted that the committee first protect him from the crowd, but they could not guarantee his safety.

"Tar 'n' feather 'im!" several shouted.

During the fracas, Paine was struck on the head, which sent his judicial wig flying. Handing it to a servant, he vowed never to wear one again, and returned home without further incident.

An amusing anecdote featuring host Timothy Paine and dinner guest John Adams dates from probably this period. When time for the toast, Paine raised his glass and declared "To the King!" The irascible Adams, snarling, raised his own glass "To the devil!" Paine glared at Adams.

His wife stepped in. "Now dear, as the gentleman has been so kind to drink to our king, let us by no means refuse to drink to his!"

Historians have recently called attention to Worcester's action against the courts as one of the earliest in colonial America to reject the authority of the king—a revolutionary act occurring eight months before the first shots at Lexington and Concord. Many local Tories, including James Putnam, the town's foremost attorney, would not wait for the next outrage, and fled to Boston. Today, on the city's west side, a narrow, twisting road, named Tory Fort Lane, runs from Tatnuck Square and meanders uncertainly toward the town of Holden. Late in the summer of 1774, near the end of the lane, some of Worcester's Loyalists fortified a rocky outcropping. With provisions on hand and weapons at the ready, a handful of men and women subsisted for three weeks, fearing for their lives. At last confident that the town's Patriots no longer endangered their safety, they retraced the four-mile path to their homes.

They received a cool welcome. A short time later, a general alarm was raised in the town, alerting the local militia to movements by British troops in and around Boston. The soldiers marched a mile or two east to Shrewsbury, where they halted upon learning that the danger had passed. Also in August, it was voted that all Tories were to be inspected for weaponry before traveling from town, and re-inspected upon their return.

On September 5, the first Continental Congress convened in Philadelphia, a gathering which had been originally proposed by long-suffering Massachusetts. The congress reiterated the rights of the colonists as British citizens, presented a list of grievances, and most militantly, agreed to ban all British imports until these grievances were addressed.

A day later, the doors to the Worcester County Courthouse were blocked by armed Patriots who refused to recognize justices appointed by the governor. The courts would not reopen until after the Declaration of Independence. Two weeks later, a convention of the Committees of Correspondence gathered, its laws now substituted for those of the suspended royal court. A request to recruit and train Minutemen was also adopted.

In October, a meeting of the General Court was canceled by Governor Gage, but the ninety representatives convened nonetheless as the Provincial Congress, with John Hancock as president. A new treasury was established to provide for a regular militia, Minutemen and weaponry. Timothy Ruggles had a paper circulated throughout the colony, denouncing these Patriots as "... bullies...a mob without order or discipline."[22]

Ruggles' letter provoked an immediate response. Late one fall afternoon, Ruggles' wife, the only family member still on the Hardwick estate, was terrorized by a band of Patriots who demanded entry. The intruders plundered the home of all its weapons, and as a parting gesture, poisoned one of the general's prize stallions.

Worcester's blacksmiths gathered in November to formally boycott any county residents still sympathetic to the king.

> We will not...do or perform any blacksmith's work, or business of any kind whatever, for any person or persons whom we esteem enemies to this country [including]... all councillors in this province appointed by mandamus... in particular, we will not do any work for Timothy Ruggles of Hardwick, John Murray, of Rutland, and James Putnam of Worcester, Esqrs., nor for any person cultivating, tilling, improving, dressing, hiring or occupying any of their lands or tenements...[23]

Capt.Timothy Bigelow, the town's militia leader and a blacksmith, recorded the boycott.

Three days before Christmas, Ruggles published in Boston an advertisement announcing his plan to organize a paramilitary organization, to counter Patriot aggression. His Loyal American Associates would

> ...assert their rights to freedom, in all respects consistent with the laws of the land from such rebellious ones as under the pretense of being friends liberty, [who] are frequently committing the most enormous outrages upon the persons and the property of such of his Majesty's peaceable subjects who for want of knowing whom to call upon in these distracted times for assistance, fall into the hands of bandits, whose cruelties surpass those of savages...[24]

On January 17, 1775, Joshua and Bathsheba Spooner welcomed a new Bathsheba Spooner into their less secure world, one of the last Bourne descendants to carry the name Bathsheba, and the Spooners' last child.

Only a decade had passed since their wedding. From the vantage point of that January, it must have seemed a century from 1765 when most colonists had been proud British subjects, and proud of their hero, Timothy Ruggles, at last returned to Hardwick. All eyes were now riveted upon the imminent cataclysm. For one family in Brookfield, the decade had left in its wake a malevolence whose darkest chapter would soon command its own audience.

CHAPTER FIVE

These Rebellious Wretches

Almost numb with exhaustion, the men dragged their way past Old South Church. It was five o'clock in the afternoon. The Worcester townspeople, in search of household fires for some relief from the early January cold, scurried past, paying no attention. Colonial towns were used to vagrants, the "strolling poor" who wandered from borough to borough in search of any work or charity the financially distressed colonists might offer.

Each man wore a brown, fringed hunting shirt or "wamus" with belt, and buckskin breeches; knit hose and leather buckskins provided the only protection for their lower legs and feet from the frost. Pigtailed wigs fell from beneath black felt tricorne hats. In fact, their clothing resembled that worn by the majority of colonial militiamen, described in one source as "shaggy hunters." Looking no different from the dozens of farmers they had passed on the road from Boston, the men marched the forty miles through Cambridge, Watertown and eventually Framingham, Southborough and Westborough into Shrewsbury. While in that last town, they "...were obliged to stop and sketch."[1] Now in Worcester, Jones Tavern lay just ahead, two hundred feet on the left.

The men entered, stomping the snow from their buckskins, the flakes scattering in clumps upon the oiled floor aglow with reflected light. Captain William "Tory" Jones looked up. "He seemed a little sour, but it wore off by degrees and we found him to be our friend, which made us very happy."[2] The men awakened Sunday morning, and prudently chose not to venture out on the Sabbath "... because of meeting...nobody is allowed to walk the streets, during divine service, without being taken up and examined...we wrote and corrected our sketches."3

That morning, innkeeper Jones proved even more hospitable, inquiring what the visitors might like for breakfast. Then he let slip the code phrase any good Loyalist would recognize.

"Could I offer you tea—-or perhaps something else?" "That", as one of the men later wrote, "was an open confession what he was: but for fear he might be imprudent we did not tell him who we were, though we were certain he knew it."[4]

Late that afternoon, as churchgoers from the village's north end returned home by horse and sleigh, they may have wondered, as they looked east, why two men who appeared to be farmers stood on the crest of Chandler (now Bell) Hill with sketchbooks in hand. The guests of Captain Jones, Captain Brown of the 53rd British regiment and Ensign DeBerniere of the 10th were surveying the village below, its layout viewed to great advantage from their lookout. General Gage, British governor, had sent them from Boston

> ...to examine the roads, note the distances from town to town, sketch the positions of the streams, heights, passes, and posts, and collect such topographical information as would be useful for the advance of a detachment.[5]

The men's reconnaissance mission included prospecting for a suitable site for a fort, one which Governor Gage hoped to build atop Chandler Hill, along the old road leading through Shrewsbury to Boston. Believing that their sketching had gone unnoticed, they returned to the tavern. About eight o'clock, Capt. Jones knocked on their door.

> "Sirs, there are two gentlemen below who wish to speak with you." "Who might they be?" one asked. "You should not worry. You will be safe with them." I would hope not," one replied, "We are only two gentlemen who have traveled to see the country—to stretch our limbs. Behaving ourselves In a proper manner, how could we meet with anything but civility?" Captain Jones interpreted their response as a refusal. "I shall return in a short while. You may, by then, have changed your minds." Jones returned an hour later. "The men have gone. They did, however, beg me to let you know—knowing that you are officers—that their fellow friends of the King in Petersham [a town in northwest Worcester County then known for an unusually large Tory population] have been disarmed by the rebels. They agreed that you should know that the same fate awaits those in Worcester loyal to the Crown."[7]

Jones shared a bottle of wine with his guests.

The conversation continued, incautiously perhaps, in a political vein. "Only a few Tories are aware of your arrival," Captain Jones offered. Brown cast DeBerniere a glance before responding, "It is very indifferent to us whether they do or not."[8] Later, however, he wrote that "We thought very differently." The men decided that they had stayed long enough, and resolved to leave early the next morning.

Shortly after dawn, Captain Jones served the men a breakfast of roast beef and rum "which was very necessary on a long march, and prevented us going into houses where, perhaps, they might be too inquisitive." Leaving by a road different from the one they had used earlier, the men were passing through Shrewsbury en route to Framingham when a rider on horseback overtook them. Pulling up closely, he examined each man "attentively, and especially me [Brown], who he looked at from head to foot, as if he wanted to know me again; after he had taken his observations, he rode off pretty hard."[9]

The rider was Timothy Bigelow (who would serve at Valley Forge, West Point and Yorktown, even one day having a mountain in Maine named in his honor), sent by the local Committee of Correspondence specifically to gather intelligence on the men. Worcester's store of rebel weaponry had been overestimated by General Gage, who was determined to march his troops to the village to seize them. A few days after they reconnoitered at Worcester, the British spies did the same in the area surrounding Concord, which also harbored contraband.

Details of the men's mission were revealed not until a discovery of a map of Worcester by Isaiah Thomas after the British evacuation of Boston in March of the next year. Which to attack—Worcester or Concord? Less than two weeks before the Battle of Concord, another British scout made his way to Worcester to verify caches of weapons hidden there. On his return to Boston, Gage asked if it were practical to march thousands of men to the village—given the difficult topography and finding "the inhabitants generally determined to be free or die that not one of them would get back alive."[10] Gage turned his sights instead upon Concord, earning that town its hallowed place in American history.

By late winter 1775, no Tory could feel entirely safe, even if, as in Brookfield, he wore a white collar. Most residents of

Massachusetts were Congregationalists, and most were Patriots (Timothy Ruggles and Peter Oliver the most famous exceptions), just as the vast majority of Anglicans were Loyalists. In a Brookfield parish neighboring the Spooners, Eli Forbes had been appointed its first pastor in 1750. By the late 1760s, his patriotism had become suspect. Called by the church council to plead his case, the majority voted against his dismissal. Their vote, however, did not satisfy the parish's radicals. One evening, they followed the pastor's chaise, hurling both stones and epithets. Shortly after, Rev. Forbes awoke one morning to find a bag of feathers and a pot of tar on his doorstop. He resigned on March 1, 1775.[11]

Two days before he dispatched Paul Revere on his famous ride, Dr. Joseph Warren, along with Worcester's Timothy Bigelow, advised America's renowned printer, Isaiah Thomas, to flee Boston with his press. As had Hancock and both John and Samuel Adams, Thomas' name had been placed on a most wanted list, and his days as a free man in Boston were numbered. Thomas, who would play a key role in publicizing the Spooner case, had been printing The Massachusetts Spy for the past five years in the over three-century-old building which today houses Boston's oldest restaurant, the Union Oyster House. British troops in the street below often shouted "Hang 'im high!" as they passed Thomas' second floor shop—few men had been so reviled by so many Loyalists for so long. Many years earlier, just around the corner, Benjamin Franklin had been apprenticed.

Activity about the British warships in Boston Harbor on the 15th of April all but confirmed suspicions in the colonists' minds that an inland expedition was imminent, with Concord as the likely target. The seizure of cannon and weapons was not the only objective. Hancock and Sam Adams were meeting at the Provincial Congress in Concord, and Gage had been ordered to arrest them.

On the moonless evening of April 16, Timothy Bigelow and others conveyed Thomas' press and types to Barton's Point on the Charles River, ferrying them to Charlestown. From there, Bigelow directed men and machine for forty miles until the safe haven of Worcester was reached, where Bigelow had the press set up in the basement of his home.

On April 18, the day before history was made, Bathsheba's father wrote to a friend in England of his plans to raise a regiment of fifteen hundred men to assist the king's cause.

> My heart leaps for joy to find the reception given by their lordships to my proposals...I have the most cordial inclination to contribute everything in my power to convince these rebellious wretches of their folly and wickedness in despising the best Government both in theory and administration that ever yet blest the earth...and if it causes me as many worrisome days and sleepless nights as five campaigns did in the last War, I pray God my constitution may endure it, and my Country will be happy if success attains his Majesty's aims, if not many of us will lose our lives, and be put out of our present miserable situation...[12]

Ruggles' son, John, also a Loyalist, had recently joined his father in Boston, fleeing the now unbearable political strife in Hardwick.

Despite sentiments so clearly expressed, one descendant claimed just over a century later that "there is nothing to show Ruggles ever crossed the line of a safe neutrality. It would have been widely known if he had."

Months later, with the backing of Major Gen. Sir William Howe, the British commander, Ruggles' ambition met with modest success, recruiting about two hundred Tories for his Loyal American Associates, most of whom were Boston merchants. Initially the associates were formed into three companies, all displaying a white sash around their left arms, with Ruggles at the helm. The second company's captain, James Putnam, was the same Putnam to whom John Adams had been apprenticed in Worcester decades earlier. The men never saw any military action.

Late in the morning of April 19, the dead and wounded lay by the Old North Bridge in Concord, repeating the scene witnessed earlier in the day at Lexington. The day's greatest carnage would be evidenced that afternoon along the road to Boston; the unusually warm April day felled many of the Redcoats not yet wounded. That evening, a total of nearly four hundred casualties from both sides were counted. Still, most colonists hoped for the restoration of their rights within the British Empire.

Those minutemen first answering the call from messengers Revere, Dawes, Prescott and others were from towns closest to the battle sites, such as Lincoln, Sudbury and Acton. As word spread and the battles subsided, men from more distant villages descended upon the British retreat. Finally, the most distant farmers and tradesmen, from Princeton, Salem and Quincy among others, joined their compatriots several hours after the last musket fire. By week's end, fifteen thousand had gathered, some destined to fall at the Battle of Bunker Hill in mid-June.

In Worcester, just before noon on April 19, rider Israel Bissell thundered through the village center, the horse dripping with sweat and bloody from spurring. "To arms! To arms! The war has begun!"

At Old South Church, the horse collapsed. Another was found, and the next day Bissell continued on toward Leicester. As the bell rang out the alarm, cannon were fired. Soon, over one hundred men were gathered. Capt. Timothy Bigelow paraded the ragtag troops about the green, then led the contingent toward Concord. En route, they learned of the British retreat, and changed their direction toward Boston. It is likely that the dispatch from Concord to Worcester, about thirty-seven miles, was the longest completed by one horse and rider that day.

Two days following the battles, twenty-nine of Worcester's Tories were disarmed, and forbidden from leaving town.

As one group of rebels headed from Worcester, another pair, John Hancock and Samuel Adams were heading toward the town, having escaped from the British only hours before the skirmish at Lexington. The men wandered between Middlesex and Worcester Counties, ignorant of the battles' outcomes.

Worcester, 24th April, 1775
Monday Evening

> GENTLEMEN [of the Committee of Safety]: Mr. S. Adams and myself, just arrived here, find no intelligence from you and no guard...Surely we ought to be supported...pray furnish us with depositions of the conduct of the troops, the certainty of their firing first...that we may be able to give some accounts of matters as we proceed, and especially at Philadelphia [at the Continental Congress]...Boston must be entered; the troops must be sent away ...Our friends are Valuable but our Country must be saved. I have an interest in that town; what Can be the enjoyment of that to me, if I am obliged to hold it at the will of General Gage, or anyone else?...Are Mr. [Robert Treat] Paine and Mr. John Adams to be with us? What are we to depend on? We travel rather as deserters, which I will not submit to. I will return and join you, if I cannot travel in reputation...Pray remember

> Mr. S. Adams and myself to all friends. God be with you. I am, gentlemen, your faithful and hearty countryman.
>
> John Hancock 13

Hancock and Adams remained in Worcester for three days before continuing on to the Continental Congress in Philadelphia. Earlier in the week, while fleeing Buckman Tavern on Lexington Green, Hancock realized he had left a trunkful of politically sensitive papers in his room. Paul Revere and John Lowell, Hancock's secretary, retrieved the trunk, now in the possession of the Worcester Historical Museum—minus the papers. (It is likely that the documents were destroyed by Sam Adams, who enjoyed a reputation for making incriminating evidence disappear).

As the famous revolutionaries lingered, their friend and compatriot, Isaiah Thomas, having briefly assisted Revere on his famous midnight ride, fought with the militia at Lexington. Following a brief visit to his family in Watertown, he walked the remaining forty miles to his new Worcester home. Within a few weeks, Thomas again had his press in operation, the May 3 edition serving as the thirteen colonies' chief source for information of the Revolution's first bloodshed.

One spring morning, soldiers broke into the Worcester residence of Timothy Paine, the Tory judge whose wig had been knocked from his head during the courthouse closure the previous November. Paine had abandoned the town months earlier, so the Patriots settled for his likeness, slashing a full-length portrait of the judge with their bayonets. On the twenty-third of May, over a year before the Declaration of Independence, when the majority of colonists still sought reconciliation, the selectmen of Worcester voted that if the Continental Congress should declare the American colonies independent of Great Britain, "we will support the measure with our lives and fortunes."[14]

Several men from the Ross family in Topsfield north of Salem, like thousands of their comrades throughout eastern Massachusetts, would answer the call on April 19. The family's youngest son, Ezra, was destined to play a central role in the Spooner saga.

On January 24, 1775, Captain Nathaniel Wade's company of minutemen signed their contract.

> We whose names are hereunto subscribed do voluntarily Inlist ourselves, as Minute Men to be ready for Military operation, upon the shortest notice. And we hereby Promise and engage, that we will immediately and each of us, provide for and equip himself with an effective fire Arm, Bayonet, Pouch, Knapsack, and Thirty Round of Cartridges, readymade. And that we obtain the skill of Compleat Soldiers, We promise to convene for exercise in the Art Military, at least Twice every week; and oftener if our officers shall think necessary.[15]

The fifty-four names undersigned included the four Ross brothers, Nathaniel, Benjamin, Kneeland and Jabez, Jr., the last substituting for an absentee. It would not be the family's first encounter with war. Jabez and Joanna lost their eldest son, Abner, sixteen years earlier during the French and Indian War. Coincidentally, his regiment fought alongside that commanded by Bathsheba's father, then Col. Ruggles, during the battle for Fort Edward.

The minutemen of Ipswich (the town to which the Ross family's land had originally belonged) and Topsfield received the call to arms hours after the first shots had been fired at Lexington.

Rather than join the retreat from Concord, already well underway, they marched the twenty-four miles south to Mystic (now Medford) into the night, to await further word.

A town historian from the late nineteenth century paints a dreamy evocation of old Ipswich.

> ...The diversity of hill and vale, of meadow and marsh, of woodland and field, of river, and pond, and brook—enhanced by the variety of the seasons; verdure and flower, the cattle upon the hillside and the husbandman in the field, the fruit...and the waving grass, the ripening apple and the purpling plum, the yellow corn and the nodding grain, and the enchanting beauty of our frost-painted forests, gratifies the eye, educates the heart and sheds over the mind a soft radiance of peperennial joy.[16]

At Newe Towne (Cambridge) in 1634, the region known as Aggawam was renamed Ipswitch "in acknowlegment of the great honor and kindness done to our people who took shipping there [the English town sharing the same name]."[17] Less than four years later, Sachem Sagamore, who had freely placed his people under Puritan rule in 1629, sold his remaining interest in the town for twenty pounds to Governor John Winthrop. A generation later, Daniel and Ezra "Rosse" were the first of the family descendants to appear in town records.

The wife of Jabez Ross, Lydia, whom he married in 1732, died a week after delivering her first child, who also died. Six years later, Jabez married his wife's sister, Joanna, and the couple settled on a farm near the Topsfield line to rear sixteen children.

Since the earliest days of New England, each colony encouraged group settlement and propagation of the faith by entertaining petitions from groups of twenty or more men who wished to resettle. A committee called the Viewers would select a site, which had to border another town's land. Once selected, the Viewers sought approval of the General Court. When approved, the petitioners then became the town proprietors, gaining title to the land. Each proprietor received his own lot, with three other lots always set aside, one each for the school, church and pastor.

In 1746 the General Court allowed some of west Ipswich and part of Rowley to become a distinct parish which, bordering Topsfield, was aptly named Linebrook. Jabez and Joanna Ross became devout members of the newly established church. In the twentieth year of their marriage, the Ross farmstead was annexed to Topsfield.

It is likely that most of the Ross farm, like most thereabouts, was a fruit orchard; any livestock and vegetables were for their own use. Fruit farms were generally profitable not from sale of the fruit, but rather its byproduct, alcohol. Besides applejack and cider (the latter New England's favorite beverage), other fruit yielded perry, brandy and wine. So valuable were these orchards of Cape Ann that a father in his will often divided the orchard among his children, even assigning specific trees to one child or another.

Typical of mid-eighteenth century homes on Cape Ann, the Ross dwelling would have been simple, each brick side laid against an inner partition, then covered with clay, and finally clapboards. Even in such humble homes, modest adornments could be found, perhaps Dutch tiles with scriptural embellishments surrounding the fireplace.

Just before the Civil War, an attorney described his native Topsfield as a village "...in a beautiful hollow formed by the rich and lovely hills, the surfaces of which are marked by that Verdancy, smoothness and uniformity which pleases the eye."[18] First settled in 1635, New Meadows (originally Sheweenemeady for native Americans) was incorporated as Topsfield in 1650, after the English town from which many of its settlers came. Linebrook, the former district of Ipswich newly named and annexed to Topsfield (and home to the Ross family), was described rather austerely by the Reverend William Bentley of Salem as he passed through in 1811.

> ...The general appearance of Line Brook is poor...We saw only an orchard and that an old one...Most of the lands were unenclosed and barren and the swamps were of no use being filled with small pines, small birches and alders... Away from the road some farms on favorite spots made a little better appearance. As we appoached the Turnpike some farms were in better condition but we soon passed to the moving sands which lay between Ipswich and this parish. It is generally considered the poorest division of Essex [County]. As it is the last place I have visited, it is the most destitute of the means of enriching a farmer...[the minds of the people] are of higher improvements than their barren country...[19]

If the reverend is to be taken at his word, it is no small wonder that the Ross brothers answered the call to arms rather than linger in so inhospitable a region. In the same entry, while asking directions to Linebrook (then popularly known as Firetown), Bentley writes "Never did I find so many opinions about the distance and course of any place."[20] Well over two centuries later, residents of Ipswich and Topsfield are still often at a loss to locate the area.

Ezra, the youngest surviving child of the Ross family, was not yet fourteen years of age at the start of the war. In a span of two weeks, the Revolution had siphoned a large share of his father's laborers.

It was a month before the planting season; pruning, transplanting, disease and insect control, grafting, and coping with uncertain weather lay in store. Likely due to his youth and the sudden lack of farmhands, Ezra would be the only son (besides eldest brother David, married and living elsewhere) not to join the soldiers' ranks in April and May of 1775. As the war dragged on and farming families bore the brunt of an increasingly smaller labor pool, military recruiters found it necessary to lower already modest standards. One ne'er-do-well was foisted upon a particular recruiter with the reminder that the hapless fellow "would do to stop a bullet as well as a better man, and as he was truly a worthless dog, the neighborhood would be much indebted...for taking him away."[21]

Four of the Rosses fought in the Battle of Bunker (actually Breed's) Hill in Charlestown on June 17, a battle that although won by the British proved the Americans to be a formidable force. A first lieutenant of the Ross brothers' company wrote home the next day.

Cambridge
June ye 18, 1775

Dear wife

I take this opportunity to inform you that I am well at Present. I would Just inform you that wee had a verrry hot ingagement yesterday. But God preserved all of us for which mercy I Desire Ever to be thankfull we have Bin Alarmed to Day But come to no Engagement it is all most Knight now. And we are going to Entrenching tonight therefore I Cannot be Pertickler. Dont be Discoredged I hope Wee shall be Carred thrue all out Diffilties and have abundant occasion to Prase the Lord together So no more at Present But remain your Loving Husband Till Death.

Joseph Hodgkins[22]

Ezra stayed on the farm through the growing season, helping further with the harvest and winter preparations, not enlisting until December of that year. Fruit needed to be picked and pressed, its juice bottled and sent to market. When snow covered the orchard, tools had to be repaired or made by hand, and livestock tended. Joanna Ross, now an elderly woman by eighteenth-century standards, would have been of little help in the orchard. Cooking, sewing, chopping firewood, slaughtering and preserving the meat, and washing and ironing kept her occupied from dawn to dusk every day but Sunday.

It must have been a trying eight months for Ezra. Not only were all of his brothers absent, but his sisters as well. Lydia, Ruth and Joanna were surely married by 1775, the youngest twenty-eight at the time, during an era when an unattached twenty-year-old woman was considered by many as past her prime. Martha, born two years after Joanna, had died in 1773 at the age of twenty-four, probably in childbirth. Except for hired hands who may have helped the impoverished Rosses, Ezra spent his days alone with his fifty-seven-year-old mother and nearly seventy-year-old father, sharing the backbreaking labor. Conscription may have looked attractive come December. Though only fifteen, it was not unusual to find boys his age as enlistees. Beyond his military history and role in the ensuing drama, little more is known about Ross. In the 1840's, Maj. Benjamin Russell of Worcester, recollecting his own childhood, recalled Ross as a handsome teen. Two brothers closest in age to him are listed in military records as average in height, and dark-complected, traits he likely shared. Also in the 1840's, another writer described Ross as "the best educated and the least hardened [of the criminals]...and altogether of the most interesting character...He was of respectable parentage...also prepossessing in his personal appearance."[23]

Ross' education was likely no better or worse than that of the average schoolboy. In his fifth year, the district of Linebrook erected its first schoolhouse, "on land two rods front and four rods deep [thirty-three by sixty-six feet], enfeoffed [freely donated] by Jeremiah Smith." Grammar, reading, spelling and "bookkeeping" were the favored subjects. Late in the century, the town fathers recommended that

> ...To read well in the Bible and spell should be necessary qualifications for entering as students in English grammar... the Chatechism of the Assembly of Divines with Dr. Watts explanatory notes and the Chatechism by the same author be continually used as much as three or four times a week according to the different grades of the scholars until... committed to memory...[24]

School was rarely in session. The schoolmaster, employed for nine months of the year, divided his time between three schools—Ross' school was open for only two months. Not until late in the next century did schools carry the cost of textbooks. As a poor farmer, the expense would have been no small burden for Jabez Ross to bear.

The first mention of Ezra Ross' name in military records is among a list of men in Col. Baldwin's regiment, men not actually in the Continental Army, but soldiers who had registered for only a year of service; the document is dated December 19, 1775, Peekskill, a town about fifty miles north of New York.[25] Ross would have seen little action or professional training until joined by Gen. Washington and several thousand troops.

Despite a political landscape that had grown increasingly hostile, many Tories managed to maintain some shred of normalcy. A few even dared to snub their noses at Patriotic convention.

In December of 1775, Peter Oliver, Jr., whose family had been scorned by the rebels, wrote from Boston to Elisha Hutchinson in London. "Your wife braves it out; by the last accounts from her in September she is President of Club comprised of eight ladies. They meet over a tea table once or twice a week, in opposition to the Rebels. They keep up their spirits strangely."[26]

Several weeks later the spirit of many Loyalists would undergo a severe test. Preparing to drive the British from Boston, the Americans accomplished their goal peaceably on St. Patrick's Day, 1776. General Howe, in the face of a severe nor'easter, chose retreat over battle. Besides the weather, the Americans had two military leaders behind the scenes to thank for Howe's retreat. In May of '75, Ethan Allen captured Lake Champlain's prize fortress, Ticonderoga. His demand that the British surrender the fort "in the name of the Great Jehovah and the Continental Congress" (as he recalled years later) was, in reality, according to vanquished Lieutenant Jocelyn Feltham, more prosaically worded as "I must have immediate possession of the fort and all the effects of George III." Duller, but more dignified than that which has come down to us from Vermont tradition, "Come out, you damned rat!"

The fifty cannon and tons of lead captured by Allen were heroically transported to Boston across two hundred miles of rough roads and thick snowdrifts by Henry Knox, an erstwhile Boston bookseller whose route took him through Brookfield and along Worcester's main thoroughfare.

Howe and the British left Boston, never to return, joined by eleven hundred of the colony's most intractable Tories. Destined for Halifax, Nova Scotia, many chose to resettle in Canada. The remainder—Timothy Ruggles, one of the most notorious—

eventually continued on to New York, which stayed safely in British hands until the war's conclusion.

Two months before his departure from Boston, per order of the Hardwick Committee of Correspondence, most of Ruggles' estate was auctioned off, a fate which befell the property of nearly three dozen Loyalists throughout Worcester County. All told, two-hundred-and-fifty Tories were the subject of some kind of official action in central Massachusetts. The Hardwick sale, held at the home of innkeeper Jonathan Warner who had served as a colonel during the Lexington/Concord alarm, disposed of twenty horses, thirty cattle, sheep and swine. Ruggles' wife, Bathsheba, was permitted to keep a parcel of the original estate, where she was joined by her son, Timothy, Jr.[27] Bathsheba Bourne Newcomb Ruggles' political leanings have never been addressed. We do know that the tavern she left behind in Sandwich, then owned by the children from her first marriage, had become that town's favorite Tory rendezvous.

The political leanings of her daughter would soon be made much more apparent.

CHAPTER SIX

An Invitation to Defile Her Marriage Bed

Late in the afternoon of July 4, Philadelphia printer John Dunlop published two hundred copies of the Declaration of Independence; early the next morning, several riders galloped out of the city, carrying a copy headed for each of the thirteen colonies. Nine days later, On July 14, a rider tore past Old South Church in Worcester en route to Boston, when he was waylaid by Isaiah Thomas. Upon hearing what news was destined for Boston, Thomas snatched the copy, and gathered the excited townspeople. Ascending the stairs of the meetinghouse, the Patriot journalist presented Worcester's citizens with the first public reading of the Declaration in New England. The town's Patriots celebrated the news at the Kings Arms Tavern, at one time the preferred gathering spot for the village's Loyalists. A grand toast was offered.

> ...George rejected and liberty protected! Sore eyes to all Tories, and a chestnut burr for an eyestone. Perpetual itching, without the benefit of scratching, to the enemies of America. May her enemies be laid at her feet. May the freedom and independence of America endure, till the sun grows dim with age, and the earth returns to chaos!"[1]

Thomas, never one to let a golden opportunity slip by, printed the Declaration in the July 17 issue of his Massachusetts Spy, adding another New England first to his credit.

General Ruggles and his fellow exiles arrived in New York in late August under the protection of General Howe and his fifteen thousand British and Hessian troops. The British set up their general headquarters on Staten Island, apparently joined by his second eldest son, John.

General Washington, immediately following Howe's evacuation from Boston, headed south to New York, expecting the British commander's arrival. The Americans were blessed to have Howe leading the opposition; over the next fourteen months, he would commit a series of missteps, any one of which if avoided might have clinched victory for George III. Ezra Ross likely took part in the months-long cat-and-mouse game in and around New York which characterized the war for most of late 1776, a dismal year for the American side. The year concluded more happily, the troops' morale reinvigorated with the surprise capture of Hessian forces at Trenton by Washington's men the night of December 26.

On the home front, rich and poor women alike continued to suffer from the lack of manpower. Abigail Adams, in Quincy just south of Boston, wrote in September

> Forty men...are now drafted from this town. More than half, from sixteen to fifty [years of age], are now in the service... how much we are thinned in this province...If it is necessary to make any more drafts upon us, the women must reap the harvests...I believe I could gather corn and husk it, but I should make a poor figure at digging potatoes...[2]

Husband John, though not drafted, waged the diplomatic fight. All but deified by Bay State Patriots, Adams was vilified by its Tories. His old nemesis, Peter Oliver, had left for Nova Scotia with the equally infamous Timothy Ruggles during the evacuation of Boston. Oliver, predictably, wrote harshly of Adams that year, citing Adams' Worcester experience as the cause for his change of character.

> ...after he was graduated, [Adams] was employed as a schoolmaster to both sexes, in a country town. This employment is generally the porch of introduction to the sacred office, in New England; but Mr. Adams chose to pass from this porch by the same way he entered and try his genius in the practice of law. He is a man of sense, and made a figure at the Bar; but whether nature had neglected him, or he had acquired, himself, and acrimony of temper by his...discipline, which he was remarkable for; certain it is, that acrimony settled into rancor and malignity—by having an absolute authority over children, he was determined to raise himself to raise himself to a superiority which he had no claim to; and he unguardedly confessed, in one of his sallies of pride, that "he could not bear to see anyone above him."[3]

Whatever deprivations Oliver may have endured in exile, they were nothing as endured by men of Ezra Ross' station. Camp conditions were atrocious. One of the best known journals from the Revolution is that of Elisha Fisher, who described a soldier's camp life in 1777, complaining of

> ...no tents, nor anything to Cook our Provisions in, and that was Prity Poor, for beef was very leen and no salt, nor any way to Cook it but to throw it on the Coles and brile it, and the warter we had to Drink and to mix our flower with was out of a brook that run along by the Camps, and so many a dippin and washin it which maid it very Dirty and muddy.[4]

At the war's commencement, it had been recommended that each soldier receive a ration of bread, beef, pork, salt fish, milk (or rice), spruce or malt beer, peas or beans, butter and vinegar, salt and molasses. Reality played the devil with such intentions. For one group of soldiers assigned to Benedict Arnold's ill-fated Quebec campaign of late 1775, the main (and only) course consisted of three dogs, including the captain's own mutt, "not excepting his entrails."[5]

For clothing, Washington suggested, in 1778, that each soldier receive "a waistcoat with sleeves, flannel, if to be had, two pair linnen overalls, one shirt, a black stock [neck cloth] of hair or leather, a small hat bound and a pair of shoes" among other necessities.[6] Written during the severe deprivations of Valley Forge, the troops' misery was likely shared by a majority of their comrades throughout the north. In Peekskill, New York, where Ross was encamped, Colonel Angell of the Rhode Island regiment wrote home to complain of the scandalous conditions. In the village, the townspeople referred to his men as "the Ragged, Lousey, Naked regiment."[7]

The camps festered with disease. As wretched as conditions were for the healthy, none suffered so greatly as the hospitalized. Soldiers had a ninety-eight percent chance of avoiding death in combat, but only a seventy-five percent chance of leaving the sickbed alive. Shelters were filled beyond capacity; sanitation was minimal, ventilation was poor (the tents' malevolent air was diffused by lighting pitch or tar), and bed straw was left unchanged corpse after corpse. Writing from Philadelphia in December of 1776, one Colonel Wayne described his hospital as a "house of carnage which Beggars all description, and shocks humanity to visit."[8]

Only the dead found reprieve, but even at its last, the body might still suffer indignities. Also in Pennsylvania, Lieutenant E. Elmer wrote in his journal of "a scene something diverting, though of a tragic nature."[9] Soldiers from New Jersey had dug two graves from the frozen earth, and returned with their bodies only to discover that Pennsylvania soldiers had used the holes to bury their own. A heated dispute ensued. The Pennsylvania regiment refused to disinter their men, so the New Jersey soldiers dug up the offending corpses, throwing them under a heap of brush and stones.

At the start of the Revolution, the study of medicine was still in its infancy; the first medical school (at what is now the University of Pennsylvania) was barely a decade old.

Home remedies were the rule, their dubious efficacy notwithstanding. One physician's wife diagnosed a soldier's ailment as "gravels in the kitteney" and prescribed "a quart of ginn and a tea dish of muster seed, and a handfull of horseradish roots—steep them together and take a glass of that every morning." It was determined that the patient "took benefit by it."[10]

Fevers of various types with ill-begotten names such as putrid, hectic and bilious were the ubiquitous diagnoses in the camps. A common diagnosis, intermittent fever, was characterized by "repeated paroxysms, returning with an evident exacerbation, and generally with shivering [followed by] complete aprexia [absence of fever]" coming and going every day.[11] The patient's symptoms, initially, included "indolence, weakness, discomfort while seated, irritable, skin cold to touch, paleness, tremors, skin as low as 74 degrees, irregular pulse, numbness, impaired senses, body aches, vomiting, thirst."[12] At the later stage, the victim experienced a fever of 105 degrees or greater [!], a strong pulse...noise and light sensitivity...delirium, nose hemorrhaging."[13] A warm bath and bed, and still warmer diluted liquors (with a dose of cream of tartar to relieve stomach distress) were encouraged to promote swelling. To further aid perspiration, James' Powder, "a mixture of crude antimony [tartar emetic], pulverized and chared bones calcinized in a reverberating furnace'" was also believed to do the trick.[14]

Benjamin Rush, as Physician General of the Continental Army, was an avid believer in bloodletting as a cure-all, a practice frequented upon soldiers whose youth was seen as especially tolerant of the remedy. The patient might lose up to eighty percent of his blood—a cure which certainly eliminated any symptoms.[15]

Ezra Ross was temporarily discharged sometime following the campaign of 1776, likely not long before the Battle of Trenton, the decisive American victory which followed the Christmas night crossing of the Delaware River by Washington. It is unclear if Ross left camp due to sickness (more fanciful accounts claim he had been wounded). But, without question, within several days of his march homeward to Topsfield, he had become seriously ill. New England winters were especially severe in the late eighteenth century, yet Ezra continued the trek in his debilitated condition. Not quite two hundred miles from Peekskill, with nearly one hundred remaining before reaching home, Ross could proceed no further.

Fate could have played its hand no more wickedly than to have chosen Brookfield as his point of exhaustion. As described by his parents in their petition to the court following Ezra's conviction, "by the lot of providence, [he was] cast upon Mrs. Spooner, in a severe fit [of] sickness, from whom he received every kind office and mark of tenderness, that could endear and make grateful a child of sixteen, sick, destitute, in a strange place, at a distance from friend or acquaintance."[16]

The Spooners, at an unknown date, had moved from their tavern to a new home further east, also in Brookfield. Only one description of their new home, written in 1843, survives.

> ...the home is still standing unchanged,, except by the waste of years. It was a plain, but large and respectable dwelling, two stories in height and constructed after the fashion of those times, when comfort was consulted more than show in the economy of living. It is situated on the north side of the old road from Brookfield to Worcester, about half a mile eastward from the meetinghouse of the South Parish.[17]

From documentation preserved following the murder, we know that the property boasted a large barn (drawing the occasional curiosity seeker until at least the 1920's). The substantial kitchen likely featured a fieldstone fireplace, its hollow base used to store wood ashes for making lye. To the back left of the kitchen stood a milk room. The home also contained a cellar, front sitting room, and at least three bedrooms. Central hall/center chimney design was common; there were as many as five fireplaces all told. The inclusion of a milk room might suggest, if not a gambrel design, then a saltbox, like that of Mrs. Ruggles' birthplace in Sandwich. Situated as it was on East Main Street, the home would have faced south to take advantage of the winter sun, the roof sloping dramatically at the rear to lessen the effects of chilling winds, as well as to conserve kitchen heat. In the front yard, just to the right of the doorway, stood the sweep-and-bucket type well.

Did Ross falter and make his way to the Spooner doorstep—or was he first spied by Bathsheba and approached by her? Surely, by this time, Ross had stopped at several farmhouses, the sight of wandering soldiers begging from door-to-door hardly unusual. Why was he welcomed so warmly by this particular household? Whatever the circumstances, Bathsheba graciously offered her hospitality, and nursed him back to health.

According to a document sworn to by Ezra at Rowley (a town bordering Topsfield), he delayed his return home until early April of 1777.[18] If we liberally allow a month's travel time (Peekskill to Brookfield, then on to Topsfield), we are left with about ten weeks spent in Brookfield. During this period, it seems, Bathsheba and Ezra restricted their relationship to that of a nursemaid and invalid.

Assuming that Ross was suffering from intermittent fever, the most common diagnosis for soldiers, how might Bathsheba have treated him? Drs. King and Foxcroft were two of Mr. Spooner's closest friends in Brookfield, and it is likely that his wife consulted them. Peruvian bark, an exotic cure discovered by the Inca nearly three centuries earlier, was nicknamed cinchona by the Spanish upon a remarkable recovery exhibited by the Countess Chinchon, the viceroy's lady, in 1640. The Jesuits brought the powder to Italy, where it was considered dangerous to the obese, causing death for some patients within a year of treatment. Nevertheless, the medication spread to England, and was soon a favorite of American troops, administered every two hours while the sufferer's fever was absent. Bloodletting, especially in colder climates, was believed to increase its efficacy. The bark's extract was boiled with water, filtered, and thickened by evaporation, its bitter flavor masked by brandy, milk or licorice.

Whatever the relationship between Bathsheba and Ezra at this juncture, it appears that Joshua took a liking to the boy, a fondness which may have blinded him to Bathsheba's eventual betrayal.

At the first sign of spring, Ezra, recuperated, returned to the family farm, as evidenced by a pay abstract which he swore to at Rowley on April 19.[19] It is unknown whether he returned willingly, was encouraged by the Spooners, or, least likely, given the erratic nature of mail delivery, was coerced by his parents. His time on the farm would be short, from just before the spring planting through the early harvest.

On July 22 in Worcester, the date which marked the first anniversary of the town's official celebration of the Declaration of Independence, the community's most prominent Patriots converged upon the King's Arms Tavern, where they demanded that its signboard be taken down and burned in the street. The innkeeper, Mary Sterne, whose hostelry had served as site of the famous Tory protest of 1774 and later as command center for the Patriots' Committee of Correspondence, cheerfully complied, not that she would have had much to say in the matter.

Summer was lovely on Cape Ann in 1777, and before it slipped away, Ross had again answered the call to arms. In early July, as Ross lingered, "Gentleman Johnnie" Burgoyne, leading his British forces south from Canada, recaptured Fort Ticonderoga from the Americans. An order was issued on August 9, requiring that one-sixth of the able-bodied men of the training band and alarm lists not already engaged, men like Ezra Ross (who had just turned seventeen) be at once drafted and marched for the relief of the northern army under General Horatio Gates. On August 15, Ross marched from home in the company of Capt. Robert Dodgde, as part of Col. Samuel Johnson's regiment.[20]

The day following their departure, Gen. Burgoyne was routed at Bennington. Jane McCrea, a frontierswoman, had only recently been murdered by a Huron-Wendat warrior under Burgoyne's charge; her brutal death heightened anti-British propaganda. Yankee farmers like Ross marched not only as Patriots, but as New Englanders determined to protect their homes and families.

Burgoyne, heading south toward Albany, had hoped to join forces with General Howe who, it was anticipated, would move his men north from New York toward the same town. The plan seemed masterful—all of New England would stand isolated from the remaining nine colonies, with the British in control of the Hudson River. In what turned out to be perhaps the most significant misstep of the war, Gen. Howe instead focused his attention upon Philadelphia. A small force under Gen. Clinton was sent to Albany, the troops never making it beyond distant Kingston. Meanwhile, a foraging expedition sent by Burgoyne suffered heavy casualties. Demoralized and near starvation, Burgoyne's men trudged southward, only to find themselves blocked by the colonists under General Horatio Gates. After enduring two defeats in battle, Burgoyne retreated north to Saratoga, where he and his five thousand men surrendered, forced to lay down their arms in mid-October. Baroness Riedesel, whose husband commanded the Hessian troops, wrote of the trials her family endured at the height of battle. As the bombs cascaded toward her property, they

> ...threw us all into alarm. Many persons...threw themselves against the door [of the cellar]. My children were already under the cellar steps, and we should all have been crushed, if God had not given me the strength to place myself before

> the door, and with extended arms prevent all from coming in. Eleven cannon balls went through the house, and we could plainly hear them rolling over our heads.[21]

At Gen Burgoyne's insistence, the British capitulation, officially speaking, was never to be referred to as a "surrender". The battle's aftermath created circumstances which would lead directly to Joshua Spooner's murder.

En route to Saratoga, in "gratitude for past favors, [Ezra Ross called] on his old benefactress, who then added to the number of kindnesses, and engaged a visit on his return."[22] It is unclear, again, how long Ross stayed with Bathsheba. In September, a company of volunteers commanded by Capt. Asa Danforth, a regiment not connected to Ross', marched from Brookfield to take part in the last major skirmish before Saratoga, at nearby Bemis Heights, on October 7. It is possible that Ross stayed on in Brookfield until that date, joining the local Patriots. Whatever the case, we know that Ross was back in Brookfield by late fall. On a deed at the Worcester County Registry dated November 1, 1777, Ross' signature appears alongside those of Bathsheba and her husband.[23]

Other evidence firmly places Ross in Brookfield that fall. One witness at the trial claimed to have seen Ross there "a little before Thanksgiving", another witness corroborating.[24] In the 1840's, Maj. Benjamin Russell of Worcester recalled as a youth watching Bathsheba and Ezra ride together, which, given Ross' earlier illness and the impending stormy winter, likely occurred during the autumn.[25]

Military records indicate that after four months of service (August 15-December 14), Ross was discharged from Peekskill.[26] The term "service" did not necessarily suggest active duty. A portion of those months may have been spent in Brookfield. Ross, not a member of the Continental Army, had instead joined a local militia; by definition his terms of conscription were informal, temporary, even non-committal. Desertion was a common problem, occurring with far greater frequency than in later wars. It would be reasonable to conclude that Ross never returned to the battlefront following the mid-October engagements in upstate New York. Like thousands of troops in the northern army, Ross' military days may have simply come to an end.

Though impossible to pinpoint, it was likely during Ross' brief stay between his last battle and final discharge (November-December) that his affair with Bathsheba began. A fascinating entry appears in the diary of Rev. Ebenezer Parkman of Westborough, who visited with the convicts in late June of 1778. Ross asked that Parkman formally record that

> I, Ezra Ross, do desire that Mrs. Spooner will take particular Notice...As she [Bathsheba] was going to Hardwick She asked me the Reason Of my being so low spirited. I made answer. It was my long absence from home. She replyed that her opinion was, I wanted someone to lodge with. I told her it would be agreeable. She asked me if such an One as herself would do. I made answer: If she was agreeable, I was (the dialect was so). Upon which she said, After she came off her Journey she would see. N.B. After her return she gave me an Invitation to Defile her Marriage Bed, Which I expected (the spelling is so).[27]

The only other specific reference available regarding their affair comes from trial testimony. Sarah Stratton, Bathsheba's housekeeper, declared that during November, Ezra and Bathsheba were in bed together when Mr. Spooner returned home from Boston unexpectedly. Bathsheba left Ross to let her husband in.[28]

By the late eighteenth century, violations of the seventh commandment had become so numerous that churches felt compelled to soften punishment if they wished to maintain their congregations. Nonetheless, fidelity (at least as practiced by women) was promoted as a high ideal, a popular example of which was found in Female Stability, a five-part novel by Charlotte Perkins. The virtuous heroine, an orphan who one writer described as shedding "light and beauty wherever she went but also accumulated property en route" professed her love to the novel's hero who inconveniently died before returning the favor. The heroine is given the opportunity to display her steadfastness to her departed in scene after scene, rejecting entreaties for her hand, ignoring temptation as she preserves her purity and enlarges her investments.[29]

Bathsheba, if she had ever read Perkins' work, seems to have benefitted little from it. Instead, she offered New Englanders a femme fatale to stand as a dark, real-life counterpart to Perkins' exemplar. The writer's heroine represented an ideal which few young women could hope to emulate. Bathsheba undoubtedly made these same women more comfortable—here was a neighbor no other wife need ever fear of becoming, a woman inspirational in her own right, whose actions on the one hand repelled the more virtuous while at the same time assuring them of their own moral superiority.

Bathsheba's geographic isolation, of course, made an already bad situation worse. Brookfield, though a substantial village for its time, offered few amusements worthy of Mrs. Spooner's status, or more to the point, sufficient to her temperament. As the nearest hub, Boston was several hours distant. Her modest but comfortable home, well supplied with servants, only increased her ennui. Largely estranged from a husband more devoted to business than marriage, a fiery spirit such as Bathsheba's might inevitably seek satisfaction elsewhere, be it from a teenage soldier, or even more recklessly, a married British officer. And, digging her own grave still more deeply, Bathsheba, so much her father's child, never hesitated to publicize her political views, which grated upon Patriot sensibilities.

Was divorce an option? Between 1639 and 1692, forty cases are recorded in Massachusetts; divorces were granted on several grounds, including adultery, bigamy, desertion, impotence, and affinity (improper intimacy with someone besides one's spouse). Over the next ninety-three years, the divorce rate increased by over two-hundred-and-fifty percent, with women petitioning slightly more than men. The grounds had also expanded to include incest, fornication before marriage with a relative of the spouse, malicious desertion, and prolonged absence with the presumption of death.[30]

Unlike the colonies of the mid-Atlantic whose Anglican divorce laws reflected the conservatism of Roman Catholicism, Massachusetts law was more liberal. In the eyes of New Englanders, marriage was a civil, not a religious contract. Two types of divorce could be sought.

Divorces "a vincula matrimonii", or absolute divorces which granted the right to remarry, were rare. Though easier to secure, divorces "a mensa et thoro", or separation from bed and board, were still uncommon. Under this category, children conceived before the separation were viewed as legitimate. Partners could not remarry, an arrangement which must have been particularly burdensome for women, who were disallowed from entering into any contract, or to sue or be sued.[31]

Bathsheba had the option of suing her husband for an absolute divorce only if it could be proven that in addition to his committing adultery, he had also been abusive (in the Spooners' case, only emotional abuse has been suggested, and never clearly demonstrated). On the other hand, as a man, Spooner only had to prove adultery.[31] Considering the circumstances as well as the law, Joshua Spooner held all of the cards. Had he successfully sued for divorce on grounds of adultery, the law would have prevented Bathsheba from receiving any alimony.[32]

Divorce, of course, was an option that neither party would have relished. Given their families' high social standing, divorce would have stigmatized all concerned; the charge of adultery would have only added to the ignominy. Further, an absolute divorce required that Bathsheba receive between one third and one half the estate, a situation which Joshua would have found intolerable. Neither would Joshua have considered, under the lesser category of separation, to continue to support Bathsheba. From almost any perspective, divorce was not an option.

Viewed within the larger social upheaval, the disintegration of Mrs. Spooner's already fragile world seems less surprising. Towns were full of women, children and old men, devoid of most males in their youth who returned only for brief periods between battles.[33] The uncertainty of the war's outcome contributed to the general malaise. An eventual British victory might make life unbearable, but an American one promised little stability. Had Bathsheba's murderous adventure occurred fifteen years earlier during a relatively calm period in American history, would the episode have drawn the same attention as it did at the height of the Revolution? Perhaps only during such a period could a scandalous murder attract such fierce interest from a population seeking to direct their war-frustrated attention elsewhere. None of the parties appears to have given a second thought to the near-hysteria their crime would unleash.

To add to the prevalent discontent, the colonists faced a daily struggle with inflation. In 1775-76, an influx of newly printed currency stimulated the economy, the gradual rise in prices further strengthening business. By 1777, depreciation had set in, so precipitously that many towns opted for a wage and price freeze. With British controls largely invalidated during war time, Americans printed even more money. Scales of depreciation were consulted in most transactions. In 1751, corn sold for two shillings a bushel; twenty-four years later it was fetching over one hundred. In a three year span, beef and veal nearly doubled in price. In the Worcester County town of Westborough, a glass of cider soared from about four shillings to more than six—in the space of six months.[34] There is little indication that Bathsheba reined-in her liberal appetite for the best which life had to offer, which likely exacerbated domestic tension.

CHAPTER SEVEN

To Take Him Off By Poison

News of Burgoyne's defeat at Saratoga in October of 1777 was cause for great joy among the colonists, none more so than Benjamin Franklin, who now had the decisive American victory he needed to convince the French to join America's struggle. Saratoga changed world history. Two of its defeated soldiers would join Bathsheba Spooner and Ezra Ross in murder.

General Burgoyne and his men, the pride of British forces overseas, had been humiliated by the upstart colonists. Chastened, the general sought to mitigate his dishonor through the Articles of Agreement (the text of the agreement used the benign term "convention", avoiding any reference to the defeat as a "surrender" or capitulation"). The terms of the convention were among the most gracious ever granted to a vanguished enemy. The Continental Congress sought to nullify the agreement, aghast at General Gates' pandering to the British. In part, the terms read

> II. A free passage to England will be granted to the troops of General Burgoyne on the condition that they shall serve no more during the War in North America. The harbor of Boston is designated as the place for the embarkation of the troops.

> IV. The troops, under [Burgoyne], will march upon the shortest and most commodious road to Massachusetts Bay, and as circumstances dictate, are to be quartered in and around Boston.[1]

The route chosen between Saratoga and Boston may have been the most facile, if not the shortest. The British were marched through the southwest of the recently formed Republic of Vermont, then Massachusetts, via Northfield and Deerfield. Rather than continuing due east, they traveled south to West Springfield, and still further south to Connecticut (Hartford). Reversing direction, they headed north through Hadley, then northeast through Leicester, and finally east via Worcester, Westborough, Marlborough and Weston before encamping at Cambridge (officers) and Charlestown (enlisted men). It is almost certain that enroute to Leicester, the soldiers passed the Brookfield Common near the Spooner home, a short walk distant.

Cambridge had already suffered in 1775-76 as the site of the American encampment. One Cambridge Loyalist described its aftermath, particularly the effects of deforestation, necessitated by the complete lack of firewood.

> Oh...that imagination would replace the wood lot, the willows around the pond, the locust trees that so delightfully ornamented and shaded the roads leading to the farm... every beauty of art or nature, every elegance which it cost years of care and toil in bringing to perfection, is laid low. It looks an unfrequented desert...[2]

Few Cantabridgians lingered for the American duration. Less than two weeks after the Battle of Concord, nearly all of the town's women and children had fled; just about everyone at Harvard College soon followed.

The hundreds of British officers captured at Saratoga had been promised comfortable, if not luxurious accommodations. They received neither, to the genuine embarrassment of the Americans. To be fair, the colonists had tried to arrange housing, but trying to do as much in wartime for hundreds of men in the span of weeks proved impossible. Space was at an absolute premium.

Twelve years later in London, Lt. Thomas Anburey, an officer under Burgoyne, published his Travels Through the Interior Part of America in a Series of Letters by an Officer.

> ...It was understood at the convention, that the troops were to be stationed on Prospect and Winter Hills and the officers were to be quartered in Boston, and the neighboring towns. On this supposition some of the officers had pushed forward and got into Boston, but were immediately ordered out. The English troops [were] up on Prospect Hill, and the German upon Winter Hill; the officers have the towns of Cambridge, Mystic, and Watertown, to quarter themselves, and a parole of about ten miles in circumference...It is no little mortification that I cannot visit Boston, for it is the second city in America, and the grand emporium of rebellion, but our parole excludes us from it...[3]

No man could be guaranteed adequate housing, not even one as imperious as the enemy commander, General Burgoyne, a poet/playwright noted for his great joie de vivre, who enjoyed the choicest French wines even while encamped at Saratoga. The journey from there to Cambridge had taken thirteen hellish days. How bitter his return to Massachusetts Bay must have seemed. As he sailed into Boston Harbor in the late spring of 1775, he sneered, "Our army cooped up in this village! Let us once land, and we'll make elbow room!"[4] Now, just over two-and-a-half years later, he and his fellow officers found themselves in miserable quarters, most of which were homes that had been seized by the Americans—ironically from fleeing Loyalists.

One British officer described Cambridge as "a town where the systematic fleecing of students has rendered the inhabitants past masters of extortion."[5] Burgoyne, after having spent weeks in a hovel, finally secured the Apthorp House which, though an improvement, was still derelict enough to inspire a letter in February to the president of the Continental Congress. Burgoyne complained that he had paid "upon a private bargain, a larger sum for an unfurnished house out of repair, than would have been required for a palace in the dearest metropolis in the world."[6]

A rich mix of fact and fiction has characterized the legends that have come down from the time of the officers' stay. Maj. Gen. Friedrich Adolph Freiherr von Riedesel, commander of the Hessian troops at Saratoga (despite their name, most of the mercenaries, distinguished by their blue cloaks, actually hailed from Brunswick, Germany, not Hesse-Kassel), was housed with his men in the college buildings. The officers' internment in Cambridge was not all misery. Baroness Riedesel's parties were among the grandest held in Massachusetts during the Revolution. In light of what she and her family had suffered at Saratoga, Cambridge must have been welcome relief. Even today, the name of Riedesel's wife, etched with a diamond, can be found on a window pane at her home on the corner of Sparks and Brattle Streets in Cambridge.

Brooks and his fellow enlisted men had a much rougher time of it, six hundred of whom were sick or wounded. Though the Articles of Agreement regarded the British soldiers as detainees, the Americans treated them as prisoners-of-war. Numbering in the thousands, the soldiers were housed in run-down barracks which had been used earlier by the Americans during the siege of Boston. Essentially oversized shacks which lacked even foundations, rain and snow passed through the buildings. As their American counterparts had done three years earlier at Cambridge, the British soldiers in Charlestown denuded the landscape of its few remaining trees. Only two years earlier, many of the town's homes had been burned to the ground, some, in fact, by the same soldiers who now even stripped some homes of their clapboarding and fences.

Lt. Anburey, our diarist, complained of the abuses suffered by his fellow Englishmen, who were subjected to

> ...the most cruel and inhuman treatment. Officers and soldiers were shot down and bayoneted in the most cold-blooded manner without the slightest provocation. If the officers resented any insults, they were sent to Worcester and treated as felons. They were charged the most exorbitant prices for food...[7]

Although Anburey was likely engaging in hyperbole, it is true that he and his fellow soldiers were viewed by the colonists no differently than any other prisoners, a fact which likely caused General Burgoyne much consternation. Those British sent to Worcester joined a number of POWs who first began arriving in the village in May of 1775. The town's small gaol (jail) at what is now Lincoln Square would have been unable to hold more than a few prisoners. Most of the British inmates were apparently incarcerated in the prison barracks erected just a couple of hundred feet up the hill from Old South Church; the stockade occupied space equivalent to a small city block. The officers were locked away in the former home of Daniel Fullerton, at the northwest corner of the stockade, a home which had been lined with bricks and otherwise fortified.

The presence of so many loosely guarded "convention" prisoners throughout Massachusetts was a growing worry among the colonists. The murder of Joshua Spooner would confirm their worst fears before the spring of 1778 arrived. The British internment in Cambridge and Charlestown, as per terms of Burgoyne's self-styled surrender, was never intended as more than a stopover before the transatlantic journey home. But circumstances had changed. The Continental Congress considered the British effectively as POWs, guaranteeing them a much longer stay. Even before the Battle of Saratoga in late 1777, the Congress had ordered the construction of barracks capable of containing fifteen-hundred prisoners, to be built in Rutland, nine miles northwest of Worcester. A lack of materials repeatedly hampered construction, pushing the completion date back many months.

Burgoyne's men had reason to fear their new designation as prisoners-of-war. Conditions in the prison camps were horrific. Lt. Col. Sir Archibald Campbell wrote to Gen. Howe from Concord in 1777.

> I am housed in a dungeon of twelve or thirteen feet square, whose sides are black with the grease and litter of successive criminals; two doors with double locks and bolts shut me in from the yard, with an express prohibition to enter it, either for my health or the necessary calls of nature; two small windows, strongly grated with iron, introduce a gloomy light to the apartment, and these are at this time without a single pane of glass, although the season of the frost and snow is actually in the extreme. In the corner of the cell, boxed up with the partition, stands a necessary house, which does not seem to have been emptied since its first appropriation to the convenience of male-factors. A loathsome black hole, decorated with a pair of fixed chains, is granted me for my inner apartment, from whence a felon

> was but the moment before removed, to make way for your humble, and in which his litter, etc., remains to this moment...[8]

From Roger Lamb, whose account of William Brooks' suicide attempt began our story, we learn of New Englanders who exhibited "a deadly hatred against the British prisoners, and rejoiced at any occasion to gratify it."[9] Sentinels had stabbed several of the prisoners at Concord; one officer "was shot as he rode in his chaise."[10] News of such degradations was likely a motivating factor in Burgoyne's decision to expedite his men's removal from American soil.

For both soldiers and officers in Charlestown and Cambridge, incarceration grew more untenable from week to week. In January of 1778, a Col. Henley, who held immediate command at Cambridge, struck out at a British officer who had treated him insolently, pricking him with his bayonet. Burgoyne was outraged, charging the American officer with "barbarous and wanton conduct and intentional murder."[11] Col. Henley was eventually acquitted by a court martial.

The move to new barracks in Rutland took on a heightened urgency.

It comes as no surprise that conditions for American prisoners were no better, their British captors reportedly starving many to death. In what may be cases of propagandistic excess, one inmate was said to have gnawed "his own fingers up to the first joint from the hand before he expired";[12] others were forced to chew bits of mortar; still others were found "with bits of clay and wood in their mouths."[13] Some tales of horror were rooted in fact. Each morning aboard the prison ship Jersey, an officer shouted, "Rebels, turn out your dead!"[14] Living and dead lay side by side in the stinking hold. Buried beneath the sand of a nearby beach, the corpses would be washed out to sea come the next severe storm, only to bake for days in the sun as they floated past the portholes. One prisoner was allowed on deck each night. Desperately anticipating their own turns, the soldiers in the hold would crowd by the hatchway's grating, through which the sentinels above thrust their bayonets, from time to time killing their charges.

Neither the British nor American high command seems to have paid much heed to the Articles of Agreement as stipulated at Saratoga. General Howe had hoped to lure the soldiers south to New York for use in later campaigns, while the Continental Congress feared that once returned to England, the prisoners would be recycled and sent back to America to fight again. The Americans' repudiation of the terms won out—only a handful of the British force ever returned home, at least during the war.

Although the first division would not arrive at the newly built Rutland barracks until April 15th, small numbers of prisoners had already made their way to that town during construction, Local farmers welcomed many of the "lobsterbacks" into their homes as boarders, an indication of the ambivalence (and desperate economy?) with which many citizens regarded the enemy, at least initially. Whether due to the lax security at their camp in Charlestown or the casual manner in which the Americans treated these "conventioneers", British prisoners-of-war roamed the Massachusetts countryside with impunity. It is also likely, of course, that many of them had simply walked away from the loosely guarded march from Saratoga to Cambridge.

Pvt. William Brooks, the thief who jumped overboard, again turns up in late 1777, as a blacksmith in Worcester. As stated in the murderers' public confession, Brooks' specialty at the forge was filing, a four-part process during which the metal's surface was made increasingly smoother. It was a skill requiring significant practice. Following the arrest of Brooks and his fellow conspirator, James Buchanan, a letter from the Worcester Committee of Safety and Correspondence was sent to the Council for the State. In the letter, Brooks and Officer James Buchanan, both later convicted for the murder of Joshua Spooner, are described as "Burgoin [sic] People" and "Convention Prisoners",[15] clearly identified as among the soldiers held at Winter and Prospect Hills in Charlestown, where both men are elsewhere documented as laborers.

Brooks could not have appeared in Worcester before November of 1777 (like many others, he probably wandered from camp) and therefore had not had the opportunity to learn his craft in America. Rather, he had likely been a blacksmith in his native Wednesbury, a town in the West Midlands, near the Welsh border. Brooks may have honed his metalsmithing skills as a member of that town's foremost industry, the manufacture of nails.

In 1811 Roger Lamb, a British infantryman, published a memoir of the Revolution. Following the British soldiers' conviction for Spooner's murder, Lamb was sent by his superior officer to offer the men solace and counsel. In his memoir, Lamb devotes a few pages to the Spooner case. Discussing the lax security at Cambridge, he relates that James Buchanan, a member of the 9th Regiment of Foot

> ...received cash from his officer, to provide shoes for the company, but unfortunately squandered it. Apprehensive

> of punishment, he went away privately to a place about forty miles from Boston, and worked at his trade [like Brooks, blacksmithing] to provide as much as he lavished, in order to make good his account. Having saved so much, he was returning to his regiment, and by accident, met with a soldier, who informed him that a sergeant was appointed in his place, it being concluded that he deserted. Being so advised, he resolved to escape to Montreal (where he left behind his wife and child) in the hope of obtaining pardon by means of Sir Guy Carleton, then Governor of Canada. On his route to Canada, he passed through Brookfield, and there, unhappily for the parties, was noticed by a Mrs. Spooner...[16]

Like co-conspirator Brooks, Buchanan, originally from Glasgow, enters our story as a thief suffering the consequences of his actions. Unlike Brooks, Buchanan planned to make restitution. The shady character they shared was one found all too commonly among their compatriots. During the French and Indian War, General Wolfe, in a letter to his father, described the British troops under his charge as "mean, corrupt, murdering, insolent, dirty, drunken, disorderly, immoral, undisciplined, slack, demoralized, easy to disorder, hard to recover, of precarious valor, tramps, loafers, jailbirds...the soldiers are very devils."[17] The situation had grown only worse by the Revolution.

Although it is uncertain at which point Brooks joined Burgoyne's forces leaving Canada for Saratoga, thirty-year-old Buchanan and family had likely been residents of Montreal since before the Revolution. Both men may have fought against the Americans while in Canada during the 1775-76 campaign, later marching south with Burgoyne's troops. In his treaty with General Schuyler at Saratoga, Burgoyne had stipulated that "All Canadians, in whatever service...are to be permitted to return to their homes, and to march at once...to the nearest British port."[18] Had that article been honored, Buchanan might have long ago headed north from upstate New York, to reunite with his family, and the tragedy about to unfold would likely never have happened.

In the confession of Ross, Brooks and Buchanan published shortly before their execution, Sgt. Buchanan indicated that he and Brooks left Worcester on February 8, 1778, heading for Springfield, fifty miles west, "with an intent...to work...we were going to Canada."[19] If the confession is to be believed (much of it corroborated), then other accounts which suggest that Brooks and Buchanan first met in Brookfield appear mistaken; the pair probably worked together in Worcester.

February 8th was only three weeks before the murder.

> We, James Buchanan and William Brooks left Worcester with an intent to go to Springfield to work [en route to Montreal]. In passing Mr. Spooner's we were called in by Alexander Cummings, who we thought was a British soldier.[20]

Alexander Cummings, a key player and observer in our drama, would give testimony crucial to the prosecution. According to the Rev. Ebenezer Parkman of Westborough, earlier cited as the man to whom Ezra Ross confided his affair with Bathsheba, Cummings was "a Scottish youth who deserting from Burgoyne's Army, lived in Mr. Spooner's house."[21] Cummings took the role of general-man-about-the-house: messenger, stable hand, servant and confidant. Following his arrest, he turned state's evidence, telling the court that he had lived with the Spooners "from the time Burgoyne's troops came down,"[22] or in Brookfield, early November 1777. Unlike Brooks and Buchanan who escaped from imprisonment in Charlestown, Cummings was an earlier escapee, likely breaking free of the marchers as they made their way from Saratoga through Brookfield on the way to Charlestown. Though ultimately serving as one of the chief witnesses for the prosecution, Cummings may have been Bathsheba's lover during his early weeks with the Spooners, possibly her first. Cummings testified that at some point in late January, Bathsheba attempted to coax him into killing Spooner.

"I will make a man of you," Bathsheba had said.[23]

Buchanan's confession continues. "Having stood sometime by the fire, he [Cummings] told us his master was gone from home, but he would go and call his mistress, for she had a great regard for the army [the British], as her father was in it and one of her brothers..."[24]

Not by chance had Cummings seen the soldiers approach. Rather, as reported by a few writers, Bathsheba requested that he welcome anyone traveling by the house. One mystery: how is it that Cummings happened to call in not American, but British soldiers? It may be that Bathsheba had asked Cummings to keep an eye out specifically for British. The sight of His Majesty's soldiers was not an unusual occurrence along the back roads of Massachusetts following the Battle of Saratoga. Even before the Revolution, New Englanders had grown used to British troops, many of whom had stayed on in America, settling upon the bounty lands granted to them in repayment for military service. Vagrancy was another widespread problem. Between the 1740's and 1760's, the number of drifters in western Massachusetts had increased five-fold.[25]

Might Brooks and Buchanan still have worn a remnant of their red uniforms? The suggestion is less ridiculous than it might seem. Although a stipulation of the treaty at Saratoga, the British POWs never received the bulk of their clothing, as promised, which remained in Canada for the duration of the war. Most of the soldiers encamped in Charlestown had worn only one tattered uniform since the mid-October defeat—(we recall Buchanan's foray to purchase shoes for his company)—some of the German soldiers had worn the same uniform for nearly four years. For Cummings to have recognized Buchanan and Brooks as British from their tatters, and during a snowstorm, does stretch credulity; perhaps he called to the men, inviting them to follow him only upon hearing their accented speech. The point is not academic. Not only had Bathsheba professed herself a Tory, but she very likely would have viewed English soldiers as more likely to join her murderous plot against a Patriot husband.

One detail of the soldiers' visit remains unexplained. Travelers to Springfield would have stayed on the main road, about a third-of-a-mile from the Spooner home. Why the detour? The storm's intensity may have disoriented them.

Buchanan and Brooks entered the home. The confession continues.

> [Cummings] called [Bathsheba], and she came down, and appeared glad to see us. She asked us whether we came down from the Hill? We told her we did, and were going to Canada, as I, Buchanan, had left my family there.[26]

By the "Hill", Bathsheba was likely referring to Prospect Hill, where Burgoyne's men were encamped.

> [Bathsheba] ordered breakfast for us, as soon as it was ready we were desired to go into the sitting room. We were very much surprised at this, for we should have thought

> ourselves well dealt by to have received any favors she might see fit to bestow on us in the kitchen. However, we all breakfasted together [as was the fashion, Bathsheba and the men likely ate from the same wooden trenches, and shared the same glass]. The weather being very bad, we were asked to stay till it cleared up. As we had but little money, we accordingly stayed. The weather continued very bad, but we stayed there day and night.[27]

In the meantime, what had become of Bathsheba's sixteen-year-old lover, Ezra Ross? In November, with Ezra as witness, Joshua and Bathsheba Spooner signed over to Spooner's brother WIlliam in Boston, the five-hundred-and-fifty acres in Princeton which Spooner had purchased from his now exiled father-in-law. The sellers may have had as little luck with the property as had General Ruggles. Although the potash works had been profitable, the parcel also contained a sawmill and gristmill, which were normally lucrative ventures.

By the mid-eighteenth century, virtually every New England town with a small river had a sawmill, whose products were in demand by several trades. Chestnut and cedar, which resisted rotting, were preferred for fence posts, cedar the favorite wood for clapboarding due to its light weight. Tanners preferred the bark of oak or chestnut. Carpenters bought white pine for flooring, and soapmakers purchased ashes. New England's shipbuilding and home construction industries kept the saws humming, saws which had to be imported from England. A pair of sawyers might produce one hundred feet of board a day, but a sawmill could churn out the same in an hour. Sawmills were expensive propositions, affordable only to merchants with capital. Even more expensive were gristmills which required grinding stones, also manufactured in Europe. A miller's work was highly specialized, and since the local gristmill was usually a monopoly, his mill was treated as a public utility. Farmers were heavily dependent upon the mills; the flour they carted off to the towns guaranteed tools and basic goods for their own use.

Joshua Spooner planned an extended visit to his Princeton property, a twenty-three mile journey, in early February of 1778, and asked Ross to accompany him, likely at Bathsheba's insistence. Although he had signed the property over to his brother three months earlier, the sale would not be recorded until March 5 (only days following his murder), until which time it was legally Spooner's.[28] The reason for his trip is unclear, but he likely wanted to prepare the property for his brother, to confirm that the mills were in good working order.

A letter written by a Brookfield native in early March details the first actual attempt made on Spooner's life, which occurred the day before he was to leave for Princeton. Ezra Ross

> ...found means to convey a quantity of Aqua Fortis [nitric acid] into some Grog in hopes of poisoning him [Spooner] therewith—Spooner drank of it, but Perceiving a disagreeable taste swore by God that had an enemy been near he should think they had attempted to poison him and at ye same time hove the remainder into the fire.[29]

Nitric acid, a pure, colorless acid, is corrosive to the eyes, skin, mucous membranes, and teeth. Had Spooner ingested the aqua fortis, within a short time he would have complained of upper respiratory irritation, which, after clearing up, would have returned with a vengeance. Mixed with liquid, nitric acid produces heat and corrosive fumes. If heated to decomposition (as it likely had been in his grog), its fumes would have been overwhelming. Spooner could not have imbibed more than the smallest sip of the poison. The fumes alone would have stopped him cold.

Despite the attempt on his life, Spooner clearly seems not to have suspected anyone of malice, least of all Ross, whom he invited to accompany him to Princeton. The taste of nitric acid may have temporarily loosed Spooner's tongue, but apparently did nothing to open his eyes.

A friend and customer of Spooner's, Loved Lincoln, visited him at home "about the first of February",[30] and asked if he could join him and Ross, at least as far as Oakham, en route to Princeton. His visit may have occurred on the same day of the poison attempt.

Spooner's motivation to travel may have been for business, but Ross' seems to have been purely malicious. From the same letter just quoted, we read "...The next day [following the near poisoning] Ross rode in company with Spooner to Princeton, where he was to seek opportunity to take him off by poison."[31] Although Bathsheba may have contemplated her husband's murder in the weeks previous, she was clearly moving toward a more active phase. The first attempted poisoning, planned for the day before Spooner was to leave for Princeton, may have been so designed to allow for a more easily explained disappearance by Spooner; after all, neighbors would not have expected him back for many days. The sudden appearance of his friend, Loved Lincoln, must have greatly complicated the situation. Whatever the case, their leather knapsacks full of frozen stew, the three men left for Princeton on the first or second of February.

Lincoln accompanied the men only as far as Oakham, about halfway. Whether or not due to Lincoln's last minute inclusion, there is no record that Ross attempted to poison Spooner at any time during the journey.

CHAPTER EIGHT

Having No Fear of God Before Our Eyes

While Ross and Spooner were away, British POWs Brooks and Buchanan enjoyed unusually gracious hospitality from Bathsheba.

> I [Buchanan] am not positive whether or not it was the first or second she told me, when by ourselves, that she and her husband did not agree—that he was gone a journey to Princeton, and that he would not be home soon—that we should not go from thence until the weather was fair, there being a great fall of snow at this time. We very readily consented, and stayed from day to day, expecting Mr. Spooner home. Mrs. Spooner getting very free in discourse with me, one day told me that she never expected Mr. Spooner to return, as there was one Mr. Ross with him, who had an ounce of poison, which he had promised her he would give to Mr. Spooner at the first convenient opportunity. The reader must needs think this a very strange circumstance, that she should make such a discovery to an entire stranger. She said at the same time, we should stay till we saw whether Mr. Spooner returned or not.[1]

It was at some point during the first week of the soldiers' stay that Loved Lincoln, who had joined Ross and Spooner for the first part of the trip to Princeton, returned to the Spooners' "to see if Joshua had done some business for him."[2] Spooner had of course not yet returned, but Lincoln's finding Brooks and Buchanan, a simple though telling detail, demonstrates Bathsheba's lack of concern (discretion?) in hiding her new friends from view.

> Accordingly, we stayed, and were never in better quarters, little thinking of the bait the seducer of souls was laying for us; we were then in a disposition to catch at it, having no fear of God before our eyes, and being entirely forsaken of him.[3]

Spooner was now alone in Princeton. Ezra Ross, having spent eight or nine days with him, and having failed to administer the new dose of poison, kept Spooner's other horse, which he had borrowed. He continued on to Topsfield through the snowstorm's wake, guiding his horse through what must have been prodigious snowdrifts given the many storms of that winter. Ross stayed on the family farm for two weeks. Questions remain. Had Ross and Mrs. Spooner planned for Ross to escape to his home once Ross had killed Spooner? Or, was the trip to Topsfield an impetuous reaction by the teenager to his having bungled again, fleeing in fear of the wrathful Bathsheba? Ross had likely not been back at his farm since his December 15th discharge. It was probably the last time his parents would see him alive.

Based upon the British soldiers' confession, as well as the testimony of Reuben Olds (another family friend), Loved Lincoln and Alexander Cummings (the Spooners' Scottish servant), what follows is a reconstruction of events surrounding Joshua Spooner's return.

Ezra Ross left Joshua Spooner for his Topsfield home as Spooner returned to Brookfield, alone. Spooner arrived back Tuesday morning, St. Valentine's Day. (There is a dating discrepancy between Cummings' recollection and the soldiers' confession; the latter, which is more consistent, will be used).

Approaching his home, Spooner, apparently suspicious, peeked in a window to discover Buchanan and Brooks. Spooner entered the house. Bathsheba later commented that she "was never so stumped," fully expecting that Ross had poisoned him while in Princeton.[4]

"How came you here?" Joshua asked the men.

"To warm ourselves," Buchanan responded, his Scottish burr unmistakable.

"Bathsheba, who are these men?"

"Sergeant Buchanan," she replied, "is Alexander's [Cummings'] cousin."[5] Spooner seems to have bought the fabrication. He left immediately for Cooley's Tavern, just down the road. While there he inquired how long the soldiers had been enjoying his wife's welcome, and no less importantly, how much alcohol had been purchased from Cooley during his absence.

Spooner did not arrive back until the evening. According to documents, he requested that the soldiers leave immediately. They protested. Spooner left the men alone in the kitchen. At some point, they were joined by Lincoln, Olds and Cummings. Cummings testified that he heard Buchanan and Brooks threaten Spooner's life, that "They would try to get Spooner out of the way."[6]

Taking Bathsheba aside, Joshua insisted that she send the men away. "If you do not, I will send for the committee [of safety and correspondence]."

After some time, Spooner relented.

"You may sit by my fire till morning," he told the British, "but you must not let me see you afterwards."[7]

The men remained in the kitchen, as Spooner opted for the safety of the sitting room rather than retire to his bedroom. Buchanan allegedly was overheard to say, "If Spooner turns me out of doors tonight, I will have his life before morning."[8]

Reuben Olds reported that Spooner spent the night at his side. Spooner also asked Cummings to join him. "I don't love to have Brooks in the house," he complained, "I don't like the looks of the man." To Olds, he remarked, "I fear that the men may try to rob me. I have not been able to find a silver spoon, and am certain that much of the pewter is missing."[9]

Reuben Olds joined the soldiers in the kitchen, and reported Spooner's suspicions. In their confession, Buchanan related that Joshua's allegations "vexed us, as we were conscious we had no thought of stealing from him. Had we been so inclined, we had as much opportunity as we desired."[10]

A search was undertaken, and the spoon was found where Joshua had laid it. Cummings convinced him that none of the pewter was missing.

Spooner went upstairs, briefly, to fetch his money box and, according to Buchanan, lay down on the floor before the sitting room fire, placing the box under his head. Olds served as liaison between Spooner and the soldiers, occasionally leaving Spooner to report his comments to the men. Eventually, Spooner dozed off, and Olds left him "to make merry together with Brooks and Buchanan."[11]

Olds testified that Buchanan threatened Spooner's life a third time.

"What is the old fellow about?" he asked Olds. "He will not come to say much to me—it won't be healthy for him, for I would put him in the well for two coppers."[12]

In his confession, Buchanan denied ever making the statement, although he does not address similar threats he made as alleged by Cummings and Lincoln. Eighteenth-century rules of testimony liberally tolerated hearsay evidence; testimony such as given by Olds could be very damaging. Buchanan's denial may nevertheless be valid. Olds' testimony, in light of its similarity to events surrounding the murder, sounds too convenient, a cynical attempt to further damn the murderers.

The next morning, Bathsheba informed Reuben Olds that "she would go through with the plan."[13] He testified that he assumed she was referring to a proposed visit to her father in New York. His claim seems disingenuous. Having just testified that he had spent a good part of the evening with the soldiers, one of whom in his presence allegedly threatened to kill Spooner, he now professes ignorance of any potentially malicious intent. In the same moment, of course, he slyly managed to further implicate Bathsheba.

In his confession, Buchanan related that it was inconvenient (read impossible, in Spooner's presence) to bid farewell to Bathsheba. Either due to Bathsheba's insistence or as an indication that he harbored no ill toward his British guests, Spooner gave Cummings the considerable sum of five dollars "to treat his pretended cousin [Buchanan] with."[14] Unwanted at the Spooners' and having nowhere else to go, Brooks and Buchanan wasted no time in indulging their host's generosity, and left with Cummings for Cooley's Tavern, at the village center. The day before, Cooley had updated Spooner regarding his guests' hefty thirst. One can only imagine Cooley's confusion as he again served them drinks (and now with Spooner's servant!), compliments of Spooner himself. As a taverner, Cooley could be held responsible for the men's excesses. Should any patrons be discovered "disguised with drink", an innkeeper could be fined, or face revocation of his license. Some towns restricted a customer's consumption to one half hour, forbade drinking after nine o'clock in the evening, or placed a limit upon now much could be imbibed when not taken with a meal.

The men's consumption of alcohol is not to be wondered at during a century when liquor was indulged to the point of excess at breakfast, lunch and dinner, and used as it was to mark every social occasion. In 1708, Cotton Mather condemned drunkenness (unlike Increase, his more tolerant father) largely out of fear that being better able to afford liquor, the wealthy would be the most likely to abuse it. "The votaries of strong drink," he warned, "will grow numerous...they will make a Party, against everything that is Holy, and Just, and Good."[15] Toward the end of his life, the plunge in rum prices in Boston (from 3 shillings 6 pence in 1722 to just 2 shillings in 1738) must have added to his grief as demand jumped accordingly. By 1730 in Boston, two years after Mather's death, one out of every eight houses sold liquor, and the rum monopoly long enjoyed by the rich was broken.

By the late eighteenth-century, the situation had grown even worse. John Adams referred to taverns as "the nurseries of our legislators"—the same Mr. Adams who downed a tankard of hard liquor at every breakfast.[16] "Is it not mortifying," he asked, "that we Americans...should exceed all other...people in the world in this degrading, beastly vice of intemperance?"[17] As a whiskey distiller,

General Washington bemoaned hard liquor as "the ruin of half the workmen in this Country," workers who, though dedicated drinkers who sought in alcohol some relief from backbreaking labor, only rarely exhibited drunkenness. "[18] Years later, expressing concern for the nation's future while reflecting upon its spirited past, a friend wrote to Thomas Jefferson "If the consumption of spirituous liquors should increase for thirty years to come at the rate it has for thirty years back we should hardly be better than a nation of sots."[19] Children occasionally joined in for a round; the sweet residue at the bottom of the glass was a favorite treat. As surgeon general of the army, Benjamin Rush thought alcohol to be a culprit in the spread of fever among the troops, and regretted that American soldiers were not more like their Roman counterparts, whose canteens, according to Rush, offered only vinegar. Rush believed that grog induced "fighting, lying, puking, tremors, bloatedness...debts, rags, hunger." Flip, an even more dangerous libation, was responsible for "swearing, obscenity, swindling... murder...pains on the limbs...dropsy...epilepsy...melancholy... madness" which could only lead to the "gallows...whipping....[and the] poor house."[20] At least in regards to one particular Brookfield home come March of 1778, his assessment could hardly have been more accurate.

Loaded with rum, Brooks and Buchanan found their way to Dr. Francis Foxcroft's home (following Edward Jenner's pioneering work against the disease, Foxcroft would open one of the first American hospitals to treat smallpox) as Cummings returned to the Spooners'. In a short while, Cummings rejoined the soldiers to let them know that Spooner had retired. All three went back to the Spooner home, where they dined—and drank some more. Buchanan and Brooks spent their first of several evenings in the barn. In the morning, Bathsheba had breakfast brought to them.

Bathsheba's sister Martha and neighbor, Mrs. Berry, had, for some reason, inquired after Buchanan the day before. The sergeant decided to visit them at the home of Bathsheba's closest sister, Mary Green, in Worcester. While there, the party drank "until late."[21] Buchanan tells of a strange episode which occurred there, providing few details. Bathsheba "...had given a handkerchief to a British soldier that had some words in anger with me, Buchanan."[22]

To whom was Bathsheba referring? Weeks later, following the murder, a British soldier identified only as a "sergeant" was arrested in Brookfield, one who "kept at the same house with [Brooks and Buchanan]...he was an intimate with Mrs. Spooner."[23] Could this sergeant have been the recipient of Bathsheba's token of affection?

It appears that Brooks was sent to retrieve the handkerchief from the mysterious soldier, but Brooks "would not deliver it, until he saw Mrs. Spooner."[24] The incident receives no further mention, although another handkerchief became the target of Bathsheba's wrath the next week.

Brooks and Buchanan spent their second night in the barn, to awaken to another day following the same pattern: hours of drunken indulgence at a local tavern (this time Gilbert's—and now likely financed by Bathsheba), later informed by Cummings that Joshua Spooner had left, when they were free to return to have dinner. They again slept in the barn, a building so bitterly cold that the men must have grown increasingly exhausted and ill-tempered. Come morning, Bathsheba kept them abreast of Spooner's movements, relating that he had "gone abroad in the country to get some oats."[25] Jesse Parker, the stable hand, had accompanied him. Wealthier colonial households often took in children like Parker, many of whom were the sons of widows grown destitute from the fragile economy. With no inheritance forthcoming, such boys worked as hired hands, until the day they might afford their own plot of land. Earlier, Parker had proposed to Brooks that upon the return of him and Spooner, Brooks should help Parker to murder Spooner. The ambush never materialized.

With Spooner away for the day, Brooks and Buchanan luxuriated before the fire as guests of Bathsheba, living "on the best the house afforded of meat and drink."[26] Spooner returned early in the evening, but the men had been forewarned of his arrival by the jingle of sleigh bells. Brooks dashed into the cellar, as Buchanan exited by the kitchen gate, pausing on the back stairs. Both men waited until Spooner had entered through the sitting room entrance, when they sneaked away to pass another dreary night with the horses.

Travel by sleigh was the favorite means of transportation in colonial New England. Its popularity made even distant Boston a welcome destination, where shoppers stocked up on clothing and delicacies. Following a storm, teams of men worked their way by shovel from outlying farms to each village green. Farmers with ox-drawn sleds followed close behind, packing the snow as they went, followed by still more shovelers who further smoothed the snow. The roads to the schoolhouse, doctor's house, and the meetinghouse were the first to be cleared—the first, that is, after the road to the tavern. When all converged at the town center, the workers marked the occasion as they did any other over a barrel of rum.

The next evening, Bathsheba sent for the men to join her for "supper and some liquor" for what would be the last during their stay in Brookfield, "to encourage another plan", according to Buchanan.[27] The plot was proposed to Brooks by the servants, Cummings and Parker. Spooner was to be murdered in his bed, and for their efforts Bathsheba would reward the men with Spooner's watch, buckles "...and as much cloth as would make a suit of clothes"—and one thousand dollars.[28]

"You can remove his body," Bathsheba suggested, "then carry it to the well. The neighbors will think he fell in while drawing water." Brooks, however, did not have the stomach for it, and the plot was never attempted.

"I did not think you so fainthearted," lamented Bathsheba.[29]

But the seed had been planted.

Bathsheba's thousand dollar offer was undoubtedly a liberal one, during a decade when the median salary was $900. However, by 1778, that sum bought much less than it might have only three years earlier, when the Continental Congress (and the states) began issuing unbacked paper money. Within a few years, inflation was rampant.

The next day, Cummings delivered breakfast to the men in the barn, and offered another plan, also of Bathsheba's making. Cummings or Parker were to tell Spooner that one of the horses had taken ill, whereupon Spooner would be killed as he entered to inspect the animal. His body would then be "...put among the horses' feet, to make people believe, when he was found, that the horses had killed him."[30] Once again, Brooks played the spoiler, taking Parker aside to ask that he not approach Spooner, requesting instead that he tell Bathsheba that once Spooner had heard of the horse's condition, he refused to follow through.

On Monday morning, February 22nd, against their hostess's wishes, Buchanan and Brooks left Brookfield in hopes of finding work in Springfield, thirty-three miles distant, the town to which they were first headed when Cummings called them in from the road. On the way, they stopped in Western (now Warren), where Buchanan worked for Mr. Marks, a blacksmith. Brooks, not having the necessary filing tools, remained idle, so after two days he and Buchanan "proposed to go to Worcester to get some."[31]

If two weeks previous the men were planning to work in Springfield, why had they made such plans, only now to reverse their direction, returning instead to Worcester? The entrance of Bathsheba into their lives may have removed any desire to venture too far from Brookfield.

Returning east to Worcester, the men passed by the Spooners' early Wednesday afternoon. Bathsheba expressed her desire to follow them the next day, "...as she wanted to see her sister, saying she was glad we had got work so near." She also informed them that she had two notes, one for twenty pounds, and another of three hundred dollars, "which she would endeavor to get changed,"[32] promising Buchanan one hundred dollars to purchase whatever he might wish. Massachusetts, following the currency act of 1751, had been restricted to issuing two-year, high-value interest-bearing notes which could not be used in private transactions, thus explaining Bathsheba's need to convert them to bills before paying Buchanan.

The soldiers stayed in the Spooner barn one last time, and left for Worcester early on Thursday. At Mrs. Walker's, a tavern, a maid named Prudence referred to in the trial notes as "a Negro woman", welcomed them.[33]

In 1778, slavery was still alive, if not as well as it had been in Massachusetts in decades past. Within five years, culminating in a Worcester case, it would be declared illegal, making Massachusetts the first New England state to do so (Vermont, a republic, had outlawed slavery four years earlier). Northern Patriots, recognizing the hypocrisy in their fight for freedom while dealing in human chattel, were especially stung by critics such as Samuel Johnson, who famously declared, "How is it that we hear the loudest yelps for liberty among the drivers of negroes?" Whereas in southern states the plantation economy depended upon slaves which comprised about one third the population in 1790, in Massachusetts slavery at its peak totaled barely two percent (in 1778, there were just over four hundred African Americans in Worcester County). Unlike plantation owners in the South, the northern colonies had neither the capital to invest in slaves, nor the agricultural economy in which to use them. In New England, male slaves served as craftsmen and laborers, performing any number of roles, from that of bookbinder to watchmaker or ferryman, often in direct competition for jobs with white workers already stung by the failing economy. Most women, like Prudence, were occupied as domestic servants. The following advertisement appeared in The Massachusetts Spy dated December 11, 1776, printed at Worcester.

> A Sprightly, healthy Negro Wench, 20 yrs. of age, born in the Country, and can do any kind of housework. She will be a valuable servant in a Country tavern, as she has lived in one several years. Enquire of the Printer.[34]

It is not unreasonable to believe that Prudence may have been the wench in question.

Distilled rum, a major New England commodity, was often exchanged for slaves newly captured from Africa, or from the Caribbean. Many had received at least a rudimentary education, and exhibited a competent level of English, as was apparently the case with Prudence. Her name suggests that she had been born a Christian, or was more likely a convert to the faith, thus accustomed to Massachusetts society. Northern slaves acclimated themselves quickly to a predominantly white world, unlike Southern slaves who formed their own large communities. Prudence's court testimony demonstrated a sophisticated use of the new language, both in listening and speaking, including the easy use of idioms, which further increases the likelihood that she was native born.

And significantly, Prudence's testimony may be the very first in the new nation by an African American in a capital case. Though circumstantial, her evidence was crucial.

Bathsheba arrived not long after the appearance of Buchanan and Brooks, and stayed only briefly. She returned from her sister's estate at Green Hill with her two nephews, and called on Buchanan, to whom she gave "as much cloth as made a shirt, and six or seven dollars, observing that they came from one M'Donald, an acquaintance of hers."[35] The last detail is of some interest; it implies that for whatever reason, Bathsheba did not have access to her husband's money (which given the circumstances seems reasonable), and needed to solicit her neighbors for donations.

According to Mrs. Walker, the innkeeper, Bathsheba also gave Buchanan "a letter which she said came from her grenadier."[36]

The contents of the letter were (as Mary Walker related) that her grenadier would meet Buchanan to go to the hill (Green Hill?) In his confession, Buchanan is more circumspect about the message, writing simply "...[Bathsheba] gave me...a note."[37] The detail was significant enough that the sergeant had not forgotten it months later (it is the only instance of one accomplice passing a note to another). Could its contents have been so damaging that, unlike Mary Walker, Buchanan chose not to reveal the note's contents?

Another strange episode followed, reported only by Prudence. Bathsheba instructed her nephew to return to Green Hill to check whether his mother was at home. Buchanan then offered Bathsheba his handkerchief.

"God damn the handkerchief!" she replied, "I will not touch it."[38]

Why so virulent a reaction? Any number of possibilities present themselves. Bathsheba may have been spurning a token of Buchanan's affection, she may have been showing signs of stress, or it may be an indication of Bathsheba's general instability, a characteristic suggested by several observers. Could the handkerchief have been the same which Bathsheba had given the mysterious British soldier, which somehow made its way to Buchanan?

Having spent much of the evening at Walker's, during which time she was frequently in and out, according to Prudence, Bathsheba finally retired to pass the remainder of the night at her sister's home in Worcester. Before leaving, she turned to Buchanan one last time.

"James, I have no paper money, beyond which I've already provided. Still, I need you to procure some poison for Joshua."[39]

Buchanan awakened early Friday to make good on Bathsheba's request, and purchased the poison that morning. Calomel, or mercurous chloride, was commonly used as a purgative, or laxative, often recommended for the treatment of fevers, following its medieval use as a remedy in returning balance to the body's humors. In later times, it proved effective as a fungicide. Like the aqua fortis (or nitric acid) with which Ezra Ross earlier spiked Spooner's grog, calomel was both odorless and tasteless, easily disguised in water or ale—unless, like nitric acid, it was heated.

As witnessed by both Prudence and Mary Walker, and as confessed to by Buchanan, as soon as the sergeant bought the calomel, he set about dividing the powder into twenty papers, in full view of the women. At some previous point, apparently as a ruse, Bathsheba and Buchanan told Prudence and Mrs. Walker of a sick child in Brookfield, for whom the calomel was destined. Both women refer only to "powder", probably having no idea as to its identity.[40] It is not clear how the conspirators had planned to administer it to Joshua. Like the aqua fortis, Joshua's grog would likely have been doctored. Buchanan himself was taking a risk, as the mercury compound is moderately toxic when absorbed by the skin.

Buchanan seems to have retired to his chamber, leaving Brooks alone. Bathsheba returned to Walker's at 10:00 AM, when Brooks let her know that Buchanan was sick (had the poison affected him—or was this a prearranged trick to get Bathsheba to his room?) Bathsheba ascended the stairs to his chamber, an impropriety which did not escape the attention of either Prudence or her mistress.

Buchanan indicated his wish that Bathsheba give her husband one of the papers "in the morning"; as it happened, Bathsheba did not.[41] The chronology is unclear. No matter where Spooner may have been, it would have proved impossible to give him the poison that morning. Did Buchanan mean the next morning? That too was impossible, as Bathsheba would not return to Brookfield until late on Saturday. For the third, and possibly fourth time (Bathsheba may have attempted to hire Cummings in January to poison his master) the conspirators failed to kill Spooner.

Bathsheba's visit to Buchanan's room involved more than wicked plans or inquiries into his health—it included one last sexual encounter. Prudence ascended the staircase to get a broom, "and saw them together."[42] Prudence would not be the only witness to Bathsheba's affections that weekend. To the dismay of Mary Walker, Brooks "often laid his head upon Mrs. Spooner's neck, and sometimes put his hands around her waist."

As Bathsheba explained to Mary, "You must not wonder, Billy [Brooks] has lived at my house and is as fond of me as he would be of a mother."[43]

As the "Belle of Brookfield", Bathsheba's behavior must have scandalized the tavern.

When not debauched or dissipated, Buchanan spent his days writing "sundry letters which he said were to [Bathsheba's] servant."[44] Does he mean Alexander Cummings? If so, it seems strange that he would have had anything to write to him that Bathsheba could not report directly. If by these letters Buchanan hoped to lure Cummings into the conspiracy, we have no evidence that Cummings ever took the bait.

Before Bathsheba left, Mrs. Walker overheard her asking Buchanan his plans. Bathsheba promised that she would "send a letter by him" (a strange comment, considering that she would see him again in twelve hours). She also informed him that she would write a letter at Mr. Nazro's general store to her exiled father "as it would not be any hurt."[45]

Bathsheba Spooner bid her soldiers good night, then rode her horse to her sister's estate, where she would spend her last evening in Worcester as a free woman.

Gen. Timothy Ruggles, courtesy Library of Congress

Marker at site of murder, Brookfield, photo by author

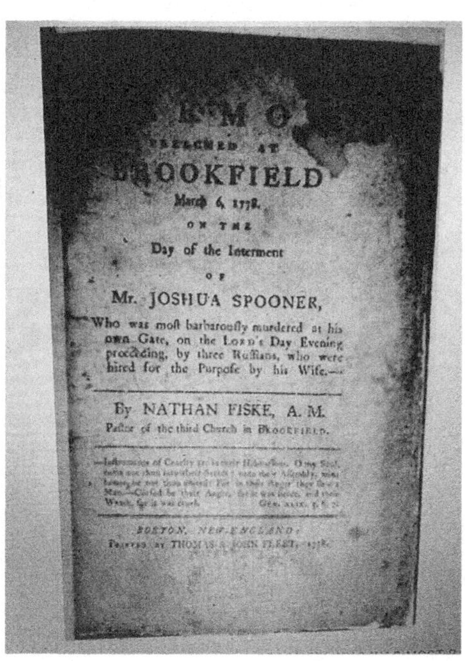

[illegible]

[illegible] AT

[illegible]OOKFIELD

March 6, 1778,

ON THE

Day of the Interment

OF

Mr. JOSHUA SPOONER,

Who was most barbarously murdered at his own Gate, on the LORD's Day Evening preceding, by three Ruffians, who were hired for the Purpose by his Wife.—

By NATHAN FISKE, A. M.

Pastor of the third Church in BROOKFIELD.

[illegible]

BOSTON, NEW-ENGLAND:

PRINTED BY THOMAS & JOHN FLEET, 1778.

Joshua Spooner's funeral sermon, courtesy Lesser Books

Gravesite of Joshua Spooner, photo by author

Second Worcester County Courthouse,
site of indictments, photo by author

Levi Lincoln, defense counsel, courtesy National Portrait Gallery

Bigelow Tavern, West Boylston, attic containing drawings of execution, photo by author

chalk drawings of execution, Bigelow Tavern, courtesy West Boylston Historical Society

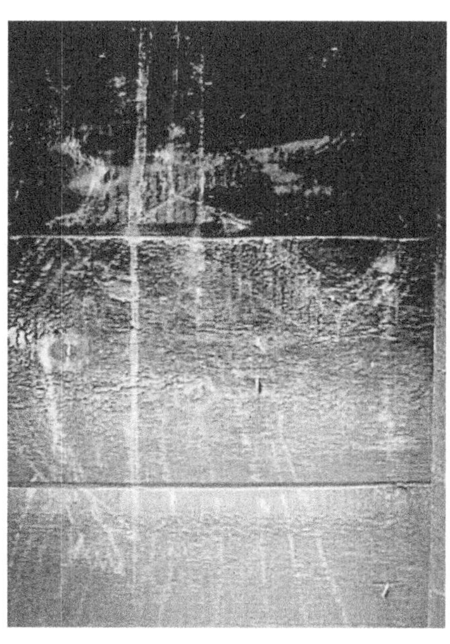

chalk drawing of Bathsheba Spooner (and Ezra Ross, extreme left?), courtesy West Boylston Historical Society

The Lives, Words and Dying Speech, etc., woodcut accompanying men's confession, (Worcester, July 1778?), courtesy American Antiquarian Society

Green Hill Park, Worcester, traditionally accepted burial site of Bathsheba Spooner, photo by author

CHAPTER NINE

Such Vile Purposes

Come, let us lay wait for blood, let us lurk
privily for the innocent without cause.

-Proverbs I:ii, from the execution
day sermon, July 2, 1778, by
Thaddeus Maccarty

The trial notes of the Spooner case, recorded by the presiding judge, Jedediah Foster, are perhaps the most complete from eighteenth-century America. What follows is a reconstruction of events the weekend of the murder.

At ten o'clock Saturday morning, February 28, Bathsheba reappeared at Walker's Tavern. To Prudence, she seemed breathless, impatient.

"Please get me the sergeant."

A few moments later, Buchanan came to the door.

"James, I have little time. I am going to Nazro's, and I want you to follow. I can get you and Billy [Brooks] some files while I'm there." Her offer was readily accepted, as the need was urgent.

"I'm staying," Buchanan said. "I'll send Billy."

She spoke quickly. "When can I expect you both in Brookfield?

"If you will sit up for us," he answered, "we will call on Monday night, at eleven o'clock."[1]

John Nazro's general store stood at the center of town, just south from the corner of today's Main and Pleasant Streets. In an advertisement from 1775 in The Massachusetts Spy, Nazro offered for sale

> India and New England rum, Wine, Brandy, Geneva [gin], Jamaica spirit [a strong rum], Loaf and Brown Sugar, Raisins, choice French and Spanish Indigo, Cake Soap, Pimento, Otter, Madder [a root used as red Dye], Coffee, Salt Fish, Flour, etc.[2]

A year later, like so many others feeling the squeeze from the failing economy, the storekeeper pleaded with his clientele to make good on their debts.

> All persons indebted to John Nazro, either by bond, note or book are earnestly desired without delay to call at his store and make payment thereof to said Nazro; the present situation of affairs, and the still darker prospect, being sufficient to influence every honest man to have nothing of that nature undone that can be done...[3]

A half block north from his shop, a colossal elm tree, with its wide-spreading branches, completely shaded Nazro's half-century-old home. With its hip roof and tiny-paned twelve-over-eight windows, corner pilasters and double entry, it was a simple, elegant Georgian structure, its gleaming white clapboarded exterior framed by brick ends. William Burr, uncle of Aaron (Jefferson's vice president and Hamilton's fellow duelist) and previous pastor of Old South Church had once resided there. In addition to the blacksmith supplies, it was Nazro who had probably sold Bathsheba the calomel which Buchanan had prepared the evening before in hopes of poisoning Mr. Spooner.

Minutes after Bathsheba left Walker's, Brooks followed. As he came within sight of Nazro's, he saw Bathsheba's horse gallop from the door. Confused, he returned to Walker's.

In the conspirators' confession, written (or more likely dictated) by Buchanan, the sergeant discreetly neglected to include his last rendezvous with Bathsheba before the murder. According to the testimony of Mary Walker, Bathsheba returned to Walker's that afternoon. Mary alludes to Bathsheba's and James' final liaison with the thinly disguised phrase, "having been in the chamber together for a few minutes, she went away on the same day."[4] As Bathsheba turned to leave Worcester for what would be her last time ever, she said to Buchanan

"Tomorrow night at eleven o'clock, remember, Sergeant."

He agreed. "Tomorrow night at eleven o'clock."[5]

Why was the Brookfield meeting changed to Sunday, (the next day) when Monday had been agreed upon earlier? In retracing Bathsheba's movements that Saturday, we know that at ten o'clock in the morning she stopped at Walker's to meet Buchanan, staying only a few minutes. From there, she rode the short distance to Nazro's, staying there briefly as well. A gap of one hour intrudes. At about noon, she made her second visit to Walker's, which ended about 12:15. Where was she between 10:45 (immediately following her visit to Nazro's) and 11:45 (by which time she en route to her second stop at Walker's)? Why the hasty exit from Nazro's before her scheduled meeting there with Brooks? Nazro may have given her news which prompted a speedy exit. Though only speculation, Bathsheba may have learned that her sister Mary Green, whose home was only fifteen minutes away, had new information regarding Joshua Spooner's whereabouts, whose home he frequently visited. Ultimately, there is no accounting for what may have occurred during this crucial hour. Robert Treat Paine, as prosecutor, presented no witness who could shed any light.

Bathsheba's sister had married into what was becoming one of the town's most prominent families, eventually one of New England's most respected medical families. Dr. John Green's great-grandfather, Thomas, arrived from England in 1635, soon settling in Malden, just north of Boston. His son, Samuel, in his forty-seventh year, joined several fellow parishioners in 1717 to settle Greenville, later Leicester, just west of Worcester. Samuel had also been an earlier settler of Hardwick, site of Bathsheba's father's estate, and his association with that village may provide the link which within two generations made possible the marriage between his grandson John and Mary Ruggles, Bathsheba's sister. John's father, Thomas, established the family's five-generation tradition of doctors.

His introduction to Worcester County presented him with the first great trial of his life. The winter of 1716-17 proved to be one of the worst in New England history. A series of ferocious storms struck the region, burying the four colonies for several weeks. Homes, even chimneys disappeared. When families could finally make their escape, they did so through attic windows. Livestock perished. Cows were seen trudging over twelve-foot drifts, feeding upon twigs—from treetops.

Come summer, Samuel Green and son Thomas arrived with others from Malden to settle Greenville. Before returning to Malden, Samuel entrusted the family farm to his son, who soon came down with a severe fever. Neighbors refused to bring him comfort; young Green "wept at their unkindness."[6] Sheltering himself under a shelving rock by a stream, Thomas tied a calf within reach, from which he nursed himself back to health. Not by milk alone did Green survive. As a child in Malden, Green had lived with two British surgeons, who had once treated pirates of the Spanish Main, and who had been granted amnesty. Enthralling young Thomas with tales of buccaneers and shipwrecks, they also shared their knowledge of herbal remedies. Now alone in Greenville, in his sickness he "made use of different roots which fell his way as medecine."[7] Other more compassionate neighbors came to his aid, and soon his father returned to take him back to Malden, a four-day journey. Thomas eventually made Leicester (formerly Greenville) his home, building the town's first grist and sawmills. When not administering to his patients' medical needs, he provided spiritual comfort as pastor of the Baptist church he founded.

Father and son later worked as a team treating the wounded during the French and Indian War. Even brother Isaac served as a surgeon at Saratoga.

In 1713, the year Worcester was permanently settled, the General Court conveyed eight square miles to the village's proprietors, a tract whose northeast corner, eventually a thousand acres, would one day form the Green estate. Thomas Green, who remained in Leicester, bought the first hundred-acre parcel, in 1754. Three years later, the land was passed on to his son John, also a physician, who moved to Worcester with his wife, the former Mary Osgood. Their modest home would grow to dozens of rooms over the next century, most of its contents sold many decades later at one of the largest estate auctions in Massachusetts history.

An early illustration shows the center-chimney colonial with fieldstone foundation which commanded the hillside above Lincoln Street. Of the two immense trees which grew in the front yard, one occupies a place of honor. Although famous as the site of the nation's first synagogue, Newport, Rhode Island had not always been kind to its Jews. Aaron Lopez and a few of his brethren, driven from that city, settled in Leicester. John Green, Mr. Lopez's doctor, received a locust branch from Lopez to use as a horsewhip. Returning to Green Hill, John stuck the branch in the ground, from which sprang the enormous tree.

In 1761, five years before the wedding of Bathsheba and Joshua Spooner, John's Green's first wife died, apparently in childbirth; only one of three children survived her. His second wife, Mary Ruggles, provided him with ten more children, the eminent Greens of Worcester aligning themselves with Timothy Ruggles, Bathsheba's father. Like so many prominent families, that of Mary and John Green must have been stunned by the pace at which political change divided their loyalties. Although the murder scandal would test their cohesion, the deference shown by the community first to Thomas, then John, would keep the family intact. John's political sympathies, firmly on the side of the Patriots, secured him favor in the village. John served on the local Committee of Safety and Correspondence as its only doctor. In 1777, he was elected representative to the General Court, after which he became town treasurer in 1778-79, then selectman in 1780 and again in 1796. John possessed all the elements for accomplishment in Revolutionary Massachusetts; brains, money, reputation, connections—and Patriotic fervor.

The landscape painting of the Ruggles estate in Hardwick, by Winthrop Chandler and now in the Worcester Art Museum, eventually made its way to the Green home. Chandler also painted pendant portraits of the doctor and his wife which, besides a portrait of General Ruggles, are the only surviving likenesses of the family.

Bathsheba Spooner had been a guest at the Greens for both nights of that fateful weekend. Before leaving Walker's Tavern for her final time early Saturday afternoon, Prudence, the slave, according to testimony, asked her "What did Mr. Green say?"

Bathsheba answered, "I told her (Mrs. Green) that I dined at Nazro's and drank tea there—it was a pretty good lie."[8]

Prudence was likely curious about the excuse Bathsheba had given her as to her comings and goings the previous evening. We know that Mary Green had made the acquaintance of Buchanan and Brooks. If ignorant of the plot being hatched, she may have been at least suspicious of the level of intimacy they shared with her sister.

After Walker's, Bathsheba left immediately for her Brookfield home. Galloping along the snowy roads, Mrs. Spooner must have looked very elegant, dressed in a riding habit traditionally-styled like that of a man's, a cutaway coat in red, moss green or blue with cuffs and collar. Over a simple dress, she likely wore a satin collar, complemented by a large beaver hat embellished with plumes and a brown ribbon band. A full skirt with sash tied into a large bow in back served as the top layer. A full, ruffled kerchief, bowed pigtail and riding gloves completed her striking, if cumbersome, outfit.

Another rider raced ahead of her, probably unaware that his lover was only two towns behind. Ezra Ross was returning from his two-week visit to the family farm in Topsfield. Given the sorry condition of the horse when Ross arrived in Brookfield, it is probable that the ninety-mile trek had been taken at maximum speed. Why the urgency? Lust may have propelled him forward, or the determination to return Spooner's horse as soon as possible. Was there a darker incentive at work? While away, Ross may have strengthened his resolve to make good his promise to Bathsheba, to at last kill Joshua, having already bungled two opportunities.

It was late afternoon. Sarah Stratton was Bathsheba's housekeeper, who, like thousands of women widowed by two wars, found in such work their only chance of livelihood. According to her testimony, she stood at the kitchen board, taking advantage of the remaining daylight to finish her ironing. At the sound of tapping on glass, she turned toward the milk room to her right where through the window she saw Ross, crouching.

"Mr. Ross—you're back—come in!"

"I can't, though I'm cold as death...I'm afraid of the master—I've borrowed his horse these two weeks, and I've hurt his back."[9] It was the first time since the Princeton journey to the mill that anyone in the household had seen Ross. The Spooner neighbor, Capt. Welden, whose horse Bathsheba had borrowed for her trip to Worcester, sent Charles (identified in the trial notes only as "Capt. Welden's Negro") to the Spooners,[10] most likely to fetch the animal. While there, Charles later testified that he saw Ross. It was dusk. Charles left without his master's horse.

Before evening, Bathsheba returned. After Welden's horse was led to the barn, it was probably Widow Stratton who informed Bathsheba of Ross' arrival.[11]

Having been apart for two weeks, Bathsheba and Ross surely indulged their passion, for what would be the very last time.

Ross was concealed upstairs all of the next day. A nineteenth-century attorney, in his analysis of the case, claimed that there was no certainty that Ross returned to Brookfield by design.

> Ross hesitated long as to the murder; and there was no positive testimony, that he knew of Mrs. Spooner's arrangements with Buchanan and Brooks, or that he had entered into their deliberations before the fatal night when he [first] met them, apparently by accident, at the house, and when he became a party to the crime.[12]

Did Ross hide from Spooner because he had injured his horse, or to lay in wait, hoping to regain Bathsheba's favor by murdering him in a surprise attack? The full culpability of the seventeen-year-old remained uncertain in the months to come, and is still one of the most tragic mysteries of the affair. Predictably, Ross has been cast as the impressionable youth led to ruin by the wicked Bathsheba. Coming to his defense, a nineteenth-century historian described Ross as one whose

> ...youth and inexperience unconsciously became the prey of the strong-minded, artful, seductive, profligate woman. Once in her toils, his youth furnished him with no power to extricate himself...This history is a solemn warning to youth, and will ever excite our sympathy and pity.[13]

Little information is available regarding events of the morning and afternoon of Sunday, March 1. Jesse Parker, the stable hand, testified that before leaving the Spooner home on Sunday, he saw Ross. Back in Worcester, Buchanan and Brooks claimed to have arrived (on foot) at the Spooner home "about eight o'clock" which contradicts Bathsheba's request that they call at eleven o'clock, putting their Worcester departure time at about 3:00 PM.[14] (It is possible that they left a few hours earlier, stopping en route at a familiar tavern in Leicester).

Many decades earlier, the eminent Cotton Mather admonished his congregation to keep holy not only the Sabbath, but Sunday evening as well.

> ...The evening that follows the Lord's Day may not be prostituted into such vile purposes as to spoil and lose all the Good of the Day, and that there may be no more be such a quick transition as there often is, from the Exercises of Godliness, to all Ungodly vanities and Lewdness. It is complained that there is more sin committed In that evening among us, than in any Evening of the week beside. Young People, where were you, and what was it that you did last Night?[15]

A reconstruction of events on the evening of the murder can be determined from the conspirators' confession as well as the trial testimony of four witnesses: servants Alexander Cummings and Sarah Stratton, their neighbor Dr. Jonathan King, and tavern keeper Ephraim Cooley.

About seven o'clock, Joshua Spooner prepared to dine with his close friends, Dr. and Mrs. Jonathan King, at Cooley's Tavern in Brookfield, nearly one-third of a mile from the Spooner home. Significantly, none of the witnesses found it strange that the party did not include Mrs. Spooner, an indication of the general disrepute into which their marriage had fallen. Joshua went on foot.

Before her husband's arrival, Bathsheba asked Cummings to return Capt. Welden's horse, which she had borrowed since Thursday. Her request seems innocent enough, but in light of events about to occur, the ever-duplicitous Bathsheba may have had an ulterior motive. The evening before, Charles, the Captain's servant, came in search of the horse. Bathsheba was still en route from Worcester. Upon later hearing of Charles' visit, we might assume that she delayed returning Welden's horse, simply because that would have left her without transportation; Joshua had one good horse, and the other (which Ross had borrowed) was still recovering. But come Sunday evening, she might have expected Capt. Welden to send Charles over a second time, and he could have made his appearance during a decidedly awkward moment as Spooner met his end.

Spooner's dinner party was characteristic of the conviviality common in New England winters before the advent of trains. The townspeople, having spent much of their day at church, now gathered before their hearths, each home's firelight illuminating the bright snow. The evening was clear and cold. Boots, sleigh runners and horseshoes had worked an intricate pattern in the packed snow, among which were the footprints of Joshua Spooner made only a short time before. It was nearly eight o'clock.

The British soldiers at long last reached the Spooner property. The men's hands, feet and ears would have been nearly frostbitten. Though eager to enter the house, they hesitated, uncertain of the domestic situation, as they confessed. Buchanan lingered for a moment by the side of the house as Brooks headed for the well, near the main door. Minutes later, Cummings returned from Welden's, and noticed the men. He entered the home, then exited almost immediately, and approached Brooks at the well, who in the dark could not identify Cummings.

"Mrs. Spooner?" Brooks called out.

"No, it's Cummings."

"Mr. Spooner should not come home a living man tonight," said Brooks. "Ask the mistress to come outside."

"I will not," replied Cummings.[16]

Brooks' warning is significant as the only clear evidence we have (from Cummings' testimony) that the murder had been planned for that specific evening. Brooks had not yet entered the home, thus no one outside could have informed him of the plot taking shape. Without doubt, either Bathsheba (or more likely Buchanan) made him privy to the plan the previous day. The rendezvous arranged between James Buchanan and Bathsheba the afternoon before ("Tomorrow night at eleven o'clock") by itself seems suggestive, but hardly explicit. There was, after all, no mention of murder. It is only in light of events about to occur, and from this comment by Brooks, that the engagement may be understood as purely malicious in nature.

Cummings re-entered the house, and found Bathsheba in the kitchen. He testified that immediately after seeing her, he went to bed. His retiring, it has been suggested, saved him from the gallows. Sarah Stratton left the kitchen to get a bucket of water, probably for the supper dishes.

Buchanan, standing alongside Brooks, asked to speak to Bathsheba. Sarah left.

Moments later, Bathsheba came out of the house.

"James—Billy—" Mrs. Spooner spoke nervously. "A Mr. Ross is in the house. He has a brace of pistols. He has promised me that he will kill Mr. Spooner when he returns from Cooley's. Come now."[17]

Bathsheba's use here of the article is significant. "A Mr. Ross..." would seem to indicate, as defense attorney Lincoln would suggest in reference to further evidence, that Buchanan and Brooks had never met Ross, and therefore could not have conspired as a team. Bathsheba's reference, however, clearly demonstrates some malice aforethought. And it obviously provides evidence of a conspiracy at least between Ross and Bathsheba. Further, although Buchanan and Brooks may never have heard of Ross, there is no evidence that the reverse was true.

The men followed Mrs. Spooner into the parlor. Ezra Ross turned to the men.

"Mr. Spooner should die by this tonight," he said, withdrawing a pistol from his coat.

"We will alarm the neighbors," Buchanan or Brooks protested.

Brooks addressed Ross. "If you will help me, I will knock down Mr. Spooner."

"I will help you."[18]

A lookout was set up by the parlor door window, as Joshua was expected at any time. Bathsheba called into the kitchen for some supper for the men. Brooks and Buchanan took a seat near Ross, helping themselves to a bowl of flip. A few minutes later, Mrs. Stratton brought them dinner.

At the center of town, Joshua was passing the evening amiably. He was, in the words of innkeeper Ephraim Cooley, "pleasant and sociable," sharing a glass of rum with Dr. King and his wife after dinner.[19] Dr. King testified that Spooner departed at the same time as he and his wife, "well between eight and nine o'clock.'"[20] The Kings, however they were traveling, unfortunately did not offer to accompany Spooner home. At the Spooners', according to the testimony of Sarah Stratton, Bathsheba took her dinner in the kitchen with a Mr. Gray and his partner, men further identified simply as "two boarders."[21] Mysteriously, outside of the few mentions they receive in the housekeeper's testimony, their names never reappear. The second unnamed boarder retired once dinner was finished. In the parlor, Stratton served rum to Buchanan, Brooks and Ross, who had been drinking for about forty-five minutes—not including any alcohol they may have consumed prior to arriving in Brookfield. Each took a turn as a lookout.

Spooner, in high (and possibly intoxicated) spirits, left Cooley's with no reason to suspect that this would be his final walk. As he had banished Buchanan and Brooks from his home two weeks earlier, he did not expect to see them ever again. He had also bid farewell to Ross at about the same time. Further, Spooner had never given any indication that he believed his wife wished him dead. The night was cold. Although only a short distance from his home, Spooner may have wished he had taken his horse. If he had, his evening might have turned out very differently.

One of the conspirators saw Joshua approach. Brooks left the parlor to stand within what was referred to as "the small gate" (entryway?) which led into the kitchen.[22] Before leaving the room, he picked up a foot-long log from the hearth.

Joshua approached, the crunching snow the only sound disturbing the silence. Bathsheba remained in the kitchen, her children asleep by the fire. It was just before nine o'clock. As Buchanan later wrote, "...and then was the time for the Devil to shew his power over them who had forsaken God."[23]

At the kitchen gate, Brooks struck out at Joshua, knocking him down with his fist.

"What is this?" Joshua cried. "Murder!"[24]

Joshua turned, pushing himself up from the snow. Brooks was upon him in an instant, partly strangling him. He raised the log, and sent it crashing onto Spooner's head, crushing his skull. Ross and Buchanan joined the murderer, all three attacking the victim viciously, "striking, beating and kicking him upon the back, head, stomach and throat."[25] Spooner bled profusely. In a feeble attempt to conceal evidence, Brooks apparently removed his jacket, wrapping Spooner's head. Brooks' breeches, as well as Ross' breeches and jacket, were bloodied. Spooner breathed his last. Ross knelt beside him, and reached into Joshua's jacket to remove his watch, which he handed to Buchanan. Before Brooks and Ross carried Spooner away, Buchanan removed Spooner's shoes. He later wrote "...I was instantly struck with horror of conscience, as well I might."[26] He stood aside as Brooks and Ross brought Spooner to the well.

Bathsheba had been at dinner, and didn't witness the murder. She left the kitchen table, and stood waiting by the staircase between the rooms. The parlor clock struck nine.

Brooks and Ross carried Spooner's body past the front door, and paused at the well. With great effort, one of the men hoisted Spooner's back upon the curb as another lifted his legs. The man nearer Joshua's head pushed the victim's upper body toward the narrow well opening while firmly grasping the shoulders, all the while working against the well curb's accumulation of ice and snow. The other struggled to raise the legs, and the two men gave a last push, sending Joshua head first into the well. Ross and Brooks peered in. The loud splash echoed off the walls, then vanished into the still winter air.

Buchanan stared at the men for a moment longer, then turned to go in. Bathsheba stood in the parlor; "she seemed vastly confused,"[27] Buchanan would write. Bathsheba lighted a candle, and left immediately to fetch her husband's money box.

Brooks and Ross remained outside. Their actions during the few minutes when Bathsheba was alone with Buchanan are unknown. Did they rest—or were they obscuring evidence? Oddly, the only blood mentioned during testimony (except the bloodstained clothing) was a few drops found on the well curb. According to the testimony of Cummings and Cooley, snow covered the ground the next morning. Did it fall that evening or had it already been there? If it had fallen after the murder, then it could have covered much of the blood. Assuming that it had not, then a clear evening with a bright moon could have assisted the men as they kicked snow over the trail, aided perhaps by a lantern. Whatever the circumstances, it seems incredible that more blood was not discovered.

Mrs. Stratton, who had not witnessed the murder, led one of the boarders, Mr. Gray, to bed, lighting his way up the stairs. He had dined with Bathsheba as the murder took place. His partner had also eaten with them, and as stated earlier, had retired beforehand.

Mrs. Stratton passed Joshua's room upstairs, and looked in to see Bathsheba holding Joshua's moneybox, which he kept in a mahogany chest. Bathsheba, apparently within earshot of Mr. Gray, approached Mrs. Stratton, taking her by the hand.

"I hope Mr. Spooner is in heaven," Bathsheba said, according to Mrs. Stratton.[28]

It would not have been the first occasion during which Mrs. Spooner used the phrase. Obadiah Rice, a neighbor, testified at the

April trial that prior to the murder, Bathsheba, in referring to her husband, had said, "I wish Old Bogus was in heaven."[29]

As Buchanan confessed, it seems impossible that Mrs. Stratton could not have known what was afoot, and Bathsheba seems to have shared the same suspicion. Mrs. Stratton and Gray entered the boarders' bedroom. Mts. Stratton testified that Gray's partner appeared to be asleep. The moneybox was carried downstairs.

Bathsheba turned to Buchanan. "Sergeant, I haven't a key to this. Could you open it for me?"[30]

Buchanan broke it open. Brooks and Ross entered. Bathsheba withdrew two $400 bank notes and handed them to Ross. "Ezra, please have these changed, and let Billy [Brooks] have all of it."[31] Searching again, she found currency in the amount of $243, which she gave directly to Brooks, taking the notes back from Ross, to whom she gave four different notes, each worth ten pounds, vestiges of British currency which would linger for years in the states.

"Ezra," she continued, "I'll need you to buy some camblet [a durable, waterproof cloth blended with silk or goat's hair] so that Sarah [Stratton] can sew me a new riding dress."[32]

In the presence of Mrs. Stratton and Bathsheba, Brooks removed his blood-drenched breeches, and tossed them into the fire along with the soiled jacket he had wrapped around Joshua's head. During this time, it is likely that the murder weapon was burned as well. Ross undressed also, giving his breeches and shirt to Brooks, but throwing his waistcoat into the blaze. Bathsheba left the room, returning with clothes of Joshua's: a waistcoat, breeches [a favorite article which, having no opening flaps, could be reversed once overworn], and a shirt and stockings for Ross. Brooks was handed stockings, a handkerchief and a second shirt. Buchanan received a ruffled shirt. Mrs. Spooner sent Sarah upstairs to find more clothes, but she returned empty-handed.

Alexander Cummings, who had retired well before the murder, awoke to the smell of burning wool. Descending the staircase, he entered the parlor to find the flames hungrily consuming Brooks' clothing as Brooks and Ross stood half-naked.

"Alex, why do you look so sullen?" someone asked.

He made no reply.

"Alex," Bathsheba wondered, "Could you go with Sarah to look for Mr. Spooner's other breeches? She can't find them." Alex and Mrs. Stratton ascended the stairs, and soon returned with them. Bathsheba stared at the victim's shoes which Buchanan had brought in.

"Alex, I'll let you have them if you'll go out and get some water to wash them with. They're all bloodied."

"I don't want them," he replied, according to his testimony.

"Oh, you and Sarah go and get some water," she insisted.[33] Under the circumstances, it was perhaps the most audacious request she could have made, calculated perhaps as a means of confronting the servants with the reality of the evening's events without having to tell them directly. More maliciously, she may have been trying to involve her servants as accessories after the fact, although comments she made later indicated her wish to leave them unimplicated.

As she spoke, Bathsheba made her last discovery in the cashbox, three eight dollar bills, which she handed to Buchanan.

Stratton and Cummings (and it could be added, nearly everyone else) were not in the habit of disobeying Bathsheba, and headed for the door. Cummings led the way to the well through the darkness. He lowered the pole and bucket, but rather than the anticipated splash, Alex felt only a dull thud as the bucket struck Joshua's feet. Dumbfounded, he paused. Mrs. Stratton beat him to the door, sobbing as she ran. Still wailing, she raced past the conspirators toward a table in the room, and grabbed the family Bible, as she would testify. Alex re-entered.

"But Alex," Bathsheba paused, regaining her equilibrium, "you didn't bring any water."

"I believe Mr. Spooner is in the well," he said.

"Now Alex, it is not true," she countered.[34]

Buchanan kept the shoes.

Cummings had been the first whom Bathsheba attempted to lure into murder, at least as far back as late January. It appears that once Cummings failed to obey, Bathsheba turned her sights on Ross. Bathsheba had apparently informed Buchanan of her desire to involve Cummings. Buchanan now referred to her attempt, when she promised to "make a man" of Cummings.

"Should you have thought my man [Brooks] would do the job for him [Cummings]?"

Alex could barely contain his outrage. "Tell me Mrs. Spooner—did they cut his throat?"

"No, they knocked him down," she responded with great understatement, ignoring his insult in categorizing her lovers as common cutthroats.[35] Alex's newfound nerve helped Mrs. Stratton regain some of her courage.

"Mr. Brooks, what have you been about this evening?"

"His time is come," was the reply.[36]

It was nearly eleven o'clock. Buchanan signaled to Brooks and Ross that it was time to make their escape. Bathsheba turned to him. According to the confession, they shook hands.

"James, when shall I see you again?"

"In a fortnight."[37] With Joshua's cash in their pockets and his clothing on their backs, the men made their getaway. Ross unhitched Joshua's good horse. Brooks and Buchanan may have traveled on foot, likely borrowing Spooner's horse from time to time while Ross walked (and less likely riding two at a time). The trio were bound for Worcester, their escape muffled on the snowy road. Although Ross chose to go with them, it is unclear whether he planned to remain with them after reaching Worcester, if he hoped to return to Brookfield, or perhaps return to his family in Topsfield.

Upstairs at the Spooners', Gray and his partner slept. In the kitchen, Bathsheba's children dozed soundly. Burning woolen smoldered in the nearby fireplace. Cummings retired a second time as Bathsheba and Mrs. Stratton lingered in the parlor.

Mrs. Stratton probably paused at the kitchen fire to fill the bed warmer with hot coals, then went up to the Spooners' chamber, followed by Bathsheba. The housekeeper testified that once in bed, Bathsheba said to her, "I hope Mr. Spooner is in heaven," repeating it through the night. At one point, Mrs. Stratton threatened to inform the neighbors.

"Please don't, Sarah. I'll pay you handsomely."[38]

Sarah testified that Bathsheba "sighed and tumbled" for hours[39]. Once her mistress fell asleep, Sarah left to pass the remainder of the evening in her own bed.

In Worcester, at four o'clock in the morning, Prudence awoke at hearing a loud rap at Mrs. Walker's door, amazed to discover Buchanan and Brooks who had left only the previous noon. In addition, there was a young man she had probably never seen before, adding to her wonder.

"Why are you back so soon?" Prudence asked.

As he later confessed, James Buchanan proceeded to tell her "a parcel of lies."[40]

"The Springfield guard is in pursuit; they're searching every home in Brookfield. Had it not been for a friend who alerted us, we should have been captured."[41]

His claim was of course nonsense. Brookfield is eighteen miles from Worcester, Springfield thirty-three miles further west, a long day's journey in 1778. Then to what was Buchanan's lie supposed to refer? Why would he incriminate himself and his accomplices in any crime? At this point, no one in the county was aware of the murder, except the criminals and the Spooner household. And surely he was not trying to suggest that as escaped POWs, they had been targeted for capture—not when hundreds of their comrades continued to freely wander throughout Massachusetts. By including the Springfield guard in the fabrication, it is possible that he wanted Prudence to believe that they had traveled as far as that town, en route to Montreal as originally planned. On the contrary, the mention of Springfield could only have aroused suspicion, as the men had been absent for too short a time to have made the over one-hundred mile round trip.

At some time she and Ezra were introduced.

"Where did you meet Mr. Ross?" Prudence asked.

Buchanan lied again. "About two miles from the tavern in Leicester [four miles west of Worcester]. [Mrs.] Spooner was there. It was she who told us about the guard."[42]

Prudence examined Brooks. "Mr. Brooks, you're not wearing your Sunday silk."

Brooks looked down at Joshua's muslin shirt, and thought quickly.

"We were in desperate want of money, and sold it."[43] Despite Brooks' stupidity which would shortly lead to the plot's unraveling, he apparently remembered to remove the bloodstained jacket given him by Ross, somewhere along the road to Worcester (probably at Buchanan's insistence). Prudence could not help but notice the general improvement in the appearance of the soldiers. She welcomed them in.

Mary Walker entered the taproom. They repeated the same story to her. She stared at the new visitor.

"Mr. Ross, tell me. Had you ever seen Mrs. Spooner before this morning?"

"I do not know that I have," he lied, then corrected himself, "but I had met Mr. Spooner—we rode to Lancaster together once." Ross was likely referring to the Princeton journey he and Spooner had made. East Princeton, formerly part of Lancaster, is about seventeen miles north of Worcester.

Buchanan opened a saddlebag, and pulled out the white shirt with ruffled cuffs.

"Mrs. Walker, could you remove these ruffles?"

Mary Walker must have found the request odd. "I suppose I could.'"

"Mrs. Spooner was kind enough to give me two pairs of stockings," Buchanan continued.

"Yes, and she gave me a shirt and stockings, too," added Brooks. It is astonishing to consider the extent to which Buchanan, Brooks and Ross went to implicate themselves over the course of the next fourteen hours.

Mary Walker again turned to Ross, who seemed moody, ill-at-ease.

"Mr. Ross, why are you so dull?"

Dazed, Ross took a couple of turns about the room, then leaned against a wall.

"Reason enough," he responded, according to Walker's testimony.[44]

It had not escaped the women's attention that Ross was riding one of Spooner's horses. The men passed all of Monday at Walker's. "In the morning we went to drinking to endeavor to drown the thoughts of the horrid action we had been guilty of," they wrote in their confession.[45]

CHAPTER TEN

Poor Little Man

Monday morning was clear and beautiful in Brookfield. Bathsheba awoke early, probably weary after her fitful sleep. She dressed quickly. The whereabouts of Gray and his partner are unknown. Downstairs, Sarah Stratton would have been already busy in the kitchen. The children stirred. Bathsheba asked Cummings to accompany her to the well.

Once there, Bathsheba paused to peer in. "Oh, Alex, I hope Mr. Spooner is in heaven," continuing her litany from the previous night.

She continued to stare.

"Do you think we could sink him?" she wondered, according to Cummings' testimony.

He made no reply. In another scenario, Joshua was to have been killed in bed, then thrown in the well to create the illusion that he had died while fetching a drink. One newspaper account suggested that Bathsheba's proposal to sink her husband's body may have been so inspired. Bathsheba thought again.

"Listen, Alex. Ride to Mr. Cooley's. Tell him that Mr. Spooner did not return home from the tavern last night, and inquire as to his whereabouts."[1]

Cummings, though no longer the ever-dutiful servant, complied, and went to unhitch the horse Ross had abused during his Topsfield-Brookfield trip, and rode to the center of town. Bathsheba went inside.

Taverner Ephraim Cooley, the town's former constable, was surely surprised to find Alex at his door so early.

"Mr. Cooley," he blurted, "Mrs. Spooner has sent me to inquire if you had seen her husband after he had left your tavern evening last."[2] The neighbors had been suspicious about the unseemly goings-on at the Spooner residence the past month, thus Alex's inquiry was received with added alarm.

"I'll bring some men over presently," Cooley promised.[3] Cooley engaged the help of six neighbors, and all rode back to the Spooners with Alex. The tavern keeper's anxiety must have been great—Joshua had been one of his closest friends. Bathsheba received Cooley in the parlor.

"Mr. Cooley, welcome. I sent Alex—"

"Is Mr. Spooner at home?" he interrupted.

"No, he isn't." Bathsheba, according to Cooley's testimony, began to sob. Ephraim and his posse stepped outside to search. Cooley noticed snow which had been pushed into a heap by the kitchen gate. He kicked something in the pile, and discovered Joshua's hat. Exasperated, he re-entered the home. Bathsheba was still distraught.

"This is Spooner's hat. What do you think now?"

"It is his hat," she confirmed.[4]

Taking the hat, Cooley left the property to continue the search, his men remaining to examine the grounds. Cooley had walked about five hundred feet down the road toward the nearest neighbor's when one of his party began to pursue him, shouting.

"Ephraim, come back. We've found something!"[5]

As they returned, the five other men stood about the well, looking in.

Cooley approached. While leaning over, he noticed two separate spots of blood on the curb, and left immediately for the constable and coroner, or "tipstave", so named for the brass-tipped, six-foot long stave that such officers always carried. If the sight of Ephraim Cooley dismounting his horse at the homes of Coroner Thomas Gilbert and Constable Elisha Hamilton piqued the townspeople's curiosity, then the sight of all three galloping towards the Spooners must have raised a general alarm.

The men arrived to find Dr. King, who with his wife had shared dinner with Joshua Spooner the previous evening. He would testify that upon hearing of the crime (from whom it is unknown), he hurried to the murder site to find the body already pulled from the well. He knelt beside it.

In the 1770's, forensic medicine was still virtually unexplored. The medical examiner of today would have noted full rigor mortis, hastened of course by the near-freezing water.[6] More than twelve hours' immersion had turned the skin grey and soft. Mottled in red in reaction to the sudden blows, Spooner was redder still due to post-mortem lividity, his blood having drained to the head and neck. Now that the body had been placed on its back, the blood was beginning to resettle and discolor his limbs as well.[7] The temple and forehead were badly bruised. King testified that the scalp had been cut about an inch-and-a-half (these bruises and scalp injury represent the only medical evidence presented during the case)[8], adding to the mystery as to why more blood evidence was not found from a head laceration which would have resulted in massive bleeding.[9]

If Dr. King had looked closely, he would have noticed hairs which had been driven into the wound, even tissue strands bridging the cut's depths. Such evidence would have strongly suggested that Spooner's wound had been caused by a weapon striking his head, rather than from a fall. Blood evidence from such a wound, however, could not make certain the actual cause of death; a head wound can cause extreme bleeding before or after.[10] It is possible that Spooner died from the strangulation which preceded the blow to the head. Although the well water may have washed away such evidence, it is likely that Spooner had vomited during the attack, which occurred but half an hour following his meal.

Dr. King, like Spooner, was a Patriot. When Brookfield's Committee of Correspondence was assembled in September of 1774, he was among its founding members, and served as captain of the local militia two years later.

The men carried the body through the front entrance into the east room, likely placing it upon the sofa. Bathsheba stood far back; neither she nor her two eldest children could be persuaded to look at Joshua. Her youngest, Bathsheba, was the only family member to approach. Water dripped from the cloak and waistcoat upon the carpet. Spooner's hair was matted and bloody, and nearly frozen, his breeches torn and bloodstained. His feet were shoeless.

Innkeeper Cooley also examined the body, later testifying that the wounds he witnessed were those as described by Dr. King, whose testimony preceded Cooley's at the trial.

The coroner, Thomas Gilbert, may or may not have been a physician, however loosely that profession was defined in early America. Whatever the case, the coroner's responsibilities during the period were mostly legal rather than medical, which may account for his apparent deference to Dr. King who performed the cursory exam. To be appointed coroner required no professional qualifications of any kind, not even medical experience. His opinion was essentially that of a layman. In fact, the only requirement was that he not be an ex-convict.

A coroner's jury of inquest would be held in the room early the next day. Within a few minutes, the neighbors departed, leaving Bathsheba, her two children, Mrs. Stratton and Cummings alone with the body. It is likely that a guard was posted.

Back in Worcester, as witnessed by Mary Walker, Sergeant Buchanan bled himself.[11] Following ancient Greek wisdom, the eighteenth century believed that the body contained four fluids, or humors: blood, phlegm, black bile and yellow bile. Bleeding was frequently prescribed to restore some balance, especially in cases of fever. It is also possible that Buchanan was suffering from mercury poisoning, which his skin had likely absorbed while preparing the calomel papers on Friday.

The means chosen to kill Spooner are equally perplexing. Besides Bathsheba's children, there were four potential witnesses to the crime: Cummings, Mrs. Stratton, and Gray and his partner, as well as a possible fifth, identified only as a "male servant" in the trial notes (likely either Jesse Parker, the stable hand, or Sarah Stratton's son who also resided with the Spooners). Circumstantially, there were at least three more: Dr. King and his wife, and Mr. Cooley, not to mention any number of Cooley's patrons that evening. Posing as robbers, Buchanan, Brooks and Ross could have easily waylaid Spooner before his return home, dumping his body within any of Brookfield's vast woodlands. Ezra might have returned to his parents in Topsfield using another horse, although the lure of Bathsheba's charms would have made that an unlikely scenario. Though an arduous trek, Sgt. Buchanan could have made his way to his wife and child in Montreal, a city within British hands. Brooks' plight was the most desperate, having no sanctuary this side of the Atlantic, although he might have joined Buchanan in Canada. In considering the extent to which the four conspirators went to incriminate themselves, they appear fatally resigned to the consequences of their amateurish plot, or perhaps remorseful, prepared for any punishment as penance.

Planning to flee Monday evening, "...it pleased God to order it otherwise," as Brooks confessed.[12] It was William Brooks, his innate gift for bungling fortified by drunkenness, who would hasten the criminals' capture. With a day's supply of rum running through his veins, Brooks left Walker's late in the afternoon, and made his way to Brown's Tavern, which being at the end of (what is now Main St.) not far from the Green Estate (and hard by the jail) likely made it a familiar spot to the soldiers.

Brown's Tavern was also known as The Hancock Arms, bearing the name of the rich, foppish John Hancock who owned a substantial amount of land in the village. A favorite meeting place of Patriots during the Revolution, the tavern was established two decades earlier by Luke Brown of Sudbury. Avaricious to one contemporary, he had few friends, and had procured his property, as rumor had it, by disreputable means. His son succeeded him, drinking up most of the profits. He died in late 1776. The tavern's disrepute was shared by its clientele. Although frequented by those having business at the nearby county court, it was generally shunned by more respectable visitors. General George Washington, en route to the troops awaiting his command at Cambridge, avoided its hospitality, opting to stay at the more genteel Stearns Tavern.

Buchanan had given Spooner's watch to Brooks, who displayed it proudly to the rapt crowd at the tavern. One patron wondered where Brooks had acquired his silver buckles, heretofore unseen. Brooks stretched out his feet to afford a better view, the shoes another gift from the sergeant. The initials "JS" were prominently engraved on the buckles, increasing the crowd's curiosity.

Rumors about the crime, unrelated to Brooks' visit to Brown's, were circulating in the town. In addition to the men's behavior which in itself surely aroused suspicion, it is likely that a rider had been dispatched from Brookfield to Worcester late in the morning—the Brookfield Committee of Correspondence would have wasted no time in alerting its Worcester counterpart, especially if a crime allegedly perpetrated by British soldiers was involved. Even if it had happened that Brooks and Buchanan had not been immediately linked to the crime, it would have required no great leap of the imagination to suspect the men, who had been seen on at least three occasions in the company of Joshua's wife.

Ensign Clark, the first in any official capacity to be alerted in Worcester, was summoned to Brown's, where he discovered that Brooks had already returned to Walker's. Clark followed. Once there, Clark informed Mrs. Walker of the men's alleged involvement.

Joshua Whitney, one of the founders of the radical American Political Society, and as captain of the militia active in drilling recruits, was another of the increasing number destined for Brown's that afternoon. The tale of the exiled general's daughter who conspired with three amorous soldiers to execute her Patriot husband would capture the imagination of New Englanders like no other. News from the distant Revolution seemed dull by comparison.

While at Brown's, another Worcester citizen (his namesake and forbear was one of the town's first settlers, in 1673) entered. According to Joshua Whitney's testimony, Ephraim Curtis announced "I heard that Mr. Spooner was murdered, and that three of the suspects are staying at Mrs. Walker's." He and Whitney left for the widow's, where they found Brooks and Buchanan.

Whitney spoke to Brooks. "I understand you've acquired a gold watch. Can I see it?"

Brooks removed the watch from his pocket. Whitney examined it, as well as the already notorious silver buckles. "Where's your young friend?"[13]

Brooks gestured toward the loft. Whitney climbed the stairs and ladder to find Ezra Ross crouched in a corner, trembling. Ross expressed surprise at being discovered. Ross and Whitney returned to the taproom.

Buchanan had stepped away. Brooks sheepishly turned toward Prudence, who then showed Whitney the gold watch which Brooks had just handed her.

Brooks confessed that it was his watch. Whitney asked the soldiers to sit while he kept guard until more help arrived, Curtis joining him.

Ross began to speak. "Sir, I wish to see a minister. I am truly guilty of the crime, but let it be known I did not strike the first blow. I helped Brooks and Buchanan...I will confess to the sorry affair once the minister should arrive...I received his jacket and breeches, and let Brooks have mine, which were bloody...I have money here..."

Buchanan reappeared. Ross dug into his billfold, and produced the four ten-pound notes, as well as three eight-dollar bills. "The cash is my own," Ross offered. "I also have the man's hose, shirt and saddlebags."[14]

Ross' uncounseled words would return to haunt him in Whitney's testimony. Brooks and Buchanan remained silent.

Brooks was led back to Brown's, followed minutes later by his comrades. Ross was committed to the care of Joseph Ball, another committee member. Ball noticed that Ross was wearing black knit breeches and a jacket of brown cloth with brass buttons. Ross' horse was equally familiar to Ball, who had seen Spooner and his wife upon it. He also testified that he had noticed Buchanan some weeks earlier at Walker's, and knew him to be a blacksmith.

John Green, Jr. (the Spooners' nephew), just shy of his fifteenth birthday, entered, dumbfounded to find Ross in his uncle's brown jacket, and Brooks wearing the silver-buckled shoes.

The same Monday evening in Brookfield, Bathsheba discussed the murder with Loved Lincoln, a long-time family friend (no relation to Bathsheba's defense attorney, Levi Lincoln). She lied liberally, if we are to believe his testimony.

"I don't know how my husband came by his death...The regulars [soldiers] went away the day before yesterday. Mr. Ross took Joshua's jacket and breeches."

"I understand Mr. Ross was in hiding," Lincoln pressed further.

"Yes, but he felt he had no other choice. After all, he had injured my husband's horse."

"When did Mr. Ross leave?"

"Saturday," she lied again, "with the regulars. They all three left together."[15]

Nothing could be done with the body until the murder inquest. Given the frosty atmosphere of New England homes in the winter, the remains of Mr. Spooner could await proper attention until the next afternoon. In a gesture of extraordinary magnanimity, Martha Tufts of Brookfield, Bathsheba's eldest sister, offered to sponsor the funeral, an event whose costs in the eighteenth-century were not unlike those of a twenty-first century wedding. Typically, the women of the family would wash and dress the deceased, although in the case of an upper-class family such as the Spooners (not to mention the circumstances of his death), it is likely that a nurse "midwife undertaker" prepared the body. Depending upon the family's means, plain linen or cerecloth (linen dipped in melted wax), cashmere or even muslin winding sheets served as the shroud. Before constructing the casket, a local cabinet maker would come by to measure the body.

In a fascinating letter dated one week after the murder, the Worcester Committee informed the Council for the State of Massachusetts Bay in Boston of the actions it had taken regarding Brooks and Buchanan.

> The Committee and many others for some time dreaded the consequences Of such members of Burgoin [Burgoyne] People passing through the Country being fearful some

> unhappy Consequences would result from it—the late unhappy murder of Mr. Spooner has shewn their fears were not groundless—the committee were so happy as to detect said murderers by accident it was told them soon after hearing of said Persons in town, who had resided there for some time, and that their was a surprising alteration of the Circumstances, from Saturday to Monday, being on Satturday quite destitute of Money, and on Monday very flush of it, as also their being posses'd of a watch and a pair Silver Buckles, these Circumstances produc'd such a Suspicion in the minds of the Committee as Induc'd them (altho there was no Order imediately respecting these Persons) to secure them as Prisoners of Warr grossly misbehaving, they were imediately apprehended but such circumstances turned up, that the Prisoners were very soon induc'd to make an ample confession—upon which the Committee sent for a Justice and delivered them to him...[16]

This letter suggests that a messenger had been sent from Brookfield to Worcester almost immediately following the discovery of Spooner's body, and that the committee may have heard rumors of the men's arrival in Worcester only hours before Brooks' drunken debacle. One newspaper account indicated that Bathsheba was soon implicated by the men.[17] It is not clear when the soldiers made their formal confession (which may have been different from the confession printed weeks later). Given the hour of the arrest, it is unlikely that they appeared before the committee earlier than the next morning.

In 1778, America lacked a formal law school. Aspiring attorneys, such as John Adams in Worcester, learned their craft while apprenticed as law clerks. Twenty-year-old Dwight Foster, a graduate of Brown University when only sixteen-years of age, was spending a few days at his family home in Brookfield on a break from his Providence law apprenticeship. Rising early that Tuesday, he galloped across town to hitch his horse alongside the many others encircling Bathsheba's home, the site of the coroner's inquest. Following British practice, a coroner's inquest in eighteenth-century America sought to determine if the cause of death appeared suspicious enough to pursue an indictment for murder. The coroner himself hand-picked the jury from his acquaintances, all white men who owned land, all likely of British ancestry, belonging to the Congregational church, and all Patriots. Each juror was paid for his trouble. While the promise of payment attracted many, the scandal's notoriety likely proved the main draw.

Thomas Gilbert had called fourteen men to serve: Richard Wellin, Moses Dorr, Seth Banister, Benjamin Jennings, John Waite, Elias Staples, Adoniram Walker, Comfort Old (a veteran of the war with France, later serving at the Battle of Bennington) and five more, all friends of the Spooners: Dr. Jonathan King, Obadiah Cooley (who more than twenty years earlier had fought alongside Comfort Old), Dr. Francis Foxcroft, James Upham (one of the state's foremost attorneys), and Asa Bigelow. Also present were Bathsheba, her children, Alexander Cummings, Sarah Stratton, her son, and several others, including our aspiring attorney, Dwight Foster. In a letter to a Mr. J. Clarke of Northampton, Foster penned some of the first words in reaction to the murder, a reaction whose tone would be echoed often in the proceeding months.

Brookfield, Thursday
March 5, 1778

My dear Sir

On Tuesday last I was present at the disclosing of one of the most horrid scenes of iniquity that ever came to my knowledge. Indeed, I can scarce believe our century ever produced its parallel...[the event] has caused a great deal of Noise and Speculation, and will undoubtedly be the subject of some conversation in more distant Parts. The character of Mrs. Spooner...is now completed as one of the blackest and most detestable ...Very little harmony and cordiality has subsisted between her and her husband for many years—She has long cherished a hatred in her Bosom...[18]

In the same letter, the law student addressed the means Bathsheba used to ensnare housekeeper Sarah Stratton, as well as the men. Stratton and Cummings, he claims "only consented...to keep ye Matter secret...in the Prospect of Pecuniary advantage..." He adds that the men had agreed to join her plot "...by the Promise of great rewards (and undoubtedly) by ye Fascination of more secret and bewitching favors..."[19]

The suggestion of sexual bribery is barely disguised. Had Foster simply been just another Brookfielder indulging in gossip, then his thought might be taken no more or less seriously than another's. He was, however, not only a future attorney, but the son of the town's most respected citizen, the Hon. Jedediah Foster, one of the presiders over the impending trial. Equally important, Dwight Foster's letter was written only two days after his attendance at the inquest, the testimony still fresh in his mind.

The coroner's jury determined that

> ...on the evening of the first of March about nine of the clock, returning home from his neighbors, [Joshua Spooner] near his own door was feloniously assaulted by one or more ruffians, knocked down by a club, beat and bruised, and thrown into his own well with water in it, by persons to the jury unknown...[20]

A custom since medieval times, the ordeal by touch, or cruentation, was a favored means in determining guilt. If the flesh of the victim discolored or began to bleed under the fingers of the accused, she would be deemed guilty. In Salem, years before the Spooner case, young John Adams found his advocacy skills tested to the utmost in trying to secure an acquittal in a sensational murder where the ordeal had suggested the guilt of his client. Historically, if the accused was a woman, her profession of innocence was less likely to be believed, thus the occasional further test by cruentation. Those believed possessed by demons were particular targets. As Bathsheba had been described in terms such as "artful" and "bewitching", her inexplicable deeds to some seemed likely to have been inspired by darker forces.

At the conclusion of the Spooner inquest, Dr. King asked that Bathsheba place a hand upon her husband's corpse. She rose, and approached his body, laying her hand upon his forehead and saying "poor little man."[21] The result of her touch is not recorded.

At the same hour, Brooks, Buchanan and Ross were being examined in Worcester, naming Bathsheba as instigator. A rider from Worcester was immediately dispatched to Brookfield, informing the officials that the daughter of Brigadier Ruggles was to be held on suspicion of murder, news so sensational in its horror that its effect on the townspeople can hardly be imagined. Asa Bigelow, foreman of the jury of inquest, testified at the April trial that a member of the jury informed Bathsheba (some hours after the inquest) that she would be taken to jail in Worcester. She confessed.

"I hired the men to commit the murder. I offered them one thousand dollars; I gave them two-hundred on deposit. The murderers include Sergeant Buchanan and Private William Brooks. We three were involved."[22] Significantly, she failed to implicate Ezra, her preferred lover.

Early that afternoon, neighbor Obadiah Rice hitched his sleigh, and joined by innkeeper Ephraim Cooley, made the short trip to Bathsheba's home, possibly on orders from the constable. As a crowd of onlookers likely milled about, Bathsheba climbed into the sleigh, joined by Alexander Cummings and Sarah Stratton, and a third unidentified "male servant", likely Stratton's son, all now under arrest. Only Bathsheba would be later detained as a suspect—her servants had been apprehended as potential witnesses who would never be formally charged with any wrongdoing.

Bathsheba waved a final goodbye to her children (there is no indication that she ever saw them again, although despite the ensuing furor, it is hard to imagine they did not visit her in prison). Most likely, the children were left in the care of Bathsheba's sister, Martha Tufts, who at the time was already providing for a daughter and four sons, all under the age of six.

Mrs. Spooner talked incessantly during the ride to Worcester (Cummings and Stratton were silent). One of her statements defies interpretation.

"It don't seem like Christmas Day."[23]

She continued. "I have a great desire to see my Daddy. If it had not been for that, this murder would never have been committed."[24]

Poignantly, Bathsheba bared her soul, imparting a sense of the desolation she had experienced during the nearly four years of Ruggles' exile from Hardwick. Heinous as the crime was, the wrath that she provoked may have been due in no small part to the contempt with which many Patriots still regarded her father. According to the testimony of the sleigh driver, Bathsheba also said, "I would suffer ten deaths for Alexander [Cummings] and Mrs. Stratton before they should suffer, for they are innocent."[25]

Arriving in Worcester early Tuesday evening, March 3, the four were taken first to Brown's Tavern, by which time Buchanan, Brooks and Ross had apparently already been brought to jail. Along with Ephraim Cooley, also present were Brookfield Constable Elisha Hamilton, and his Worcester counterpart Samuel Bridge, deacon at Old South, and of the few Loyalists in attendance. Despite his allegiances, he was much admired, described in his obituary as one who had "filled his station with honesty and honor, and supported his Christian profession by a constant observance of the offices of piety and an habitual exercise of the active virtues of the Gospel."[26]

Bathsheba freely acknowledged her complicity. She wept openly.

"I am the whole means by which the murder was done. I bribed them to say and do everything. As I've told Mr. Cooley, Sarah and Alex are innocent."[27]

When asked about her accomplices, she replied, "If I could see the persons face to face, I could give you satisfaction. You know, this is the effect of bad company,"[28] possibly an attempt by Mrs. Spooner to allay some of her guilt, neglecting to address the fact that as far back as the fall she had been trying to involve first Cummings, then Ross as her hired killers, many weeks before any appearance by Brooks and Buchanan.

"Were it not for this thing, I could meet my judge. This happened by means of Ross being sick at our house."[29]

Bathsheba's steadfast belief in God's mercy would find its last expression in her prayer at the gallows. And here, typically, Mrs. Spooner cast her actions as under the nefarious influence of others.

All four suspects were jailed. It was their only option. Under Massachusetts colonial law, murder defendants could not post bail, although bail was allowed in cases of manslaughter. The Worcester prison would be a crowded shelter that week, housing yet another resident of the Spooner household up to this point unmentioned, one Sam Woods who, according to the same earlier cited letter from the Worcester Committee, was, like Buchanan

> ...a sergeant...who kept at the same house with these murderers...he was an intimate with Mrs. Spooner who was at this House the most of Frayday and part of Satturday before the Murder of the others. The Justice as there was no direct proof was inclined to release him, but the Committee apprehending he might throw some light upon this matter committed him as a prisoner of war misbehaving...[30]

To rattle the nerves of the county's residents even further, one additional Spooner boarder had been captured, also transferred by the Brookfield Committee to Worcester. Five days following Bathsheba's arrest, he was

> ...charged with gross misbehavior being very quarelsome declaring he had [imbued?] his Hands in american Blood, and would do it again, [the committee] at the same time expressed their uneasiness at such Numbers of these Persons passing through the Country...we committed this Person whose Name is John Rains to gaol...[31]

Grudgingly, the harsh days of winter retreated. News from the battlefield came to a stop, significant hostilities not recommencing until the summer. Three months earlier, delighted to hear of the British defeat at Saratoga, Louis XVI of France recognized the United States. On February 6th, a formal Treaty of Alliance was signed; George III heard the distressing news six weeks later. The treaty made its formal arrival in America in early May, a treaty which helped to ensure eventual victory for the new nation.

Rumors were rife—Georgia and Connecticut were planning to defect, the British were hoping to arm Catholics, Native Americans and the enslaved against the Patriots—not to mention the fifty thousand Russian Cossacks about to arrive who would join His Majesty's troops. The wilder the story, the more likely its dissemination. But no tale was as prized as a true one. About New England's hearths that early spring, no news would be related with such fervor and frequency as the story of the general's daughter and her murderous lovers.

CHAPTER ELEVEN

A Most Horrid Piece of Villainy

News unfolded at a breakneck pace—the murder, the soldiers' arrests, and finally the shock of Bathsheba's involvement. New England awoke each day to learn the latest gossip of what had become by mid-March a cause celebre.

Eight years before the Revolution, Stephen Salisbury arrived from Boston to establish his hardware store near Worcester's courthouse. In Boston, he and brother Samuel had operated a similar store for many years, and determined that the villagers from surrounding towns moving to and fro the county seat of Worcester would provide a substantial market. North and west of the business at what would become Lincoln Square (named for Governor Levi Lincoln, son of Mrs. Spooner's attorney), Stephen Salisbury bought a large farm adjoining land owned by John Hancock. Salisbury and Hancock were among a handful of prominent Bostonians who recognized the village's potential as a new frontier welcoming sons of farmers whose land in towns nearer the coast had either been overfarmed or dispersed to older brothers. Salisbury's farm would become the site of Worcester's first factory, the first of one thousand, and his descendants would be among the city's richest and most philanthropic. Writing to Salisbury from Boston, brother-in-law Samuel Barrett penned one of the few letters in reaction to the murder which survive from that first week.

> Dear Sir
>
> Boston
> March 6, 1778
>
> ...Surely nothing more diabolical was ever perpetrated in New England than Spooner's murder—I am glad the authors and assassins are likely to be discovered...[1]

News of the "authors and assassins" and their apprehension had apparently not yet reached Boston, but only four days after the discovery of Spooner's body, reports of the murder were reaching the capital, nearly seventy miles from Brookfield. A couple of days earlier, a close follower of the case, Reverend Ebenezer Parkman of Westborough, eleven miles east of Worcester, wrote in his diary of a friend's visit, at which time he heard of "...a fresh story of an horrible murder. One Mr. Spooner was murdered by two soldiers lately, at Brookfield—he was knocked down and thrown into a well...said they were hired by his wife, who is a daughter of Brigadier Ruggles..."[2]

As the arrests occurred only two days before his diary entry, it appears that the reverend was privy to the freshest gossip.

In another letter, one Mr. Savage passed on less accurate rumors to his wife. "...It seems a certain British officer lodged at [Mrs. Spooner's] house, when he came down with Gen. Burgoin [sic]—he rose early it was on his way...she informed him she had a husband very disagreeable to her..."[3]

In Bathsheba's native town of Sandwich, on Cape Cod, Benjamin Percival noted in his diary of March 14, 1778

> My brother John got here today from Lennox [sic, a town near the New York border] a very unnatural murder in Brookfield, a woman hired two Russians to kill her husband.[4]

Russian hired guns certainly would have added an air of exotic intrigue to the tale. Mr. Percival apparently confused "Russians" with "Hessians" (or perhaps "Prussians"), the mercenary soldiers whose hiring by King George two years earlier outraged Americans. The fact that Hessian soldiers were imprisoned in Charlestown, where Brooks and Buchanan had been encamped, may have added to his confusion.

Dwight Foster, the young Brookfield attorney, wrote in a letter dated March 5

> Mrs. Spooner (who appears to be destitute of every sensation) with her own hands cast Brooks' breeches, covered with Blood, into the Fire... Brooks offered to turn State Evidence...I believe a similar Piece of Iniquity was scarce ever perpetrated in North America since settled by the English...Their unaccountable stupidity...Quos Deus volt perdire priusquaam dementato [Those whom god loses first go mad]...[5]

In his own diary, he wrote

> ...On Sunday evening the 1st instant a most horrid piece of villainy was committed in this town in the murder of Mr. Spooner, who was barbarously massacred by three hell-hounds at the instigation of Mrs. Spooner...[6]

Newspapers weren't immune to the lurid prose. A week earlier, the Boston Gazette and Country Journal referred to the case as "...the most cruel, inhuman and unheard of Murder..." and wrote of the "particulars of the diabolical Plot."[7]

The enormity of Bathsheba's crime may not be readily appreciated by the twenty-first century reader. Murder was a very rare event in colonial Massachusetts. One plotted by a woman against her husband scandalized even the most sanguine citizen.

Shocked New Englanders viewed the crime as an attack upon a social fabric already frayed by revolution. And its sensational details only added to the outrage.

Although the most enlightened minds considered marriage an equal partnership, in the popular imagination, the wife joined to and abided by her husband's direction. The death of a wife and mother did not cause the same ramifications as that of a husband and father. Young mothers died at an alarming rate, chiefly, of course, from childbirth and its complications. Widowers seeking to remarry were commonplace. If a wife died, her place was often quickly taken by another. With a father's death, the family's position died along with him, its identity lost. Seen in this light, Bathsheba's crime was described, understandably, in extreme terms. Her attorney was the first to explain the murder as a consequence of insanity. It was beyond the imagination of early Americans why a woman would kill not only her sole means of survival (by colonial law, Bathsheba could inherit only one third of her husband's estate, assuming her innocence), but the very identity of the family itself.

For Worcester's citizens, The King's Arms Tavern, on what is now north Main Street, was the clearinghouse for gossip. For twenty-five cents, a meal could be enjoyed in the dining room, or a drink in the taproom opposite, whose shelves of bottles, glasses and decanters reflected the fire's glow. Landlord Patch, who owned the town's largest farm and finest herd of sheep, welcomed fellow farmers who debated weather and politics over a glass of flip. In the great room above, children danced the Virginia Reel as the days of winter waned.

Town officials, striving to keep the fragile government on a steady course, found particular reason to worry following the murder. The Brookfield Committee was as alarmed as its Worcester brethren, mistrustful of security at the Worcester gaol. In a letter to the Worcester Committee the day before Spooner's funeral, the committee wrote

> ...We are in doubt whether the Perpetrators of the late Horrid Murder Committed in this Town whose Persons are committed to the Gaol, will remain therein until the Time of there Trial...which is not very far distant. Voted as the opinion of this Town that a good and sufficient Guard be kept round the Gaol of this County to secure those Murderers Till they can be brought to Justice...[8]

A day earlier, the legislature of Massachusetts Bay, by now familiar with the murder, expressed their own fear of these "Burgoin People" encamped across the Charles River.

> The Committee appointed to consider the Expediency of removing the British troops now in Cambridge farther into the Country, and what was proper to be done to know whether there are any Fire-Arms secreted among said Troops...(and elsewhere)...respecting the remaining Troops of the Convention, and of their present Situation, and the dangerous Situation of the Town of Boston on their Account...[9]

In the centuries-old opinion of western Massachusetts, Boston and its lawmakers have regarded their part of the state at best dismissively, at worst with condescending arrogance. The suggestion here that the troops should be removed "farther into the Country" smacks of supreme insolence—"the Country", of course, meant Rutland, where many of the British would be incarcerated within six weeks—only a few miles from the scene of the crime!

As the sole media of the eighteenth-century, newspapers had a profound impact. In the popular imagination, Benjamin Franklin comes first to mind as the foremost journalist of his day, but few remember his fellow printer from Worcester, Isaiah Thomas, the journalist-entrepreneur par excellence whose Massachusetts Spy would become the most influential Patriot mouthpiece throughout the colonies. By early 1775, just before the outbreak of hostilities, Thomas' paper had reached a circulation of 3,500, delivered to its readership by a complex system of post riders. Undoubtedly, the riders served an equally vital function as liaisons between the many Patriotic Committees of Correspondence.

Providing he maintained other business interests, a professional printer could succeed. His list of worries, shared by most businessmen, included unpredictable supplies, and even less reliable sales. The scarcity of rags, the chief raw material for the manufacture of paper, was at times so great that newspapers regularly advertised for them.

In 1775, Thomas estimated that a weekly such as his required six hundred customers and a generous number of advertisements to stay alive. Less than a year after the start of the Revolution, revenues had become so depleted that Thomas and his apprentices were forced to subsist on bread and milk. In March of 1776, Thomas suspended publication. In order to resume in April, Thomas found it necessary to raise the subscription price, as his creditors had attached the paper. Beginning in June, Thomas leased the newly named Worcester Spy to other printers while he traveled the colonies to collect money owed him. He returned to Worcester only for brief periods during the next two years to keep tabs on his business.

The closing of Boston Harbor had prevented the arrival of ships from Europe bringing news from overseas. A sensational murder in Brookfield filled the gap. The developing story's twists and turns undoubtedly made Thomas' visits to Worcester more frequent than they might have been. This "...most extraordinary crime ever perpetrated in New England" kept printers close to their shops throughout the spring and early summer of that year.[10]

For scoops on the Spooner case, Thomas likely found no better source than the Worcester jail, where the suspects had been imprisoned since March 3. Worcester's first gaol could only charitably be referred to as minimum security—it offered the village little more protection from its malefactors than a door latch might secure a home against intruders. Built in 1733, it was one of the town's earliest public buildings, following Worcester's permanent settlement by only twenty years. The grandest of Worcester's earliest buildings, its jails and courthouses, were dedicated to serving its least worthy citizens.

The first prison soon outlived its usefulness, and a new gaol, thirty-eight by twenty-eight feet (about the size of a modest colonial home) was erected in 1753, just south of its predecessor. The south end faced Back (now Goldsberry) Street and its gallows. The prison's walls were studded with joints six inches square, set five inches apart, and filled between with stone and mortar. The top, sides and floor, inside and out, were covered with oak plank fortified with seven posts, and secured by hundreds of iron spikes. Doors and windows were heavily grated with iron. Despite its formidable appearance, the wooden structure, largely populated during the Revolution by British prisoners-of-war and Tories, facilitated a number of escapes. In 1784, it too was superseded by a new granite prison, the state's largest stone building, after King's Chapel in Boston.

Incarceration is mostly a nineteenth-century idea. In earlier times, prisoners were either political detainees, convicts awaiting execution, or debtors facing the dilemma of gaining release only upon payment of their debts, prevented from earning any income while languishing behind bars. Those awaiting trial could also be jailed. Massachusetts Bay forbade bail for suspects charged with a capital crime, as were Bathsheba and her three soldiers, who were almost immediately remanded to jail upon Mrs. Spooner's arrival in Worcester on the evening of March 3. Despite their notoriety, the men were likely treated little differently from their fellow inmates (although guarded more heavily). Bathsheba, however, was an anomaly—not only female, but very much out of her social element. She received at least one concession, that of a personal jailer, a Mrs. Curtis, who Bathsheba described as very kind and obliging toward her.

There was another who attended to Mrs. Spooner while in prison, one more obliging than any, the Reverend Thaddeus Maccarty, pastor of Worcester's Old South Church. Son of a successful merchant and captain, Maccarty was born in Boston in 1721 and, expecting to follow his father's career, joining Capt. Maccarty on several voyages. A delicate constitution, however, frustrated his father's ambitions for him, and the land-loving son opted for a life in the ministry. In 1742, Maccarty was ordained to the church in Kingston, near Plymouth.

The first three years of Maccarty's pastorate were peaceful. The young clergyman, however, started his vocation during an era destined to become one of the stormiest for New England Christianity, the Great Awakening. A reaction to the church's sterility and uninspired conformity, what began as a revival meeting in New Jersey in 1719 intensified over the next twenty years until by the early 1740's, New England was aflame with the spirit of renewal. Aside from the Boston Mathers, no minister would achieve such renown as Jonathan Edwards of Northampton, whose Faithful Narrative of the Surprising Work of God of 1737 spread word of his miraculous conversions, including that of an infamous harlot. Not since the 1692 witch hysteria had the colony's churches witnessed such frenzy. The dry, death rattle style of more conservative pastors offered little to counter the impassioned revivalists. Even more than Edwards, it was the celebrity of the British preacher, George Whitefield, and the resulting pandemonium (a word whose etymology, "all demons" coined by Milton as the name for hell's capital, would have happily matched the opinion of opposing ministers) which best characterized the movement. No histrionics were beyond Whitefield and his followers, not scenes of Christ Crucified, nor even sinners enduring hell's torments, acted out before the congregation.

Maccarty invited Whitefield to preach at Kingston in 1745, which for Maccarty's career proved disastrous. In a letter written the same year, the pastor defended his invitation.

> I can't but think Mr. Whitefield is a man eminent for his piety, and that he has done vast service to the kingdom of Christ in this land more especially; and that if ministers and people would let him have a free course throughout the Land, he would be instrumental of bringing about a very glorious reformation. And no one that is in such a thought, can help being grieved, to think he meets with such opposition among ministers and people.[11]

Had Maccarty asked the then current pope, Benedict XIV, to preside over baptisms the next month, the reaction might have been less virulent. The church's windows were covered, its doors nailed shut. Maccarty's invitation was withdrawn, and the pastor was asked to resign.

Aaron Burr's uncle, the Rev. William Burr, had served for twenty years as pastor of Old South. In 1740, the fiery Whitefield, to great acclaim, was invited to preach on Worcester's common, an invitation which had received a lukewarm endorsement from Burr. Pro-Whitefield circles were taken aback at Burr's ambivalence, and a campaign was begun to remove him from his post, which did not occur until 1745. Over the next several months, however, an anti-Whitefield faction gained the upper hand, and while searching for a new pastor, the congregation agreed "...that the church will esteem it an offence, if any member thereof, shall hereafter countenance itinerant preachers."[12] Luckily for Maccarty, within a couple of years the Great Awakening had cooled, and he was welcomed to Worcester as Burr's successor.

Historians have made much of the formative influence of the Great Awakening upon the rebellious spirit which gave birth to the Revolution. It was no coincidence that preachers allied with Whitefield later proved to be among the most patriotic. Maccarty preached several sermons comparing the plight of the Israelites under pharaoh to that of the colonists under King George III. The pastor's son, William Greenough Maccarty, would serve as quartermaster of Col. Timothy Bigelow's Minutemen regiment. It is inaccurate, however, to include Rev. Maccarty among the town's fervent Patriots. As one historian has written, Maccarty's politics were "...decided and firm, ranking, however, with the moderate

Whigs. His printed sermons are more characterized by judicious thought, good sense, and piety, than elegance or eloquence."[13]

As pastor of Worcester's only real church, and whose political sympathies, though moderate, were aligned nevertheless with those strengthening their grip on Worcester's government, it was natural that Rev. Maccarty should have been assigned as spiritual adviser to the conspirators. It is unclear when he was chosen. While he may or may not have counseled the suspects before their indictment, he certainly did so shortly thereafter. Bathsheba soon came to rely upon him as her most trusted aide.

CHAPTER TWELVE

This Complicated Scene of Wickedness

Layers of snow, piled deep since November's first storm, characterized the unusually snowy winter of 1777-78. White clapboard homes hugging each village green were distinguishable only by their black shutters and occasional brick end. The east parish of Brookfield would have seemed no different from its hundreds of New England neighbors that first week in March, had it not overnight become a center of pilgrimage. On foot and horseback, by coach and sleigh came friends, family, and the merely curious, overwhelming the county's inns. Private homes handled the overflow crowds, determined, despite the abominable travel, to take some part in one of the biggest funerals in the county's history, that of Joshua Spooner.

If death was everywhere in eighteenth-century America—children and mothers in childbirth, war, smallpox and diphtheria—murder was exceedingly rare. Funerals of any kind were major social events, but the funeral of a murder victim from the social elite, brought to his fate by his wife—this was a once-in-a-lifetime spectacle. For families with means like the Spooners, funerals provided an opportunity to lavish sums of money Americans would never dream of spending on weddings or baptisms.

In 1741, the General Court attempted to regulate funerary extravagance.

> No scarves, Gloves (except six pairs to the bearers and one pair to each minister...of the church or congregation)... [and no] wine, Rum or Rings be allowed to be given at any funeral under the penalty of fifty pounds....[1]

The black cloth normally worn as funeral attire, of British manufacture, was no longer available; in its place, a band of black crepe was worn on the hat, or as an armband. Each member of the deceased family received a pair of white gloves, and often a gold ring enameled in black, engraved with either a skull or skeleton encased in a coffin; mottos such as "Prepared Be to Follow Me" might be included (although in the case of Joshua Spooner, such sentiments might have been unsettling to the more literally minded). One Salem doctor was said to have owned a tankard full of such rings. Rev. Andrew Eliot of Boston's Old North Church boasted nearly three thousand pairs of mourning gloves.

Typically, the body was waked at home the evening before, during which time liberal quantities of alcohol were consumed. Attendance at a funeral was by invitation only, usually conveyed by the church sexton. In the case of Joshua Spooner, the sexton had likely traveled to Boston the day following the murder to inform members of the family. The long journey ahead would have necessitated a funeral worthy of such trouble and expense. Although the Revolutionary period generally witnessed a decline in funerary extravagance, the Spooner funeral was likely an exception.

On the morning of Friday, March 6, Nathan Fiske, who had served as pastor of Brookfield's third church for twenty years, stepped up to the pulpit as the bells finished tolling: three times for a man, and thirty-six more for Spooner's age. Funeral sermons were a favorite of both preacher and mourner, and Fiske's sermon, like so many others, was published only days later by the Boston firm of Thomas and John Fleet. In a letter written about a week after, Dwight Foster, whose father would preside at the trial, observed that "Mr. Fisk [sic] preached a good discourse on the Occasion—great number of people collected."[2] The lengthy title read "A Sermon Preached at Brookfield March 6, 1778 on the Day of the Interment of Mr. Joshua Spooner, Who Was Most Barbarously Murdered at his Own Gate, on the Lord's evening preceding, by three Ruffians, who were hired for the Purpose by His Wife."

Echoing sentiments written by Dwight Foster the day before, Fiske, through his grand phrases, imbued the crime with an almost cosmic significance. "Such a murder must not be spoken of in soft terms; it ought rather to be painted in colours, could such colours be found, black as the crime itself...So premeditated, so aggravated, so horrid a murder was never perpetrated in America, and is almost without parallel in the known world..."[3]

Fiske admonished the standing room crowd to consider Bathsheba, a woman for whom affluence meant only tragedy.

> What is the possession of wealth, without domestic peace, and the sweets of conjugal affection and confidence? What are elegant apartments, what a house full of silver and gold to a man, if his house will not afford him a quiet retreat, nor a safe shelter, nor a single friend! —And what will it avail persons to set their hearts on rich attire, and to be able to dazzle the eye with a profusion of ornament, if under that gaudy dress, there be the foulest heart, the most shameful behavior, and a body hastening to the dungeon and the gibbet?[4]

Following his description of the perpetrators as whited sepulchers, he continued to assail their misdeeds as folly of the highest order.

> ...the devil, to whom they have devoted themselves, wily and cunning as he is, will only lead them into a snare and befool them...he that leaves the paths of uprightness to walk in the ways of darkness, will stumble and fall, will be snared and taken. All sin is folly; and a complication of wickedness is a complication of folly, as not to be in continual danger of discovery and dissolution...[5]

Fiske concluded his sermon by asking the faithful to reflect upon the fate of those most affected by the tragedy, including the suspects. His last words cast this world as properly outfitted for such evil.

> The virtuous friends of the murderers, as well as of the murdered, deserve our compassion, and our prayers. The innocent children, so suddenly, so awfully, bereft of their father, yea, I may say of their mother, too, demand our pity; and ought never to be reproached with the infamy of their mother, much less with the tragical death of their father. And sure I am, the condition of the unhappy murderers loudly bespeaks our anxious concern and earnest supplications at the throne of grace, that they may not, after their hardness and impenitent hearts, treasure up unto themselves wrath against the day of wrath, but be brought to a pungent sense of their deep and aggravated guilt, may abhor themselves and repent as in dust and ashes, that their souls may be plucked as brands out of everlasting burnings. Finally, this complicated scene of wickedness should make us all weary of such a world, which is a theatre for such bloody tragedies to be acted upon, and to long after that better, that heavenly country, where all is security, all is harmony, all is perfection, and all felicity...[6]

In early New England, the bereaved attached laudatory verses to the funeral bier. The procession to the place of burial, about a quarter mile west of the parish church (just over a half mile from the Spooner home) was oxymoronically, austerely splendid. The hatchment, a square tablet set diagonally which bore the Spooner coat-of-arms, consisted of canvas stretched upon a black frame. First placed in front of the deceased's home, it was now attached to the hearse. Escutcheons, or shields featuring the coat-of-arms, would have decorated each horse, each animal also wearing black stockings, and housings decorated with painted death's heads and coffins. Four men carried the funeral bier, above whom a large black cloth of linen or velvet was held aloft by six pallbearers. Spooner's cloth-lined pine coffin, an irregular hexagon, included a single top piece, nailed into place, and ornamented with hundreds of coffin nails and white tacks.

Following a brief prayer (more elaborate petitions were considered "popish"), Joshua Spooner was likely laid to rest in a receiving vault at the cemetery, a structure used to temporarily house the remains of those who had died during the winter, when burial had to wait until the spring thaw. It must have made for a starkly dramatic scene, the hearse, the mourners and horses dressed entirely in black, their steamy breath disappearing into the expanse of snow and headstones all about them.

The family's cash outlay did not end at the cemetery gate. The guests expected a funeral dinner, which though often held at the deceased's home, in this case was surely given at a building attached to the church, which served the function of today's parish hall. Bathsheba's sister and sponsor of the funeral, Martha Tufts, need not have worried over the awkwardness of attending such a dinner; women were not welcome. Prodigal funeral feasts were a long established tradition which maintained themselves well into the next century. In 1797, one Caleb Dawes of Boston was sent off in a sea of rum, beer, gin, brandy and wine (over one-hundred-and-twenty bottles worth), as well as lemons and oranges (costly in early America) and sugar (for the punch), beef, ham, bacon, foul, fish, oysters, twelve dozen eggs, peas,onions, potatoes, cheese, fruit and sweetmeats. Extra crockery, dozens of chairs and a cadre of waiters were provided.

The conspirators were to be tried during an awkward period of colonial justice, between one era dominated by British tradition, and another seeking to establish a distinctly American system.

Less than two years after the Declaration of Independence, the British system still prevailed.

Jurisprudence aside, what complicated (and as will be seen, perhaps poisoned) the legal proceedings against Bathsheba and accomplices was the fact that by the spring of 1778, many of the judges, attorneys and court officers who had remained loyal to the Crown had been either expelled from the colony (such as Bathsheba's own father), or voluntarily exiled. The proportion of Tories to Patriots in the legal professions varied widely throughout Massachusetts. In Boston, just prior to the war, a balance between the two seems evident. Three years' worth of the rebellion had decimated the legal system. As its practitioners fled, vacant positions were filled by Patriots, appointments frequently made after much difficulty in locating qualified, interested candidates. Just before the Revolution, among Worcester County attorneys and judges, Tories had clearly outnumbered Patriots (an anomaly considering the openly seditious leanings of much of the population). Ultimately, of course, it was the powers in Boston that established the colony's general tone. Whatever one's political sympathies, it is unfair to presume that an individual's impartiality was necessarily impaired. Under such circumstances, would not the most liberal thinker struggle even more mightily to maintain his impartiality? In 1770, in what is remembered as perhaps the most celebrated case of a Patriot's magnanimity in pre-Revolutionary Massachusetts, John Adams represented the British soldiers indicted for manslaughter in the killing of five colonists, an incident referred to by the Patriots as the Boston Massacre. Adams' outrage over what he viewed as an unjust charge helped to acquit the majority of the defendants. At the same time, we must accept the existence of prejudice against Loyalists which inevitably colored the decisions of an occasional judge or jury.

What were the foundations of eighteenth-century jurisprudence? The basis of civil and criminal justice in Massachusetts Bay Colony rested upon Britain's Law and Liberties of 1648. Although in the 1680's the royal charter which had guaranteed greater autonomy had been nullified, the 1648 document continued to exert great influence. Though much of medieval civil law reflected church law, in Britain a more independent system had evolved. But since its founding, Massachusetts Bay Colony had pursued a new alternative, drawing its inspiration directly from the law of Moses, particularly regarding capital offenses. Rather than increasing the number of crimes punishable by death, this led to the elimination of petty crimes which had encumbered English tradition. Besides murder ("But if any man hates his neighbor, and lies in wait for him, and attacks him, and wounds him mortally so that he dies, and the man flees into one of these cities, then the elders of his city shall send and fetch him from there, and hand him over to the avenger of blood, so that he may die" Deut. 19:11-13), crimes designated as capital now included certain types of manslaughter, killing "by guile", by poison, even sodomy and adultery. A child over the age of sixteen could be put to death for cursing his parents if unprovoked—or the parents could seek the death penalty if they deemed him rebellious or incorrigible. Just as the influence of Puritanism had waned since the early seventeenth-century, by the mid 1700's its impact upon the judicial system had greatly diminished. As British tradition reasserted itself, it was perhaps natural that the most celebrated series of law lectures ever to come from England should, in the 1760's, do much to expand and sophisticate the legal system. In 1753, the first university lectures in law were delivered at Oxford by William Blackstone, and published between 1765 and 1769.

Blackstone's Commentaries were ardently debated by his colonial counterparts. By 1776, nearly 2,500 copies were in circulation, mostly of the 1772 American edition. Blackstone's work exerted the greatest influence yet upon the evolution of American legal practice during the reign of George III.

In our age when almost anyone of means instantly seeks counsel if accused of even the pettiest crime, it is difficult to imagine an era when only the most serious offenses necessitated an attorney. Blackstone's popularity helped to change that. Observing British practice, he wrote that it was the custom of judges

> ...to allow a prisoner counsel to stand by him at the bar, and instruct him what questions to ask, or even to ask questions for him, with respect to matters of fact: for as to matters of law, arising on the trial, they are in-titled [sic] to the assistance of counsel."[7]

Blackstone's model portrays counsel more as adviser than advocate.

In 1701, Massachusetts Bay officially recognized attorneys as officers of the courts, requiring from them an oath of office once admitted to practice. Competent, honest lawyers were the exception, outnumbered throughout New England by bumbling crooks who encouraged the proliferation of writs. Litigation abounded. John Adams derided "The dirty dabblers in the law."[8] By mid-century, sheriffs and deputies were prohibited from filing writs or offering legal advice, and by 1769 the Massachusetts Bar was founded, in an attempt to standardize practice while professionalizing the discipline.

Despite gaining some hard won respect, the profession continued to face a steady stream of criticism, even ridicule from a public weary of endless litigation. John Adams bemoaned the increasing number of litigious hopefuls seeking admission to the bar: "They swarm and multiply."[9] The town of Salem soon mandated three years of study with a barrister before admission to Inferior Court, two more years of practice before admittance to Superior Court (as solicitor), and finally still two additional years of practice of the same before achieving the status of barrister. Lawyers and judges superficially enhanced their status by adopting immense British wigs, and black gowns ornamented with scarlet.

Slow to recognize the many honorable members of the bar who had struggled to secure the country's liberty, public criticism continued unabated through the Revolution. Only weeks after the Declaration of Independence, a Yale professor of divinity discouraged graduates from pursuing a legal career, characterized by

> That meanness, that infernal knavery, which multiplies needless litigations which retards the operation of justice, which, from court to court, upon the most trifling pretences, postpones trial to glean the last emptying of a client's pocket, for unjust fees of everlasting attendance, which artfully twists the meaning of law to the side we espouse, which seizes unwarrantable advantage from the prepossessions, ignorance, interests and prejudices of a jury.[10]

The professor recommended that the graduates shun the profession more assiduously "than death or infamy."[11]

A decade would pass between the last British edition of Blackstone's Commentaries and the establishment of the first American law professorship, at the College of William and Mary. Five years later, the country's first law school was founded by Tapping Reeve in Litchfield, Connecticut. Prior to the Revolution, an aspiring attorney had two avenues open: travel to England to study at an "inn of law", or apprenticeship to an established American lawyer. The inns were unique institutions dating back to the fourteenth-century, where students lived and practiced with barristers, while engaging in mock hearings and trials. When not at the inn, students attended sessions of the High Court. The inns, nevertheless, were not genuine law schools, having no university affiliation nor offering any classical training. Most Americans who enrolled hailed from southern families. By the eighteenth century the inns were ghosts of their former selves, reduced to little more than social clubs. Only fifteen Massachusetts men had attended the inns, the last in 1733. At the outbreak of hostilities, they were closed to the colonists, a move which dealt a severe blow to southern justice.

Meanwhile, prospective attorneys from New England, following graduation from Harvard College (more rarely, Yale) instead opted to train as apprentices to established lawyers. Each attorney might have several apprentices paying for the privilege, a demeaning and demoralizing one whose duties included copying forms, filing, entering motions in court, and preparing a pleading or two. Adams referred to his own training as "a dreary ramble"—and this despite an apprenticeship more thorough than many of his colleagues.[12] On August 1, 1756, John Adams signed a contract drawn up by James Putnam, which stipulated a two-year period of study for a fee of one-hundred dollars. Putnam, Worcester County's most prominent attorney, and a Loyalist, was destined to become the last attorney general of Massachusetts under the Crown.

William Livingston, the future governor of New Jersey, described his own legal training in the harshest terms, denouncing it as "an outrage upon common honesty...scandalous, horrid, base, and infamous to the last degree!"[13] He argued that it was impossible to learn the law "by gazing on a number of books, which the [apprentice] has neither time nor opportunity to read; or...be metamorphos'd into an Attorney by virtue of a Hocus Pocus...If [lawyers] deserve the imputation of justice and dishonesty, it is in no instance more visible and notorious than in their conduct towards their apprentices…[the young law clerk] trifled away the Bloom of his Age...in a servile drudgery, nothing to the Purpose, and fit only for a Slave."[14]

Written in 1745, Livingstone's scathing words, endorsed by scores of his peers, did little to discourage interest in the profession, which expanded dramatically in the next generation. In Worcester, Joshua Eaton was the first to put up his shingle. His limitations as advocate proved no hindrance to a successful career, guaranteed as it was by his local monopoly. Many early Worcester attorneys were forced to supplement their income, as storekeepers, even codfish and molasses salesmen—or in Eaton's case, as a minister, indulging his fervent passion to preach (likely reinvigorated by the Great Awakening) in neighboring Leicester.

Although Worcester was the county seat, more substantial towns in central Massachusetts provided most of its attorneys prior to the Revolution, influential men like Timothy Ruggles, Bathsheba Spooner's father, who was leader of the Bar and eventually Chief Justice of the Court of Common Pleas, and Joshua Putnam of Brookfield—both Tories, as were virtually all attorneys in the county before the war. Upham's tragic end, like that of Ruggles, was typical of Loyalists. In 1776, he was compelled to abandon his practice and flee to Boston, then New York. His property seized, he at last settled in New Brunswick, where he died. The Revolution destroyed not only the strong professional collegiality which had been dearly attained, but further divided families with two or more sons as attorneys. Statewide, most of the lawyers who were Tories—about half—were exiled to England, Canada or the Caribbean. Despite the schism, the legal system recovered quickly following the war. By 1785, all of the Tories had been replaced. Six years later, the state boasted more than twice the number of attorneys active in 1765.

In late 1774, the Worcester courts were closed, by which time only eight attorneys were practicing. Five were Tories who abandoned the county. Adams' Tory mentor, Joshua Upham, stayed only a short while longer; another, a Patriot, moved his practice to Maine. Only one attorney, a lukewarm Patriot, remained to develop a successful practice.

In December of 1775, Levi Lincoln (a distant cousin of the president) arrived in Worcester. Though a newcomer, he was anything but a stranger. Drawn not only by the opportunity to establish a practice in a town now virtually devoid of lawyers, Lincoln had been promised a greater prize, that of Clerk of Courts, attained, undoubtedly, as much through talent as political connections. Less than two-and-a-half years later, he was hired to represent Bathsheba Spooner and her co-conspirators.

Levi, the third son of Enoch Lincoln of Hingham (south of Boston), first served as a blacksmith's apprentice, spurning the trade of glazier as practiced by his father and grandfather. A local school teacher, Joseph Lewis, as well as Dr. Gay, his pastor, revealed another path to him.

"[Lincoln's] books were his companions day and night. He generally appeared as if in deep thought, and by some was considered distant and reserved in his manners."[15]

Following his graduation from Harvard in 1772, Levi moved to Northampton, studying law under Joseph Hawley, and joined the Hampshire County Bar. His choice of mentor was politically prophetic. As a cousin of Jonathan Edwards, the most celebrated/reviled minister of the previous generation, Hawley had studied theology with the fiery reformer, and went on to serve in the French and Indian War as chaplain during the siege of Louisbourg. Returning to Northampton, Hawley quickly established a reputation as the most prominent radical of western Massachusetts, one of the first to encourage independence from Great Britain. In 1776, mental illness forced an end to his career, if not his voice, and continued to work, as an advocate for liberal causes. Eight years before his death in 1788, he refused to serve in the state senate, protesting the religious test imposed upon its members.

Upon word of the Battles of Lexington and Concord, Lincoln immediately took up arms, and marched seventy miles to Cambridge, where he seems to have remained until his move to Worcester before Christmas that year. Although his legal practice was chiefly preoccupied with mundane matters, his virtual monopoly combined with a strong Patriotism and position as court clerk guaranteed a rapid ascent. In 1777, he was Judge of Probate, in the meantime refusing an appointment to the Continental Congress, citing overwork. However, in 1780, he welcomed the opportunity to serve as a delegate to the convention charged with drafting a state constitution.

Having played a central role in the abolition of Massachusetts slavery, his career culminated with the election of Thomas Jefferson, who appointed him US attorney general, even serving briefly as secretary of state.

Despite his political sympathies, it is no surprise that Lincoln was chosen to represent Mrs. Spooner. Lincoln was a member of the Worcester Committee of Correspondence, Inspection and Safety, whose role was to maintain the peace, as well as to maintain contact with fellow Patriots throughout the colonies, while keeping a close eye on both Loyalists and Redcoats. Dr. John Green, Bathsheba's brother-in-law and the county's most prominent physician, was also a member. It is likely that Green approached Lincoln. How could a young ambitious attorney refuse such a case? Money, however, had likely little to do with his acceptance. In the eighteenth century, the client typically paid a statutory fee of only ten or twelve shillings, or about three dollars. Of course, given the case's high profile, and the fact that Lincoln would represent four defendants, it is possible that John Green sweetened the pot. The extensive trial notes prepared by Lincoln stand in evidence of the many hours he devoted to the case. Like John Adams' defense of British soldiers accused in the Boston Massacre, that of Lincoln, an avid Patriot, would demonstrate a firm impartiality, a defense which, unlike Adams', would prove unsuccessful.

In the colonial era, counsel was usually retained following the indictment, not after arrest as happens today. Lincoln had little time to carefully consider the finer details of the case—the state supreme court, riding circuit, was making its first of two visits to Worcester that year, requiring that the trial follow fast on the heels of the indictment. Justice would be swift.

CHAPTER THIRTEEN

A Matter of Surprise and Amazement to All

On April 21, just over seven weeks following the murder, twelve jurors returned an indictment against the four suspects. In part, it read

> ...William Brooks...James Buchanan...and Ezra Ross, not having God before their eyes, but being moved and seduced by the instigation of the Devil, on the first day of March last past, with force and arms, at Brookfield... feloniously, willfully and of their malice aforethought, in and upon Joshua Spooner then and there in the peace of God...an assault did make...William Brooks, with his right fist the said Joshua Spooner to and against the Ground...did strike down...with both his hands and feet...in and upon the back, head, stomach and sides of him...did strike, beat and kick...of which said several mortal bruises the said Joshua Spooner there instantly died...[1]

The indictment continued

> James Buchanan...and Ezra Ross...feloniously and of their malice aforethought, then and there were present, aiding, assisting, abetting, comforting and maintaining...William Brooks, to the felony and murder aforesaid...[2]

Finally, Bathsheba Spooner's alleged involvement was cited.

> And that Bathsheba Spooner, of Brookfield, in the county of Worcester, Widow, late wife of the said Joshua Spooner, not having GOD before her eyes, but being seduced by the instigation of the Devil, before the felony and and murder aforesaid...on the twenty-eighth day of February last past... maliciously, willfully, and of her malice aforethought, did incite, move, abet, counsel and procure, against the peace of the Government and people aforesaid...[3]

The indictment is signed by Robert Treat Paine, prosecutor, and Samuel Denny, foreman.

Paine left Boston on April 20, traveling via Lancaster en route to Worcester, where he dined. He spent the four days until the trial's completion at the home of Elijah Dix, a prominent Worcester physician who had studied medicine with Bathsheba's brother-in-law, John Green.[4]

Reverend Ebenezer Parkman of Westborough had been named pastor of that town's Congregational church in 1724, a position he would hold for nearly sixty years. Following the ethnic cleansing of French Acadians from Nova Scotia by the British and their New England compatriots in the 1750's, a few families settled in Westborough. Though Roman Catholic, Nova Scotians were made to feel at home by the Parkman family. In his diary (one of America's most complete from this period) for April 24, he writes

> ...rode up to Worcester...the Tryal of the murderers of the late Mr. Joshua Spooner...the criminals...Bathsheba Spooner...Dux Femina Facti [the female instigator of the deeds] were arraigned in the Afternoon and then remanded to Jayl.[5]

The arraignment read

> Worcester Superior Court, April Term 1778
>
> The said William Brooks, James Buchanan, Ezra Ross and Bathsheba Spooner, were brought and sit to the Bar here, by the Sheriffs of Worcester County, and arraigned; and upon their arraignment—they severally plead, that they are not guilty, and thereof they put themselves, for trial, on God and the County...[6]

The arraignment was held in the only building directly connected with the case which still stands in Worcester, the second Worcester County Courthouse. The gracious Georgian hip roof, with four brick chimneys (now painted white) at each corner and nine "six over six" windows surrounding an elegant entry capped by a narrow fanlight, was constructed in 1751. Its thirty-six-by-forty foot dimensions were a marked improvement over those of its predecessor. The first floor housed the county offices, while the upper floor served as the courtroom. Here, a pair of fireplaces stood along one wall, paneled wainscoting gently enhancing the low-ceilinged chamber. Originally located at Lincoln Square, it is perhaps Worcester's most historic building, having been forcefully closed by Patriots prior to the Battle of Concord, and years later, serving as one of the sites of Shay's Rebellion, the first armed revolt against the US government. The building was moved in 1791 to make way for a still larger court house, designed by Charles Bulfinch who, having recently completed his first designs for the new State House in Boston, was the architect of the moment.

In the eighteenth century, the hill behind the courthouse served as the location for public humiliation and punishment, excepting the rare execution which took place a half mile southeast. The stocks, pillory and whipping post rose from the crest of the hill. The stock's staging, elevated several feet above the ground, included a post at the center. The cross pieces (with holes allowing for the placement of head, hands and feet), when brought together, encircled heads and wrists at the same level. If the prisoner failed to stand upright during his several hours of public torture, he risked suffocation. Whipping was an alternative. The malefactor, stripped to the waist, had his hands tied to the crossbar. The officer then lashed the prisoner with a cat-o-nine-tails (a foot-and-a-half long handle with several small knotted chords). Years after the event, a witness recalled one such flogging in Worcester, during which the sheriff shouted to his officer, "Cut harder, or I'll cut you!"[7] The punishment completed, the blood continued to run freely as the attendants rubbed the wounds with soft soap. Branding, though rare, was occasionally ordered by the judge. Placed upon his back in a crude box, the victim's limbs were secured, the letter "T" (for thief?) then pricked into his forehead with indelible ink—a more stubborn, less attractive stigma than that endured by Hester Prynne.

As fearsome as these retributions seem, none were deemed suitable for the "Brookfield Four", for whom only the ultimate sentence would suffice.

Five men presided over the trial: William Cushing as Chief Justice, and Jedediah Foster, Nathaniel Peaslee Sargent, David Sewall and James Sullivan as associate justices. Best remembered are Cushing and Foster, Cushing for his pre-eminent role, and Foster for his legacy—some of the most extensive notes culled from any American eighteenth-century trial, including the testimony of virtually every witness.

The son of Justice John Curry, William Cushing was born in Scituate (south of Boston) in 1732. Closely paralleling the career path of John Adams, his junior by three years, Cushing graduated from Harvard in 1751 (ranking third in a class of thirty-six). Like Adams, he first served as schoolmaster (at Roxbury, now part of Boston) in 1752 before beginning his law apprenticeship. As the site of his eventual practice, Cushing chose Pownalborough, Maine, the first trained lawyer to establish himself in that region, then part of Massachusetts. While in Maine, Cushing earned a substantial portion of his income from the cargo trade between Maine and Massachusetts, lent money at interest, and as did many of his colleagues, took the debtors to court for payment. Although reticent to discuss politics, his Patriot leanings prevented his accepting a grant from the Crown. In 1772, he succeeded his father as Judge of Superior Court, and served for five years. Battered by political turmoil, the Supreme Court was reorganized during the first year of the Revolution. John Adams was appointed Chief Justice, but never sat on the bench, and a year later he relinquished his seat to Cushing. After the Spooner trial, Cushing remained in that capacity for nearly a dozen more years, when his illustrious career culminated with an appointment to the US Supreme Court, where he served for over two decades.

Justice Jedediah Foster was praised by a Brookfield historian (in 1869) as the first among any citizen who "has ever dwelt among us, [one] who held so many local trusts, [who] lived in such intimate sympathy with people, cared for and served them so abundantly and excellently—and yet so far excelled them in station and character."[8] Hyperbole notwithstanding, Foster does seem to have been Brookfield's premier citizen of the eighteenth century, a name as celebrated as Bathsheba's was scorned.

Justices Sargeant and Sullivan had both served as members of the provincial congress only a few years earlier. A decade after the trial, Sergeant was appointed Chief Justice for Massachusetts. Sullivan, at the end of the war, was elected to the Continental Congress, and later served as the state's attorney and governor.

The political sympathies of at least three members of the twelve-person jury are known, all three of whom were active Patriots. Forty-nine-year old Ebenezer Lovel (who would outlive nearly everyone associated with the trial) was a colonel in the local militia, having served as ensign during the march to Lexington. He was a member of the Committee of Inspection, examining "from time to time the merchants and traders of the town, [to] see that no imported goods were offered for sale in violation of "the solemn league and covenant"' (banning goods imported from Britain).[9] He had only recently been chosen as selectman, and the previous year was named representative to the General Court in Boston—and was one of the founders of the American Political Society.

His junior by one year, Benjamin Stowell was a lieutenant during the French and Indian War, and had also been appointed selectman in 1777, a sure indication of his Patriot leanings. Lastly, and most famously, David Bigelow, brother of Worcester's best-known Minuteman, Timothy, had been one of the drafters of the resolution which enforced a blacksmiths' boycott against the most vocal of Worcester's Tories; the name of Timothy Ruggles, Bathsheba's father, was singled out. A year later, Bigelow was named delegate to the Concord convention, called to adopt emergency measures to counter the effects of a ruinous economy. The same year, he joined Levi Lincoln at another convention charged with framing a state constitution.

No specific information may be available regarding the political loyalties of the remaining nine jurors, but it is almost certain that the majority, if not all, were Patriots. Not only were Tories now a rare breed in Worcester, but they lacked most of the political muscle and connections which would have secured them a place on the jury.

The Regulating Act of Parliament, news of which arrived in Boston in the summer of 1774, withdrew the citizens' right to select juries, that power now given to the county sheriff. Any sheriff deemed unsympathetic to the Crown was removed from office. Gardner Chandler, Bathsheba Spooner's brother-in-law, and a member of one of Worcester's most prominent Tory families, remained in his post until 1775, when the Patriots had their turn, expelling him in favor of Simon Dwight of Western (now Warren). At his death in 1778, another Patriot, William Greenleaf of Lancaster, assumed the position. The regulation by which the sheriff selected the jury, introduced to stifle Patriot participation, was maintained and now used against the British.

The fate of Brooks and Buchanan was in the hands of not a single true peer. As an American soldier, Ross may have been better represented, but by association he probably garnered little sympathy, despite his extreme youth. And as the only woman, and a Loyalist at that, Bathsheba Spooner found herself in the most precarious position of all.

In the eighteenth century, even trials involving capital crimes lasted barely more than a day, and the Spooner trial was no exception.

The indictment and arraignment had taken place at the courthouse at (now) Lincoln Square. For the trial itself, the venue was changed from the courthouse to the meetinghouse (Old South Church), a change made necessary by the great numbers who had made their way to Worcester.

At the time of the trial, Old South Church was but fifteen years old. Its history as a parish, however, nearly stretched back to the town's settlement. Deciding that their homes could no longer accommodate the burgeoning faithful, the first citizens built a small meetinghouse of logs, in 1717. A historian from Brookfield, reflecting upon a time when his town was larger than Worcester, described the church's founders as "...a little hardy, brave band of men, fearless of danger, true to Puritan principles, and loyal to Christ...[they] stood absolutely isolated and alone, surrounded only by a broad and desolate waste infested by wild beasts and savages..."[10]

Two years later, a larger church was built, this time on the common. The town's first minister, Rev. Andrew Gardner of Brookline (neighboring Boston) was installed the same year. An avid deer hunter and equally enthusiastic practical joker, his pastorate was widely criticized almost from the beginning, and Gardner was asked to leave three years later.

Bathsheba's grandfather, Shearjushub Bourne, among others, preached in his place for a short time. Isaac Burr was tapped for the position in 1725, who was followed by Thaddeus Maccarty in 1747. Burr's home, the future site of Nazro's General Store (where Bathsheba would procure poison) had never been a proper parsonage, and with Maccarty's appointment a home was bought just southeast of the church to serve that purpose.

Sixteen years into his term, Maccarty was given a new church as well, built at a cost of just over fifteen hundred pounds. The pride of the village, it featured sixty-one square pews, and as with most New England congregations, the pews were purchased by member families, the choicest pews running along the pulpit's west side. Jacob Hemenway, the church's builder, had purchased a pew to the left of the pulpit, under which a door led to a storeroom where he kept his home brew stashed, shared with the worshippers during the midday break on Sunday. Two long pews were placed in front of the pulpit, where the deacons and elderly sat. Beyond were the "free" seats, men to one side, women on the other. Porches were constructed along the south, east and west entrances, with a one-hundred-and-thirty foot spire crowning the north side. Over the next several decades, the pulpit would feature several notable orators, John Quincy Adams and Daniel Webster among them. Preaching during the summer months proved a special challenge, the church's eastern windows overlooking the "pound for the reclaiming of disorderly beasts."[11]

Those not in sympathy with the practices of Old South worshipped instead at Second Church on Summer St., not far from the jail. Its pastor was the Rev. Aaron Bancroft, father of George, perhaps America's most eminent historian of the nineteenth century.

Another orator to grace the pulpit of Old South, who would prosecute the Spooner case, was Robert Treat Paine, the commonwealth's first attorney general following the Declaration of Independence, a document he had signed. The son of a minister turned merchant, Paine graduated from Harvard in 1749. Not long after, his family lost its fortune. Like his lifelong colleague and rival, John Adams, Paine first served as a schoolmaster in Worcester County, in Lunenburg to the north. A merchant in North

Carolina, the Azores and Spain, Paine had even joined a whaling voyage to Greenland in 1754. He moved back to Worcester County (Lancaster), and served as preacher in Shirley for several weeks. A regimental chaplain at Crown Point, he began to practice law in 1757. He and his wife Sally raised eight children, a famed poet among them. In short time, Paine solidly regained his financial footing; contemporaries were taken aback at his profligate spending.

In 1774, Paine was one of five representatives from Massachusetts named to the Continental Congress which, once war broke out, was instrumental in supplying the troops with cannons and saltpeter (potassium nitrate) for gunpowder. Elected Speaker of the House in 1777, he was appointed attorney general shortly after, during which tenure he prosecuted the Spooner trial. As the state's top law official, one of his chief responsibilities was the seizure of Loyalist estates, the proceeds used to defray the war's costs. By late 1777, few Loyalist estates remained, and little money was ever collected.

The two Harvard alumni, Paine and Adams, both beginning their professional lives as schoolmasters, also began practicing law at about the same time, and were soon rivals. In 1770, Adams defended the British soldiers in the Boston Massacre trial, with Paine as prosecutor for the Crown in what was the most publicized trial of the 1770's prior to the Spooner case.

In the late 1760's, the two young attorneys confronted each other in Doane v. Gage, a maritime law case which sought to determine who owned a whale which had been struck by harpoons from two different ships, Adams representing one captain, Paine the other. There is no record who won, but a petty dispute between the attorneys provides a glimpse into their respective characters. Adams, very sensitive about competition, observed that "Bob Paine is conceited and pretends to more knowledge than he has."[12] At one point, Adams informed Paine that he was reading Vinnius, a Dutch legal commentator who specialized in marine law. Paine only sneered "Vinnius...you can't understand one page of Vinnius," Paine the ex-whaler dismissing Adams' inexperience. Adams noted "[Paine] must know that human behavior is disgusted with such incomplaisant Behaviors. Besides, he has no right to say I don't understand every word in Vinnius, for he knows nothing of me."[13] Adams' intellectual vanity must have been sorely wounded by Paine's condescension, an opponent four years Adams' senior, and more cosmopolitan.

Less than eight weeks separated the murder and trial. Given the demands of their schedules and the complicated nature of the conspiracy—murder involving four defendants of different gender, age, nationality, political sympathies, social status and motivation—even degrees of culpability—neither Paine nor Lincoln had much time to prepare. The public's fevered interest combined with the need to chart a judicially tortuous path during political crisis must have added greatly to their burden.

Due to the number of Loyalist judges who had been exiled, the governor himself, John Hancock, was tasked with organizing the trial.

In England, before the seventeenth century, the jury's role was to guarantee that the trial proceedings operated within the guidelines of the applicable laws; the judges' role was to offer instruction as needed. Unlike later practice, the jury was not expected to determine, or even necessarily understand, the facts of the particular case. The trial was essentially a battle between the accuser and the accused, the accuser serving as his/her own prosecutor, who was expected to prepare the state's case. (The defendant was not permitted to present his own case). Defense counsel was allowed in non-capital cases only. In capital cases, ironically, it was often treated as a foregone conclusion that the accused was guilty; the trial took place to ensure that the defendant was tried according to the law. In one famous case from 1649, the presiding judge advised the jury "I hope that the jury hath seen the evidence so plain and so fully, that it doth confirm them to do their duty, and to find the Prisoner guilty of what is charged upon Him."[14]

The British legal system was inherently suspicious of defense counsel, who would only befuddle the truth. One British officer of the court, as late as 1721, noted that "Everyone of Common Understanding may as probably speak to a Matter of fact, as if he were the best lawyer...the very Speech, gesture and Countenance, and Manner of Defense of those who are Guilty, when they speak for themselves, may often help to disclose the Truth, which probably would not be so well disposed from the artificial Defense of others speaking for them."[15]

Of course, in speaking for themselves, defendants were open to self-incrimination, which was encouraged, implicitly, under seventeenth-century British law.

Despite inheriting much of its judicial practice from the mother country, colonial America very early on established its own tradition regarding self-incrimination. In 1637, the Rev. John Wheelwright of Massachusetts Bay was accused of heterodoxy, like his more famous sister-in-law Anne Hutchinson, believing that salvation was earned through faith alone, not good works. The General Court asked him to clarify "some controversial [statements] in [your] sermons." Gov. Winthrop assured him that such inquiries were being made "...not to draw matter from himself whereupon to proceed against him,"[16] suggesting the accused had the right not to incriminate himself. In the years following, the right was never formally acknowledged, however, and when it was, it had to be first invoked by the defendant. By the mid-eighteenth century, the right had become firmly recognized in Massachusetts. Such recognition served the state's purpose in at least one aspect, as it was believed that asking the accused to testify for himself only encouraged perjury.

The Spooner trial was virtually free of the legal maneuvering so taken for granted in sensational trials of our day. Typical of contemporary court proceedings, anyone could join in the fray at any time: jurors, attorneys, and judges. These were proceedings far removed from today's rigid formality, more closely resembling New England's town meeting format. Severe time constraints necessitated as well that the legal haranguing be kept to a minimum.

Levi Lincoln's role as defense counsel was a relatively new one which, according to recently established procedure, did not begin until after the indictment. It would seem, then, that Lincoln only had between Tuesday, April 21st and the date of the trial, the 24th, to prepare.

Although not formally named as counsel until after the indictment, it is very likely that he had been assigned as their lawyer at the time of the arrest several weeks earlier.

Dwight Foster, the young Brookfield attorney who followed the case closely, made a tantalizing reference to a missing document, the discovery of which might cast further light upon Bathsheba's motivation, as well as the true nature of the relationship with her husband.

> To Mr. Clarke: April 24, 1778
>
> ...I have the copy of a journal kept by the unfortunate [Joshua Spooner] of her malice for near two months before he was killed—found amongst his Papers—[17]

Foster's mention of "malice" could have simply referred to Bathsheba's ongoing attempts to kill Joshua (the attempted poisoning by Ezra Ross, and the aborted plan to dispatch Joshua while he and Ezra visited the Princeton land)—or was there discussion of other attempts, or more generally of marital discord? If its specifics remain unknown, it is likely that the generally negative impressions of the Spooners' relationship made after the trial by different sources were at least in some part based upon that journal. There is, however, no indication that it was entered as formal evidence. And although pure speculation, it could be that Joshua finally came to the conclusion (despite his seeming refusal to publicly acknowledge as much) that his wife was determined to kill him, and that she would eventually succeed. The journal might have given Joshua an opportunity to speak beyond the grave to firmly implicate Bathsheba. Why the journal was never entered as evidence, and how Foster somehow gained possession of it (perhaps during his attendance at the inquest?), remains unknown. It is of further interest that as an attorney not involved with the case and as the son of the Hon. Jedediah Foster, young Foster should be the keeper of the diary.

Rev. Ebenezer Parkman of Westborough, an enthusiastic follower of the case, attended the trial, and recorded in his diary

> [April] 24 Attended the Tryal. It was at the Meeting House. A great Throng! A most sad Sight!—Many evidences were sworn. Three were brought from jail who were made use of as witnesses, Namely, the widow Stratton [sic] and her son, and Alexander Cummings, a Scottish youth who deserting from Burgoyne's Army, lived in Mrs. Spooner's House. The Court continued till past Midnight during the whole time I continued at my Seat...The Court was adjourned to 8 o'clock next morning....[18]

Though lasting only sixteen hours (including recesses), twenty-two witnesses testified. The short duration is even more impressive considering the complicated nature of the indictment (one instigator, one murderer and two abettors), which must have required lengthy instructions to the jury from the tribunal of judges.

To highlight only the key points of the testimony—evidence which went beyond the circumstantial—Ephraim Cooley, the Spooners' neighbor (and innkeeper who saw Joshua Spooner only minutes before his murder) testified that he was present at Brown's Tavern in Worcester the day after the murder, when Bathsheba claimed that "she was the whole means of this murder being committed."[19] Joshua Whitney was also at Brown's, where he heard young Ezra Ross request "a minister, for he was really guilty of this crime, but he did not strike the first blow, although he was aiding and assisting."[20]

Neighbor Ruben Olds recalled that about two weeks before the murder, Buchanan approached him at the Spooners, warning that Joshua "will not come to say much to me, or it won't be healthy for him, for I would put him in the well for two coppers."[21]

It has been suggested that three witnesses: Alexander Cummings (the first British prisoner-of-war Bathsheba allowed into her home), the housekeeper Widow Stratton, and her son (never named), turned state's evidence to avoid their own indictment.

Cummings recalled that Bathsheba, upon first meeting Brooks and Buchanan, told the men that "she wished Mr. Spooner was out of the way; she could not live with him...Buchanan [added] he wished he was out of the way..." Days later, Brooks told Cummings that Spooner "should not come home a living man that night." He testified that a month earlier, Bathsheba "desired the witness to kill Spooner and she would make a man of him." Cummings related that before accompanying Spooner on the trip to his land in Princeton, Ross "dropped some aqua fortis into some toddy to poison [Spooner]. Spooner said if he had any enemies in the house he should think they intended to poison him."[22]

The widow Stratton and her son presented less damaging testimony. Neighbor Asa Bigelow testified that during the coroner's inquest, Bathsheba "confessed that she hired the people to concert the murder; was to give them one thousand dollars, and had paid them two hundred. She mentioned the names of Brooks and the sergeant; she said they were all three together."[23] Brookfield's constable, Elisha Hamilton, using hearsay (acceptable as evidence in the eighteenth century), heard Bathsheba say she told Cooley (the innkeeper) "that she did not blame anybody, for this was all her own doings. She said Mrs. Stratton and Alek [Cummings] were innocent. She had briefed them to do and say what they had done."[24]

The final witness, William Young, Justice of the Peace, formally presented the piece of evidence which had been gossiped over for weeks, the confession of Brooks, Buchanan and Ross made to him upon their arrest. Young testified that "...the murder had been committed by them at the instigation of Mrs. Spooner..." Although Bathsheba had not taken part in their confession, Young indicated that while in prison she "...had confessed that she consented to the murder."[25] None of the defendants took the stand.

The men's formal confession was without question the key piece in determining their guilt, as well as Bathsheba's duplicity. At no point in the four-month ordeal following her arrest did Mrs. Spooner formally confess her culpability. During the trial, no one, not even Cummings or Stratton who were present several yards from the scene of the murder, could describe any details. Circumstantially, of course, the amount of evidence was overwhelming: Buchanan and Bathsheba whispering over their rendezvous in Brookfield at the appropriate hour, Cummings' report to Bathsheba that Joshua was in the well, Brooks displaying Spooner's shoes and buckles the next day, bloodied clothing, etc. No fingerprints were presented as evidence—they were not recognized as unique until 1788, and not admissible as evidence until many years later.

Despite the stark notoriety of the case and the weight of evidence presented against his clients, Levi Lincoln did what he could to present mitigating evidence which might lessen the full culpability of at least two of the party, namely Ezra Ross and Mrs. Spooner. The notes which Lincoln had prepared for the trial are among the Lincoln family papers.

While there is no indication that Robert Paine made any closing remarks, Levi Lincoln, as defense counsel, may have viewed his summation as the last chance to save his clients' necks.

Lincoln opened by noting that it was the first capital trial since the country's founding less than two years ago, and asked that the jury deliberate without letting their political sympathies interfere. This barely hidden reference to Mrs. Spooner's father was surely lost on no one, no less than Bathsheba's Loyalist leanings nor Joshua's Patriot convictions.

In the case of Ross, Lincoln questioned the degree of his guilt; as per the indictment, had Ezra Ross "feloniously, willfully and of [his] malice aforethought" killed Spooner?[26] The testimony made no reference to Ross as complicit beforehand, but depicted him as one who happened to show up at Spooner's the evening of the murder. Lincoln offered that Ross might rather be guilty of misprision of felony, that is, failure to prevent the act of murder, or the reporting of it.

Lincoln emphasized that although Ross had had plenty of opportunity before March to murder Spooner, be it in his home, while in Princeton at Spooner's sawmill, or on the road, he had failed to make any attempt. Or at least, wholeheartedly—the fact that he had served grog laced with aqua fortis to Spooner, at Bathsheba's behest—may have badly weakened Lincoln's argument. Inversely, Ross could have been excused for later indulging Bathsheba in taking poison along on his trip with Joshua to Princeton, which he never used. Lincoln's portrayal of Ross as hapless bystander may have suffered further from Buchanan's description of events in the confession during the hours immediately before the murder. "Mrs. Spooner came out to the front yard, by the well, and told us [Buchanan and Brooks] that one Mr. Ross was in the house, who had a brace of pistols loaded, and that he had promised her he would kill Mr. Spooner as he came home from the tavern. She desired us to come in, which we did. He [Ross] shewed us a pistol and said Mr. Spooner should die by that tonight."[27]

The confession goes on to relate that Brooks said if Ross would help him if he would knock...[Spooner] down, accordingly it was agreed on. During the actual murder "Ross and Buchanan came out; Ross took Mr. Spooner's watch out and gave it to Buchanan; Brooks and Ross took [Spooner] up and put him into the well head first."[28] At no point during the trial did the subject of Ross' youth come up, who was seventeen at the time of the murder. The tendency to view the juvenile offender differently did not really develop until the early nineteenth century. In Puritan Massachusetts, sinners came in two varieties, young and old. In 1642, a sixteen-year-old was found guilty of bestiality with a cow and a horse, and paid for the crime with his life. At age seventeen, Ross could marry, serve in the military, drink, or own property. From the perspective of his compatriots, he could also hang.

Lincoln's chief client was of course Mrs. Spooner, and most of his closing argument addressed her plight, specifically her mental competence and how it had colored her decisions over the past several months. Lincoln wondered how one so high born and comfortable could find any profit in engaging in so sordid an enterprise. Her husband's death would leave her children fatherless, at the same time leaving her with but one third of the estate; should she be found guilty, the children would also, of course, be left motherless.

How could a sane person devise such a plan? If she could not live with her husband, why not separate from him, and go live with her brother or friends—or better yet, he wondered, with her father, "whose favorite she was"? In such circumstances, she could attract any "gallant" she desired, one more suitable to her status than Ross.[29]

Lincoln considered that for the criminal mind, the "hope of impunity" served as "the source of wickedness [and] the incentive to guilt."[30] In Bathsheba's case, how could this be so? The blatant nature of the crime, the number and nature of the criminals, and the utter lack of any plans following the murder spoke, for Lincoln, of a woman not of sound mind. Why secure calomel the evening before, if an ambush was in the works? Why give her husband's clothing to the murderers, to be displayed in a tavern the next evening? "Was this," Lincoln wondered, "the conduct of a person in the exercise of reason? Would it have been less rational to have written on their foreheads, in capitals, the murderers of Mr. Spooner?"

"The distraction, the disorders of the mind operate variously—mark the difference between a fool and a man disordered—the fool draws wrong conclusions from right principles—the disordered mind argues right from wrong principles."[31]

Lincoln further questioned Bathsheba's entrusting the crime to foreigners who, had they escaped, would likely boast of their deed in their homeland. If she were of sound mind, wouldn't she have made arrangements with a confidante who would have worked to conceal the crime? And to perform the deed among neighbors likely to hear the commotion and discover the body—and to have it done while other members of the family stood nearby?

"Whom did she trust with the management of a villainy, that so nearly affected her reputation, her safety, her life, her children, the lives of others, and the happiness of her friends? The answer was, to prostitutes, tories, regulars, deserters, strangers and foreigners. Was a woman that is admitted to have sense, so stupid, if in the exercise of her reason, as to trust all that was valuable to her and to hers, in the hands of such persons? Could there be a doubt, in the minds of the jury, that this woman was not in a state of mind which rendered her guilty in the eye of the law, of a most horrible crime, which would subject her to the last infliction of human power and vengeance?"[32]

The insanity defense would not be established in American law until well into the nineteenth century. In an early seventeenth-century trial in England, known as "Beverly's Case", Lord Cole cited non compos mentis (not of sound mind) as reason enough to find a defendant not guilty. "The punishment of a man who is deprived of reason and understanding cannot be an example to others...[he is] not able to form the felonious intent."[33] Beverly's Case, however, was to have little impact on American colonial law. Puritan Massachusetts preferred to view the insane, as with so much else, through a biblical prism. The Book of Genesis excused children under the age of seven, children who "knoweth not of good and evil", and by extension, Puritans excused the insane as well. But the spirit of Puritanism had been on the wane in Massachusetts for several decades, and further, Lincoln apparently made no convincing case for Bathsheba's insanity. To be fair—he had neither the expertise nor would he likely have been given the time to do so.

In ancient times, demonic possession was an alternative for those acting "non compos mentis", a view which continued through the Middle Ages, in fact well into eighteenth-century America. In the popular imagination, the devil may have made them do it (as evidenced by such epithets as "sorceress" and "artful witch" directed at Bathsheba—tellingly, the male conspirators were never referred to by similar terms). Misogynistic perceptions of women as heirs to Eve's sinfulness—women beguiled by the devil, women as inciters of men's lust, thereby leading all to an infernal death, had been popular in Christian art and literature for centuries.[34] In Bathsheba Spooner, Revolutionary Massachusetts found a readymade archetype.

In England, in 1847, Daniel McNaughton was acquitted for his botched assassination attempt against Prime Minister Robert Peel, the court concurring that the defendant could not be guilty of a crime if, he either didn't know what he was doing, or didn't know that the action was wrong. It is pure speculation to consider what verdict might be rendered in a twenty-first century courtroom. During the entire time following her arrest, Bathsheba was consistently described as calm, emotionless, unruffled. Even if by today's standards she was seen fit to stand trial, it is hard to imagine that considering her behavior before and immediately after the murder, she would not be acquitted on grounds of insanity.

Rev. Ebenezer Parkman, among the most devoted observers of the tragedy, wrote in his diary for April 25, 1778, reflecting on the previous day:

> I was kindly found in the dark at the Meeting House Door by and spoke to the friendly Mr. Richard Pratt and wife...[the next morning] The Criminals were brot—the Jury brot in their verdict, Guilty!—upon which the awful and shocking Sentence of Death was pronounced—and were remanded to Jayl...[35]

Young law student Dwight Foster of Brookfield in his own diary entry of May 15 reflected on the demeanor of Mrs. Spooner.

> On Tuesday the 21st of April....[trial] lasted...till 10 o'clock the next morning...Mrs. Spooner, the most vile of the criminals appeared in a great Measure unmoved—Never

> did I see a more unaccountable composition in my life than meets in the character of that [abandoned?] Wretch—We are also yet told she continues in the same careless unaffected condition—[36]

About a week earlier, in the May 7th edition of The Massachusetts Spy, Isaiah Thomas reflected on the trial he had undoubtedly attended, paying particular attention to the character and motivation of Bathsheba.

> Mrs. Spooner had, for some time, conceived a great aversion to her husband...His only fault appears to be his not supporting a manly importance as head of his family, and not regulating the government of It...it is probable she cherished a criminal regard for some other persons, until, having followed the blind impulses of wicked and unchaste desires, she lost all moral sensibility, disregarded reason and conscience from her breast, and gave herself up to infamous prostitution, and finally became determined to destroy the life of her husband, who seemed to check her wanton career in no other way than by preventing her wasting his whole estate as she pleased, in pursuance of this horrid design...[37]

Dwight Foster, a few days earlier, in a letter to a Mr. Cornelius Linds of Cambridge, wrote from Brookfield

> The hardness and Insensibility of the Criminals (during the trial), of the Woman more especially, is a matter of surprise and Amazement to all...[38]

CHAPTER FOURTEEN

A Lewd, Artful Woman

June 4 was set as the day of execution.

Poignantly, five weeks following the trial, Ezra Ross's parents petitioned the authorities in Boston to spare their son.

> ...We have been called by providence to suffer a large and uncommon share—That at the commencement of hostilities, of seventeen children, six sons and three daughters alone survived to your aged and distressed petitioners, whose footsteps from that period have been marked, with anxiety, and whose sorrows, from the melancholy fate of their youngest son, have received a tinge of the keenest kind.[1]

After listing the family's military service, Jabez and Joanna Ross addressed the manner by which Bathsheba had ensnared the hapless Ezra.

> On his return from the first year's campaign, [Ezra] was, by the lot of providence, cast upon Mrs. Spooner, in a severe fit [of] sickness, from which he received every kind office and mark of tenderness, that could endear, and make grateful a child of sixteen, sick, desitute, in a strange place, at a distance from friend or acquaintance. [In the fall of 1777] gratitude for past favors led him to call on his old benefactress, who then added to the number of her kindnesses, and engaged a visit on his return. With a mind thus prepared and thus

> irresistibly prepossessed, by her addresses, kindnesses on his tender years, he for the first time heard the horrid proposals; tempted by promises flattering to his situation, and seduced both from virtue and prudence, a child as he was, by a lewd, artful woman, he but too readily acceded to her measures, black as they were.[2]

The Rosses portray their youngest son as an unwilling conspirator.

> But [he] never attempted an execution of the detestable crime, notwithstanding repeated solicitations, and as frequent opportunities, until on an accidental meeting, he became a party with those ruffians, who, without his privity, had fixed on a time and place for that horrid transaction, of which he now stands justly convicted.[3]

Jacob and Joanna make their final, pathetic plea.

> Your petitioners by no means attempt an extenuation of guilt, or measures inconsistent with the safety of the community and the preservation of individuals. But if it is consistent, if the criminal, who is thoroughly impressed with a sense of what is past, present, or to come, can be spared, and his guilt condemned; if he has been a valuable member of society, and fought in her cause, although from the inexperience peculiar to youth, the strength of some momentary impulses, and alluring seducements, he gradually erred until he arrived to the violent act of wickedness; if upon recollection he has found repentance, confesses his life a forfeiture to the law, looking up to heaven for that forgiveness which none can find on earth...if youth, if old age, the sorrows, the anguish of a father, the yearning of a mother, the compassion and wishes of thousands can avail...restore him to his country, to himself, his sympathizing friends, to his aged, drooping and distressed parents;-it will console them under the weightiest afflictions, and turn the wormwood and the

gall into something tolerable; and your petitioners in duty bound will ever pay.[4]

The Ross family's minister, George Leslie, who also signed the petition, was very likely its author, given both its consistent spelling and scholarly style. But it was all in vain; the general court did not relent.

Several days earlier, on May 20, another petition for reprieve was placed before the Council for the State of Massachusetts Bay, this time from all four convicts.

> ...[We are] fearfull of [our] unpreparedness to appear before [our] Maker and judge...[grant us] some longer time...which...through the divine assistance and blessing upon the means used, trust they shall improve it to the most valuable purposes, it being a matter which concerns their everlasting salvation....[5]

Thaddeus Maccarty, the Worcester minister named as their spiritual counsel, added in his own petition that he

> ...has found the men all along, and especially since their condemnation, to be much affected with their deplorable condition; freely acknowledging their heinous guilt, and the righteousness of the sentence pronounced against them. They appear to be very humble and penitent—to be much in earnest that they may make their peace with their Maker—much engaged in acts of devotion, and eager to embrace all opportunities, both public and private, for religious counsels and instructions.[6]

Roger Lamb, the British officer assigned to Brooks and Buchanan during their last days, also wrote of the men's change of heart.

> Buchanan was deeply impressed with the justice of the capital atonement they were doomed to make, and by his

> means chiefly, his guilty partners became truly penitent. Buchanan addressed letters to his officers, full of religious contrition.[7]

It is not surprising that a convict under sentence of death might find religion, if they hadn't already discovered it. In earlier times, such a discovery could have practical benefits beyond those of grace and comfort—it could save the convict's skin. 'Benefit of clergy', which first evolved during the Middle Ages, originally applied to members of the clergy, whose offenses, even capital ones, were instead tried in the much more lenient ecclesiastical courts. There was only one requirement for the change of venue, the defendant's ability to read the Miserere (Psalm 51: Have mercy on me, God, in your kindness. In my compassion blot out my offense...) "Clergy" was broadly defined—so broadly, in fact, that over time it was assumed that if one could read, one must be clergy. Proving literacy was difficult, as the psalm was routinely memorized by even illiterate convicts, and became known as the "neck verse."[8] In 1487, a statute distinguished between literate laymen and actual clergy; laymen could claim the benefit only once. The offender's thumb was branded to make him readily identified the next time around (women were not granted the right until 1692).

In 1576, "murder of malice prepensed" was no longer "clergyable."[9] That is, for the first time, a legal distinction was made between premeditated murder and manslaughter, only the latter still eligible for benefit of clergy. In Britain, in 1705, the practice was abolished. Why, legalist Blackstone argued, should the uneducated suffer while the literate go free? At the time of the Revolution, all but one of the colonies recognized the benefit. In 1771, the benefit was most famously applied to the pair of British soldiers defended by John Adams at the Boston Massacre trial, both of whom were convicted of the lesser charge of manslaughter, and burned on the hand.

Apparently, the male convicts' religious fervor dated from shortly after the time of their arrest. Might they, despite the unlikelihood, have been hoping that the indictments would read manslaughter? Six weeks later, the murder indictments came down, and any hopes of leniency were dashed. Through the trial and beyond, the men's spiritual devotions continued, so it would appear that their remorse and piety were genuine.

Bathsheba, however, remained impenitent. As her counselor, Maccarty had come to know Bathsheba intimately during her confinement. A man of integrity, he could not include her name among the remorseful. Nevertheless, he would have done all in his power to buy Spooner some time, even if but a few weeks' delay of execution.

To that end, he concluded the request for reprieve with the following.

> ....And as to the unhappy woman, [I] would beg leave further to represent, that she declares, she is several months advanced in her pregnancy, for which she humbly desires, that her execution may be respited till she shall have brought forth.
>
> Worcester May 20, 1778.
>
> The above application is made at my most earnest request.
>
> Bathsheba Spooner[10]

Under British law, a convict claiming pregnancy was entitled to a "writ de ventre inspiciendo". A jury of twelve matrons and two male midwives examined the criminal, and if quick with child, her execution was not to occur until she had delivered, or should the examiners have been mistaken, until the appropriate time had passed. Two of the guilty during the Salem witch trials were granted a temporary stay of execution under the same provision. Misson, an eighteenth-century French traveler, who had reported on conditions in English prisons, noted that

> ...the women or wenches that are condemned...never fail to plead they are with child. Very often, their pleas were substantiated. Though they never come so good virgins into the prison...there are a set of wags there that take care of these matters. No doubt they are diligent to inform the very moment they come in, that if they are not with child already, they must go to work immediately to be so...Who would not harken to such wholesome advice?[11]

From time to time, infants were delivered in the condemned's cell.

On May 28th, the State Council granted the convicts a reprieve from the June 4 day of execution, addressing Worcester County Sheriff William Greenleaf

> It hath been represented to us, that the said William Brooks, James Buchannon [sic], Ezra Ross, and Bathsheba Spooner, are desirous of further time being allowed them to prepare for Death—We of our special grace and favour do hereby direct and Command you to suspend and delay the execution of the Sentence of our said Court until Thursday, the Second Day of July next...[12]

On the same day, the Council granted the writ de ventre inspiciendo.

> Being desirous of knowing the truth [of Bathsheba's claim], do commend you...taking with you two men midwives,

> and twelve discreet and lawful matrons of your County... and cause [Bathsheba] diligently to be searched by the said matrons, in the presence of the said men midwives, by the Breasts and Belly...at or before the 25th Day of June next...[13]

Two days later, Rev. Ebenezer Parkman of Westborough, whose diary reveals an avid interest in the case, received a visit from Rev. Maccarty "...on his journey from Boston [who] came and has Reprieve for the criminals, to July 2."[14]

Several months earlier, John Adams had accepted the appointment of commissioner to France; ten-year-old John Quincy joined him on his February voyage. On June 10, Abigail wrote to her son in Paris "...the Modern History of our own times furnishes as black a list of crimes as can be paralleled in ancient time, even if we go back to Nero, Caligula, or Cesare Borgia..."[15] The Spooner scandal cannot have been far from her mind.

Sheriff Greenleaf assembled the two male midwives (Elijah Dix and Hosiah Wilder, local physicians) and twelve matrons on June 11, who included Elizabeth Rice, daughter-in-law of the town's first permanent settler; and Mary Stearns, innkeeper of the former Tory nerve center, The King's Arms Tavern, renamed the US Arms Tavern. After what was apparently a brutal examination (the matrons did the actual exam; the physicians' role was supervisory), the examiners concurred that Bathsheba Spooner "...is not quick with child."[16] Twelve days later, Sheriff Greenleaf endorsed their finding, and forwarded it to the Council in Boston.

In the meantime, a reporter with The Worcester Spy wrote that the prisoners complained to him of "the multitudes that crowd in upon them. They therefore induce that none may come to see them out of a vain curiosity, or merely to gaze at them, but leave them to enjoy their short time in as profitable a manner as may be."[17]

Bathsheba petitioned the Council further. An extraordinary document, it is included here in full.

> May it please your honor, with unfeigned gratitude I acknowledge the favor you lately granted me a reprieve. I must beg leave once more, humbly to be at your feet, and to represent to you that though the jury of matrons that were appointed to examine into my case have not brought it in my favor, yet that I am absolutely certain of being in a pregnant state, and above four months advanced in it, and the infant I bear was lawfully begotten. I am earnestly desirous of being spared till I shall have been delivered of it. I must humbly address your Honors, not understanding my great unworthiness, and take my deplorable case into your compassionate consideration. What I bear and already perceive to be animated is more of the fault of her who bears it, and has, I beg leave to say, a right to the existence which God has begun to give it. Your honors' humane Christian principles, I am certain, must lead you to desire to preserve life, rather than to destroy it. suffer me, therefore, with all earnestness, to beseech your honors to grant me such a further length of time, at least, as that there may be the fairest and fullest opportunity to have the matter fully ascertained, and, as in duty bound, shall during my short continuance pray.[18]

Bathsheba makes the startling claim that "the infant I bear was lawfully begotten." By her calculation, the fetus was conceived in late February, days before Joshua's murder. Her adulterous relations with Ezra Ross are an indisputable fact, part of the testimony of her housekeeper, Sarah Stratton. In the trial transcript, we read

> Sarah Stratton, She lived at Mr. Spooner's at several times. The first time she saw Ross there was in the fall of the year, between the two Thanksgivings. Spooner came from Boston after they were in bed; Mrs. Spooner got up and let him in.[19]

(In honor of the American victory at Saratoga, the Continental Congress proclaimed a Day of Thanksgiving to be observed on December 18 that year, weeks after the traditional Thanksgiving holiday, thus "between the two Thanksgivings"). To be examined more in depth later, their affair would be confirmed by Ross himself only a week before the execution.

Ross, of course, was not her only illicit partner. As testified by Prudence, who worked at Mary Walker's tavern where Brooks and Buchanan had been lodging, she on one occasion went up to Buchanan's room where she "saw them [Bathsheba and Buchanan] together."[20] "Together" is clearly, in the context of eighteenth-century courtroom discretion, a euphemism for "in bed." Mary Walker herself reported seeing Brooks with his head upon [Mrs.] Spooner's waist. Bathsheba commented, "You must not wonder, Billy [Brooks] has lived at my house and is fond of me as he would be of a mother."[21]

In truth, there is no way of knowing precisely how many lovers Mrs. Spooner had. To further complicate her claim that the infant was "lawfully begotten", Worcester County had been rife with rumors that she and Joshua Spooner had not shared intimacy for several months before his demise.

In her second request for a reprieve, Bathsheba remained consistent in refusing to admit any guilt. She speaks of her "great unworthiness" and refers to her case as "deplorable", but confesses no culpability. However justified she may have felt, she was surely trying the patience of the court in her obstinacy, and could not have advanced her cause by suggesting that the child was Joshua's.

Rev. Maccarty, who almost certainly hand-delivered the petition, added

> ...it is with deep regret that I think of her being cut off...I should be very sorry if your Honors should consider me over-officious in the matter. But principles of humanity and a desire that righteousness may go forth as brightness, and judgment as the noon day, have powerfully prompted me to make this application on her behalf.[22]

However impartial the Council may have thought themselves, Bathsheba was placing her fate in the hands of men who at the very least found her politically abhorrent, her personal morality another issue altogether. It has been noted that John Avery, Jr., the Council's secretary, was Joshua Spooner's stepbrother, and that his relationship to Joshua helped to turn the Council against Bathsheba.[23] Certainly, it would be naive to suggest that Avery could have viewed Bathsheba's petitions with much impartiality, if any. And yet, it should be recalled that he signed both the original reprieve, delaying the execution by one month, as well as the writ de ventre inspiciendo, granting Bathsheba's initial request to be examined for pregnancy. Could it not be argued that, rather than wishing to see Bathsheba executed, he may have been equally determined that the Council should in light of his personal interest exhibit no bias against Mrs. Spooner, permitting her every recourse available?

Avery shared one key trait with virtually every other member of the Council, his Patriotism, a shared outlook that, despite however fairly they may have viewed their decisions, inevitably guaranteed the conspirators' destruction. To consider just three members: Walter Spooner (apparently no relation) had been president of the Council on three separate occasions, during the stormiest period of all, 1775-76, when only the most fervent of Patriots could have survived such a role. Artemus Ward of Shrewsbury (just east of Worcester) had served as commander of the Continental Army before Washington was named his successor in June of 1775. A descendant writing of Ward's unshakeable Patriotism, described him as "...rather over stern in demeanor...inflexible in his ideas, and full convinced that the Massachusetts Bay Colony were the Chosen People."[24] A third member, Jeremiah Powell, had served as a lieutenant colonel in the French and Indian War, and would become the first president of the Massachusetts senate under the constitution, a man described as a "zealous patriot."[25]

The Council ignored Mrs. Spooner's request that they reconsider whether or not she was indeed pregnant.

Nevertheless, Bathsheba underwent a second exam, without official approval. On June 27, three male midwives, a female midwife and two matrons examined her; a plurality concurred with Bathsheba.

> May it please your honors, we, the subscribers, have examined the body of Mrs. Bathsheba Spooner (by her desire) to find whether she is quick with child or not; and altho' it was our, and the Jury of Matrons' opinion, on the examination of ye 11th instant, that she was not quick with child at that time, yet, upon this further examination, we would inform your Honors, that we must give it as our opinion, that we have reason to think that she is now quick with child.[26]

The opinion was signed, as before, by Josiah Wilder and Elijah Dix. Hannah Mower, as the only female midwife (not part of the earlier exam), concurred. And there was a fourth name in agreement, Worcester's most prominent physician and Bathsheba's brother-in-law, John Green, who also played no role in the first exam. We can only speculate about his participation, but it's reasonable to assume that his wife Mary, Bathsheba's sister, insisted upon it at this critical juncture. She may have even suggested he play a part in the initial exam, which he may have refused in the name of impartiality.

But even now, agreement could not be reached. The two dissenters added

> Whereas we, the subscribers, Matrons, on the examination of Mrs. Bathsheba Spooner, on ye 11th instant, did give it as our opinion on oath, that she was not quick with child at that time, have again this day, at her request, examined her present circumstances, and give it as our opinion, that she is not even now quick with child.[27]

It was signed by Elizabeth Rice, one of the original matrons, and by a new matron, Molly Tatman.

The Council, as with Bathsheba's second petition, did not respond. They had fulfilled the letter of the law in granting the first exam, and had accepted the initial finding. They saw no need for a second exam, and surely attached even less importance to its results; although only speculation, the Council may also have viewed the results of the second exam more dismissively, the first exam unanimous, the second divided.

Maccarty persisted, calling upon still another midwife who examined Bathsheba informally, and believed that she was in fact pregnant. He again petitioned the Council, to no avail.

Only days earlier, on June 25th, Isaiah Thomas printed the following notice in The Massachusetts Spy

> The selectmen of the town of Worcester, taking into consideration the large concourse of people who will probably attend the execution of the unhappy persons under sentence of death here, and also that there are several hospitals in this county for the reception of persons having the small pox, DO, in behalf of the public, caution and request all Physicians and Nurses, concerned in such Hospitals, and persons lately having had the small-pox, not to appear in the assembly of spectators unless sufficiently Cleansed. Otherwise their attendance may prove fatal to many, and render the execution, which is intended for a warning and benefit of All, a public detriment.
>
> By Order of the Selectmen,
> William Stearns, Town Clerk[28]

As one author noted, "With the exception of the war itself, smallpox was the greatest upheaval to afflict the continent in these years."[29] Eventually, 130,000 perished; hundreds of thousands more were stricken but recovered. As a contagion, the variola virus is unmatched it its communicability. The smallest droplets of the infection, even scabs and bodily secretions can transmit the disease. The air of sick rooms which had been swept could be full of potentially lethal particles. Those enduring the worst ravages of the plague faced the torment of excruciating, foul-smelling postules as a prelude to their death. In Worcester, Dr. Green, Bathsheba's brother-in-law, as well as the Spooners' neighbor in Brookfield, Dr. Foxcroft (who inoculated two-hundred patients) were among the nation's earliest pioneers in its treatment, a disease for which Dr. Jenner's vaccination was a generation away.

That same day, Ebenezer Parkman of Westborough paid an extraordinary visit to the convicts. Parkman notes that while at the jail, he met Ezra Ross' brother, Timothy, and "Lucy McDonald (who was with child by Ezra)..."[30] Given the date of Ross' arrest, this mysterious Lucy McDonald was therefore at least four months pregnant, since Ross could not have seen her after February. Only feet away, Bathsheba sat in her cell, also expecting a child likely by Ezra. In his diary, Parkman shared his talk with Mrs. Spooner.

> ...The Criminals are very penitent and behave well. I questioned them concerning the first beginning of the woeful proceedings. They said Mrs. Spooner began them. Each of them affirmed it, but on visiting Mrs. Spooner, I found her of no different mind from time past, unless it was in more evident denyl of the Legality of her Condemnation. She was free and friendly in Converse, offered me Wine, which I drank. She answered me as heretofore she took it kindly that I came to see her... but when I asked who was foremost in the horrid and cloody acts, she laid this on Ross which, being contrary to what I had met with the Prisoners below, I enquired whether she would say this before them if they were together. She said she would be willing to with Ross, but did not want to have the other two present. We went down to prayer..."[31]

Why now, for the first time, only a week before their execution, did Bathsheba characterize Ross as the murder's instigator? Is this but another example of Mrs. Spooner's erratic personality, even mental illness? Ross had visited his parents' farm in Topsfield only days before the murder when he may have been intimate with McDonald. Had Mrs. Spooner just become aware of Lucy McDonald's pregnancy, in a fit of jealousy lashing out by casting Ross as the murder's mastermind? Whatever the reason, her suggestion was extraordinary.

Parkman continues

> 'Will you ask for me?' says she. 'Yes, readily.' I did and she had leave. I went to ye men, a little while before she came: for the Guard waited on her. A paper was delivered me, which Buchanan had drawn up from Ross' mouth, and Ross had signed it, while I was in the Chamber. When we were together, Ross by my desire read the paper containing the First of her promoting her Husband's Death.[32]

In his statement to Parkman, Ross makes the claim (see chapter three) that on one trip to the Ruggles estate in Hardwick, Bathsheba asked him if he would be willing to be her lover. As a "nota bene", he added

> NB. After her return she gave me an Invitation to Defile her Marriage Bed; Which I excepted. (The spelling is so). And after that she proposed constantly Every skeam for her husband's death.
>
> Ezra Ross[33]

Parkman's diary continues, noting that Ross had provided him with more details, which Parkman chose not to include. Before returning to Westborough, he rode his horse a half mile down Main Street to the parsonage of his friend (and confidant of Mrs. Spooner), Rev. Maccarty, who "shewed me another Testimony of Ross". In it, Ross spoke of being strongly urged by Bathsheba to poison not only her husband, but also to "give the Poison to Mr. Crosby also [a neighbor of theirs at Brookfield] But [he positively refused]."[34]

More details of Mr. Crosby remain a mystery.

CHAPTER FIFTEEN

A Necklace of Gold or Diamonds

Repent of all your Errors past
and eye the Stroke of Fate
Lest you should come to Shame at last
And mourn when tis too late

And that all who read this verse
Would warning take by them

That so they may avoid the Snares
That they were taken in

Before young men do you attend
To what the Scripture says
"That he that's wicked overmuch
Shan't live out half his days."

And let this warning loud and shrill
Be heard by ev'ryone,
Oh do no more such Wickedness,
As had of late been done.

– from "A Mournful Poem" by Isaiah Thomas,
broadside printed July 2, 1778

Following British tradition, an execution day sermon would be preached early on the afternoon of July 2. In earlier times, on the eve before, an Ordinary (minister assigned to the condemned) preached to the criminals as they sat around a coffin. Later, this evolved into a church sermon at midday open to all.

Rev. Thaddeus Maccarty's sermon followed the centuries-old format, a sermon which served to comfort the condemned, while reminding the faithful of their own waywardness and the need for repentance. All but one of the convicts would attend; Bathsheba was still incapacitated from her brutal exams only days earlier.

The men had at least two visitors beforehand. The Rev. John Lesslie, pastor of Linebrook parish in west Ipswich, had traveled to Worcester to attend the execution of his parishioner, Ezra Ross. A native of Ireland, Lesslie assumed the pastorate upon graduating from Harvard College, a position he held for thirty years at a salary of one hundred pounds and twelve cords of wood. Described by one contemporary as "essentially Scotch—strong, courageous, active, efficient, stable, true,"[1] his steady character would be tested that afternoon as he led the youngest child of Jabez and Joanna Ross, three weeks shy of his eighteenth birthday, to the gallows.

John Lesslie and Ezra Ross likely joined Maccarty and the British men in devotions. In his History of Ipswich, Felt described the west Ipswich parish as stricken with profound grief, which had declared a day of fasting, humiliation and prayer, to be solemnly kept.[2]

Another visitor attending the visitors that Thursday was Roger Lamb, a British officer who had served at Saratoga. As a Convention prisoner, like Buchanan and Brooks, Lamb was marched to Cambridge, and after a few weeks transferred to serve again in New York as a member of the Regiment of Royal Fusileers (a fusil was a flintlock musket). Once again, Buchanan wrote to his superiors of his predicament, and Lamb was chosen to offer what moral assistance he could in the soldiers' last hours. Considering the men's much proclaimed piety, it is probable that most of the final morning was spent in prayer.

Rev. Ebenezer Parkman of Westborough was undoubtedly already in Worcester. Hannah Breck Parkman, his second wife, taking a respite from the relentless heat, wrote in her diary

> 2 July People are a moving very early in the morning to go to Worcester they go 10 or 12 persons in a Coverd Waggon The weather is so hot and there is like to be so much company I do not go[3]

The day's demeanor was not one of grave solemnity; rather, hangings provoked the citizenry to raucous, unruly behavior. One source even traces the origin of the word gala to gallows. For people dullened by war and deprivation, a quadruple execution was high theater.

Before noon, at Old South Church, the condemned would have been seated in one of the two long pews immediately before the pulpit on the west side, pews usually reserved for deacons or the elderly. Many hundreds filled the church, the crowd spilling out from all doors.

In 1774, the British closed the port of Boston in retaliation for the Boston Tea Party. Rev. Maccarty delivered an impassioned, patriotic sermon which until today's oration would be regarded as his finest. He opened his execution day sermon by quoting from Deuteronomy XIX, xiii

> Thine eye shall not pity him, but thou shall put away the guilt of innocent blood from Israel, that it may go well with thee...[4]

Maccarty continued in a similar vein at some length, developing the theme of blood sacrifice as elaborated throughout the Bible.

> You know the instance I refer to, Cain's imbuing his hands in the innocent blood of his brother. Of the old world in the days of Noah, it is said that the earth was filled with violence. Violence of this kind...It is a crime that is peculiarly foul and black in the esteem of God.[5]

Maccarty continued, assuring the pious of their need to punish the prisoners.

> Thou shall put away the guilt of innocent blood...but that there is law violated in the present case, is plain beyond all dispute. Among the laws or commandments given at Mount Sinai this is one—Thou shalt not kill. The apostle John, among other heinous transgressions, mentions murderers, who shall have their part in the lake which burneth with fire and brimstone, which is the second death...[but] it may be observed here, that as black a crime as murder is, it may be repented of, and in virtue of the great atonement by Jesus, be pardoned by God...The blood of Abel cried for vengeance; But the blood of Jesus, the lamb slain, cries for mercy...if the guilt of blood is not put away, it will be displeasing to God, and expose the land to distressing judgments...[6]

Maccarty's perspective, perhaps a casualty of the week's suspense, suffered from at least one instance of extreme hyperbole.

> It was a most shocking, cruel murder, and, taken in all its circumstances, such a instance as has never happened in this land from the first settlement of it, and indeed it is scarcely to be paralleled in all history...[7]

Maccarty implored those present to be merciful to the innocent victims of the tragedy.

> And pity and pray for their afflicted distrest relatives, whether parents, brethren, and sisters, and others that are near to them by the bonds of nature. Let them never be

> upbraided and reproached by the ultimely, ignominious death of these four prisoners. This would be cruel and brutal. And particularly would it be so to the orphan children of Mr. Spooner... May they never be made to suffer, for what has happened to their parents [and may they find solace in the words of] Psalm xxii, 10 "When my father and my mother forsake me, then the Lord will take me up."[8]

Nearing his conclusion, the reverend addressed the person most conspicuously absent.

> When we consider your sex, the respectable figure that in times past you made in life, your connections, and your many agreeable qualities, it is with pungent grief that we behold you a prisoner of death...though you have not been disposed to [repent of your sin] to man, I hope you have done so upon your bended knees to the omnipresent, who cannot be deceived.[9]

Maccarty had been preaching nearly forty minutes. He exhorted the convicts (especially Bathsheba) to plead for God's forgiveness.

> It is thus with you poor dying woman!...Call upon him even at the last, lie at his feet, beseeching him that his tender mercy and compassion be extended to you; that he would not leave you to perish forever, but give you a name and place among the redeemed and saved in his eternal kingdom...And so we bid you a solemn and final farewell![10]

The men were returned to prison. A short time later, Maccarty found his way to the Worcester gaol, likely accompanied by several church brethren, who joined the condemned in prayer. The minister (in the printed appendix to the sermon) noted that Mrs. Spooner "appeared very calm, humble and penitent [professing] her faith in the great savior and her dependence upon him."[11]

According to the appendix, Maccarty broached the subject.

"Would Mrs. Spooner consider baptism in her last hour?"

"Yes, of course," she replied.

About this time, Sheriff Greenleaf appeared carrying four nooses, which he had likely weighted with bags of cement the previous evening to lessen their elasticity. After measuring the men, he re-entered Bathsheba's cell.

"Mrs. Spooner, I'll need to fit this about your neck for a moment."

According to Maccarty, Bathsheba responded, "Sir, I esteem it as much as though you had placed a necklace of gold or diamonds about me."[12]

It was nearly two o'clock. The throng of five thousand (over three times the town's population; it would be perhaps another half century before a crowd of equal size filled the town) choked the streets. By now, viewers had chosen their preferred vantage point: by the jail to watch the prisoners exit, or along Back (now Summer) Street to observe the morbid procession which would stop at the gallows.

Substantial profits were reaped from the pressing crowd, and not only by the innkeepers. Isaiah Thomas was busy at his press, cranking out the weekly edition of The Massachusetts Spy. He had returned to Worcester only very recently, having spent weeks traveling the colonies in his attempt to collect overdue subscriptions to his paper. Being the newsman and businessman that he was, this was an opportunity he could not miss. Without doubt, the July 2 edition enjoyed the distinction of having one of the largest circulations up to that time. Although the issue contained no current news related to the affair, it did include two notices of direct appeal to the throng.

> This day was published, price two shillings. The Dying Declaration of James Buchanan, William Brooks, Ezra Ross, who are to be executed at Worcester, this day, being Thursday, July 2, for the murder of Mr. Joshua Spooner, late of Brookfield.
>
> Also, this day published, a poem on James Buchanan, Ezra Ross, and William Brooks, who are to be executed at Worcester, this day, being Thursday, July 2, together with Bathsheba Spooner, for the barbarous murder of her husband, Mr. Joshua Spooner, late of Brookfield. Sold at the printing office, in Worcester, and by I. Thomas, in Londonderry.[13]

The selection of Londonderry, in southern New Hampshire, gives further evidence of the regional interest generated by the scandal. Surely, the streets of Worcester were full of boys hawking the weekly paper, directing the curious to the printing office but a stone's throw from the jail.

The execution of Bathsheba and her three accomplices was the most infamous, but certainly not the only eighteenth-century hangings in Worcester; about a half dozen preceded those of July 1778 (though unlike here, individual cases), although these were the first since the Declaration proclaimed a new nation. Throughout New England, indeed all of the colonies, hanging was the preferred means of capital punishment. Those guilty of whatever crime typically did not receive jail time for their offenses. Following Great Britain's lead, New England punished a majority of offenses, however trivial, by hanging. The mother country, however, indulged the practice with a ferocity encountered only sporadically in western history. In the sixteenth century, it is estimated that Henry VIII dispatched as many as seventy-one thousand (many political opponents), enthusiastically continuing an eight-hundred-year tradition. In the eighth century, hanging replaced the earlier method of capital punishment, boiling in oil, which was discontinued not for humane reasons, but because hanging was a much cleaner, less tiresome affair.[14]

Women suffered a different fate. Until the eighteenth century, a woman convicted of "petty treason" (husband murder) would be burned alive. Come the reign of George I, the criminal was first hanged as sticks were piled upon her, then incinerated once dead. Such executions did not always work as planned. In 1726, Catherine Hayes was convicted of husband murder (like Bathsheba, she had enlisted the help of accomplices). Her neck was placed in the noose when, mistakenly, the sticks were lighted. As the executioner tried to hang her, the flames scorched his hand, and with a yell let go of the rope, burning her alive Three hours passed before her body was reduced to ashes.

Death by strangulation was often a long, drawn-out process, taking sometimes several minutes. The most primitive method entailed throwing a rope over a tree branch; in America, the writhing victim was often put out of his misery with a gunshot. (In England, spectators were sometimes allowed to pull on the criminals' legs to shorten the suffering). Eventually, a simple crossbar or triangular gallows replaced the tree, with or without a platform. As evidenced from at least two contemporary drawings of the executions, Mrs. Spooner and her cohorts were hanged from a crossbar.

The practice of public execution was, of course, a long-sanctioned one, endorsed by the ancient Romans. Writing in the first century, Quintilian explained that "when criminals are executed the most public places are chosen, where there will be the greatest number of spectators, and so the most for the fear of punishment to work upon them."[15] His contemporary Seneca added that "the more public the punishments are, the greater the effect they will produce upon the reformation of others."[16] Their fallacious reasoning, which resulted in little reformation over the next eighteen-hundred years, was not rejected until the late nineteenth century when executions were thereafter carried out within a prison's walls

Whether or not the executions of Spooner, Ross, Buchanan and Brooks were to serve as a deterrent, the village was overwhelmed by thousands eager for the opportunity. Hangings were referred to by the term "turning off", a reference to the manner in which the criminal mounted a ladder (in still earlier times) which was turned around, leaving him dangling in the noose. The turning off of the Brookfield Four would be the largest group executed in Massachusetts since September of 1692, when eight Salem "witches" were hanged together.

The waiting mob stretched for a third of a mile down Back Street. Those not lucky enough to secure a spot near the gallows (likely today's Washington Square) or jail lined the street. Mrs. Spooner and Rev. Maccarty exited the jail. Bathsheba wore a black hat, extravagantly accented by a white plume, probably provided by sister Mary. Still weak from the midwives' exams, she turned to the crowd with a wan smile as she and Maccarty stepped into the carriage. One hundred guards had been assigned to Worcester for the execution, many of whom likely surrounded the four caskets making their way down Back Street. The three male prisoners marched behind them, followed by Mrs. Spooner and Rev. Maccarty in the chaise. For the duration of her ride, it was reported that Bathsheba smiled at the curious, acknowledging her friends with a wave of farewell.

As recorded in the addendum to his sermon, Maccarty stared ahead to the gallows, then turned to Bathsheba, who also fixed her gaze upon the stage. "Does the sight of it strike you?" he asked gently.

"No more so than any other object," she replied.[17]

Further to the southwest, perhaps even from Brookfield, then Spencer and Leicester, lightning bolts flashed from cloud to cloud. Roger Lamb, Buchanan's escort, wrote in his memoirs of the Revolution, "although the former part of the day was serene and fine, of a sudden, as they approached the place, the sky was covered with clouds."[18] The gallows, only a hundred feet ahead, towered above all, its stark outline framing four nooses against the now dark sky.

"The awfulness of it was great indeed," Lamb marveled, "and the truly contrite feelings of the culprits were calculated to turn vicious spectators to virtuous and pious ways...Mrs. Spooner... seemed impenitent a good deal." Only nature itself could have enhanced the scene. "A storm of thunder followed," Lamb recalled, "following with copious rain [attaching] additional terrors to their ignominious catastrophe."[19] Isaiah Thomas wrote in The Massachusetts Spy

> Just before they reached the place of execution a black thunder cloud arose and darkened the Heavens; here followed an awful half hour! The loud hallooings of the Officers, amidst a crowd of five thousand, to MAKE WAY! MAKE WAY!...The fierce corufications athwart the darkened horizon, quickly followed by loud peals of thunder, conspired

> together, and produced a dreadful scene of horror! It seemed as if the author of nature was determined to add such terrors to the punishment of the criminals as must stagger the stoutest heart of the most abandoned...[20]

The men were led up the steps, each then positioned aside the other by Sheriff Greenleaf of Lancaster, the executioner. The trio likely stood atop a three square foot box shaped structure (maybe 18 inches tall) on the raised platform, which was designed to collapse into the scaffold, leaving the criminals suspended. According to an eyewitness, many of the horses reared and cried, stomping violently. Buchanan and Brooks bowed their heads, lost in private devotions as the youngest, Ezra Ross, prayed aloud. According to Thomas, as the death warrants were being read, Bathsheba sat calmly in her chaise with the pastor, listening to the sheriff "as she would the most indifferent matter."[21]

Maccarty alighted from the carriage, stepping aside as Bathsheba, shaken, clutched both his hands, appearing otherwise undisturbed, ever smiling, as she surveyed the mob. Faltering before the steps, she let go of Maccarty, then gingerly lowered herself until her knees touched the bottom stair. Stretching out her limbs to pull herself up the steps, with great effort she pushed herself erect upon reaching the stage. Proceeding to the end of the platform, she stopped behind the last noose, likely next to Ezra Ross.

Greenleaf approached Brooks to fasten the noose, slippery from the rain, then secured his hands with rope, and covered his face with a black hood, repeating the procedure with Buchanan and Ross. The men's feet had likely been menacled to prevent wild thrashing.

The sheriff would have knelt before Bathsheba, modestly securing her dress at the ankles with rope, before tying her wrists behind her back.

Bathsheba indicated her desire to make a final statement.

"My dear sir! I am ready! In a little time I expect to be in bliss; and but a few years must elapse when I hope I shall see you again."[22]

Isaiah Thomas observed that the criminals were calm, and "almost smiled at the approach of death, considering the king of terrors but as a kind messenger to introduce them to the regions of eternal joys."[23] As the storm withdrew, a light shower blessed their final moments. Greenleaf secured Bathsheba's black hood before the levers were pulled.

Despite the day's extraordinary events, prosecutor Robert Treat Paine wrote tersely in his diary "2 July....very hot."[24]

One witness from Groton (thirty-seven miles distant) had left his home early that day. Amos Farnsworth, commissioned as a lieutenant in the Continental Army three months later, had enlisted less than a week after the Battles of Lexington and Concord, entering the regiment of Colonel William Prescott, commander at the Battle of Bunker Hill. Farnsworth's diary of the Revolution was published over a century ago. He wrote

> 2 July Thursday Sot out Early in the morning and went to Worster and saw fore Persons Hung for the murder of Mr. Spooner of Brookfield...all young persons and o what a solam sean it was: to Behold Persons launching into the world of spirits. O Lord keep me from falling into Sin which exposes life to publick justis [25]

Each corpse would have been held by a soldier as the nooses

were cut, halters removed. The bodies were dragged aside, each laid next to the other as more soldiers removed the coffin lids. The heat returned, the storm having offered only a brief respite.

The bodies of Buchanan and Brooks were carried down the stairs, each deposited in the waiting coffins, never again to be disturbed. The British men were likely buried beneath the gallows; Ezra Ross' body was returned home (despite an arduous trek of many hours in severe heat), interred in an unmarked grave on the Ipswich-Rowley line. Bathsheba would undergo one last trial before her final repose.

CHAPTER SIXTEEN

Multiple Acts of Unfaithfulness

Facing the common at Westborough, Reverend Parkman sat at his desk that evening to reflect on the day's events eighteen miles to the west.

> The sun very burning—the Wind abated and Heat after 4 P.M. arose a storm of Thunder, Lightning and Rain. My thoughts have been much employed upon the Case and Condition of the Criminals whom I have commended to the infinite Mercy of God and hope the penitent are removed to a New Life. Concerning the poor Woman, it is with me uncertain whether she's hanged or not, or what has become of her...The storm renews; the Rain continues.[1]

Once the bodies were cut from their nooses, the intense heat required a quick burial. Internment at the execution site was common, and it is likely that the two British men were laid to rest under what is now Worcester's Union (train) Station.

In west Ipswich, in the parish of Ezra Ross, ther day was "kept as a season of fasting and prayer for his untimely end."[2]

The body of Bathsheba Spooner, abused and degraded over the past six weeks, would undergo one more trial, at her own request—an autopsy to confirm her pregnancy. It is not known where the autopsy took place, but in all likelihood it was back at the jail, which was the nearest public building, even if it meant transporting the victim's body through the lingering mob.

Nor do we know who or how many were present at the autopsy, although the names of three are certain: Bathsheba's brother-in-law Dr. John Green, Sheriff Greenleaf, and the only eyewitness who recorded the procedure (however briefly)—her confessor, Rev. Maccarty. (Bathsheba's sister, Mary Green, despite having been badly traumatized by the day's events, may also have been present). In the appendix to his execution day sermon, Maccarty wrote simply "she was opened the evening after execution...[a male fetus was found] of the growth of five months or near it."[3]

Though never verified, local legend has maintained that Bathsheba's remains and those of her five-month-old fetus were claimed by her sister Mary, who then had the victims interred somewhere on her estate just a half mile north. The scene can only be imagined—Mary Green and husband John in their chaise winding its way to the Green estate, Maccarty likely accompanying them. Behind, Bathsheba and son lay in their coffin, the cart creaking slowly up the hill, the early evening still stifling. Certainly dozens, perhaps hundreds who had attended the executions swarmed the entourage.

The procession's desolate solemnity was contrasted by the merrymaking found that evening among the village's overcrowded taverns; still thousands more, unable to find a room, headed home to towns throughout New England. Breck Parkman, from his father's parsonage in Westborough, wrote "...at evening a severe Thunder Storm people return all wett from Worcester."[4] The next day, his father noted simply "Hear that all four Criminals were hanged yesterday," and still a day later, the second anniversary of the Declaration, "the conversation is wholly upon the Case of the Criminals, especially respecting Mrs. Spooner and her Behaviour."[5]

A short time after, Rev. Parkman was asked by Rev. Maccarty to present a sermon at Worcester's Old South, reflecting upon the events of the past several months. Parkman entitled his sermon "The Adultress Will Hunt for the Precious Life."

> What horrendous scenes have been open! What tragical executions have ensued! The horrors of bloody and cruel murder have issued in public, infamous strangling and Death—and such cruel, unnatural and loathsome Murder has been preceded by detestable uncleanness, by repeated if I say not multiple acts of unfaithfulness to conjugal bonds and defiling of the Marriage Bed. these atrocious Acts accompanied with many other[s] of Profanery and Iniquity. But what this course of Iniquity produced? What fruit does this bale-full Tree bear? Were these questions put to those persons who have the most experiences (ah, what sorrowful experience!) what must the reply be from you but mournful and sad!...The Adultress!—how can we conceive of one who shall be so metamorphosed, or changed into such a Monster![6]

Reflecting further on Mrs. Spooner's depravity, he continues that she

> ...not only hates him [Joshua], but allows her loose imagination to range and wander after others; and instigated by both her own wanton, salacious Desire; and by the wily arts of the Devil...to pollute and defile the marriage Bed...[murder] by the help of how many persons! And by how various Means! —If Poisons, if Pistol you fail—horrid, impetuous...invincible Violence and Outrage succeeds. But now an End! behold an End is Come!

Most contemporaries ascribed Bathsheba Spooner's motives to immorality. Only one dissenting voice has come down to us, that of her attorney, Levi Lincoln. As her legal advocate, it was natural that he should try to explain away her culpability. His attempt to allay her guilt by resorting to a kind of insanity defense was, of course, doomed to fail. Such a defense was several decades away from public or legal acceptance, and further, the seven weeks Lincoln was given to prepare the case put him under severe restraints—in fact, his time to prepare may have been much shorter. (In 1778, there was of course no expert witness in psychology to call upon; had he fully committed himself to portraying Bathsheba's insanity, Lincoln's arguments would likely have been viewed by prosecutor, judges and jury as mere opinion, having no more or less validity than their own). And aside from any time constraints, the case was already cluttered. Three other defendants and all the inherent considerations of status and especially politics left no room for any serious debate over Mrs. Spooner's psychological competence. Lastly, a trial which was predetermined to last no more than a day—including deliberations—precluded any such treatment.

If attracting little notice in 1778, Bathsheba's mental competence has more recently become an issue of some fascination. Today's psychologist might be tempted to draw conclusions based not only on her behavior, which ranged from the erratic to the delusional, but from her family's history of mental illness as well. A century after the murder, two descendants, in different accounts, noted that various members of the family had suffered from mental illness.

In a paper read at Worcester's American Antiquarian Society in 1888, Samuel Swett Green, convinced that Bathsheba was insane at the time of the murder, noted that her daughter, also Bathsheba, had suffered similarly. The second source describes the younger

Bathsheba as having been "hopelessly insane many years before her death, the same woman who as a three-year-old was the only family member to approach her father's corpse at the inquest." Green also noted that Bathsheba's most beloved sister, Mary Green, who had claimed Bathsheba's body, "was made temporarily insane by the troubles which preceded and accompanied the trial and execution."[8]

In his History of Hardwick (1883) another descendant, Lucius Paige, refers to Bathsheba's uncle, John Ruggles (Timothy's brother) who had been "very eccentric, perhaps partially insane, but harmless." We recall also contemporary rumors of raucous arguments between Bathsheba's parents, and the occasion when Mrs. Ruggles supposedly served Gen. Ruggles his favorite pet dog for dinner. Paige considered how his fellow Victorians would have handled Bathsheba Spooner's trial. "Under such circumstances [her deranged behavior during the murder] a verdict of "guilty" could not be expected from a jury, at the present day; but "not guilty by reason of insanity" would be recognized by the jury and the whole community as a righteous decision...confinement in a lunatic asylum would seem to have been a more appropriate result than death on the gallows—involving, as it did, the death of her unborn child."[9]

Mrs. Spooner may have engaged in sexual relations with at least five different men in a three-month period between 1777 and 1778. Victorian sensibilities would have considered her a likely candidate for what we might today call sexual addiction; one late nineteenth century writer, using the term "erotomania" (which is more aptly applied to the sexually delusional) wrote

> "...a very intelligent lady...tormented from infancy with the most inordinate desires. Her excellent education

> alone saved her from the rash indulgences to which her temperament so violently urged her. Arrived at maturity, she abandoned herself to the gratification of her desires frequently, she saw herself on the verge of madness... [she confessed] "Everywhere...I see nothing but the most lascivious images—the demon of lust unremittedly pursues me at the table and even in my Sleep. I am an object of disgust to myself, and feel that I can no longer escape either madness or death."[10]

The writer adds that "there is almost invariably great depression of vital energy: it is one of the most direct roads to dementia."[11]

Portraying women as the sex more vulnerable to such desires, and consequently the more likely to suffer as a result, was of course a common bias. In the 1990's, one writer noted the interest of feminist scholars in the insanity defense, "especially as it relates to cases in which traditional stereotypes of women's behavior have traditionally been reflected in judicial decision making, where the defense's uses are purportedly connected "to notions of women's frailty, mental confusion, emotional instability, defective reasoning capacities, and receptivity to manias."[12] Gender bias aside, Bathsheba Spooner exhibited enough bizarre behavior before, during and after the murder that, were she to be tried in a court of law this century, her attorney would have likely secured for her a verdict of not guilty by reason of insanity.

As her attorney, Levi Lincoln had hoped his playing the "insanity card" might free his most prominent client. And although he never overtly made reference to Bathsheba's gender as being more susceptible to derangement, it is interesting to note that another client, William Brooks, was never viewed by Lincoln as insane, despite the fact that only two years previous, he had thrown himself overboard while en route to America (Lincoln may never have heard of his attempted suicide).

About sixteen months after the Spooner executions, Robert Young was hanged for raping eleven-year-old Jane Young (relationship unclear) of Brookfield. Young's execution was one of the last in Worcester not to involve murder; after 1786, only killers would pay the ultimate price. A couple of decades later, the gallows were dismantled. Down the street a few blocks, one of America's first mental asylums was constructed, its water gravity-fed from the estate pond of the Green family, less than a mile to the north. Across the street, the Worcester County Jail was built, the old gaol at (now) Lincoln Square having outlived its utility. Inside its walls, a new gallows had been raised; though the executions were still public, eventually Victorian sensibilities prohibited the old-fashioned public square hangings, a sign, perhaps, that the much-vaunted deterrence factor of such spectacles was losing credence.

The last hanging to occur in Worcester was that of Samuel J. Frost of Petersham, guilty of fratricide. He was executed in the jailhouse on May 25, 1876. "Frost was a small man, and when the drop fell his head was nearly severed. Many in the gathering fainted, and from that day there has been a sentiment in Worcester against hanging."[13]

In the larger sphere, it has long been held that the execution of Bathsheba Spooner, and the shame which followed the discovery of her unborn child, prevented any court in Massachusetts thereafter to sentence a woman to death. However, we know of at least two executions of female criminals in Massachusetts not long after. And yet, it may be that Spooner's execution while pregnant eventually caused the state to move against capital punishment for women.

In 1857, despite overwhelming evidence, a woman in Plymouth County was released after being tried on the charge of murdering her husband with arsenic; the jury hopelessly deadlocked. A few months later, the Massachusetts legislature redefined its murder statutes, for the first time creating a distinction between first and second degree murder, the latter requiring a mandatory life sentence. During hearings for the bill, it had been argued that no jury in the state would convict a woman of murder, not wishing to see her hang for the crime, a pattern of acquittals which traditionally has been attributed to the tragic aftermath of Bathsheba Spooner's hanging.

The woman from Plymouth County was retried, and after some clever evidentiary restructuring, as well as clarification of the defendant's intent, she was found guilty of second degree murder and sentenced to life.

Three decades later, Sarah Jane Robinson was convicted on six counts of first degree murder, and sentenced to death, but even in her case, the sentence was commuted to life, apparently due solely to her gender. The most vocal women's rights activists saw no contradiction in pressuring the governor to commute her death penalty.

Most infamous, of course, was the case of Lizzie Borden, indicted for two counts of first degree murder in the grisly slayings of her father and stepmother in Fall River in 1892. Despite compelling evidence presented against her, Borden was found not guilty, and it has been suggested that the memory of Bathsheba's execution influenced the jury's finding.

Elizabeth Cady Stanton, considered the driving force behind the first women's rights convention held in Seneca Falls in 1848, which inspired the first national convention at Worcester two years later, had by her mid-80's become an invalid. In 1899, now blind, she often dictated letters from her New York apartment. In one letter to the editor of the New York World, she addressed the imminent execution of a female convict, and referred to the Spooner case.

> This is not a question of "maudlin sentiment", but of justice to a class of citizens that have no voice in the laws, no representation in the government ...Women are dragged into the courts to be tried by men, the jury all men, advocates men, judges men, and in cases of capital punishment, to have their heads shorn, dress adjusted, and to be strapped in the chair, for electrocutions by men in the presence of men, to watch their death agony. Men make and administer their own laws, sustain them by their votes and their moral powers in the halls of legislation, the pulpit and the press, and are responsible for the criminals of their own class...Women's position is entirely different. Justice for the two classes must be viewed from a different standpoint...After reading the following sad account of the last woman executed in the old Bay State, more than a century ago, I hope our Governor will use his influence to end the barbarism of capital punishment in the great state of New York. This would indeed be the crowning glory of his brilliant public career.[14]

Stanton's plea failed; Martha Place became the first woman in the world to die in the electric chair, under Gov. Teddy Roosevelt.

The American Revolution would grind on for more than three years following the Spooner executions. After the British embarrassment at Saratoga in the fall of 1777, in which Brooks and Buchanan had fought, the French entry into the war helped to weaken British strength in the West Indies. The northern war had by now come to a stalemate, the British instead focusing their energies to the south, winning important victories at Savannah and Charleston, with the Patriots suffering the additional loss of the treasonous Benedict Arnold at West Point. The British attempt to further secure their domination of the south by capturing the Carolinas resulted in their disastrous defeat at Yorktown in 1781.

The fate of the surviving participants in the Spooner case was closely aligned to the direction the war would take. For printer Isaiah Thomas, the month following the trial represented his professional nadir. Eventually, his fortunes made a dramatic recovery, and in time became, along with Benjamin Franklin, the new nation's most successful publisher. The 1812 donation of his complete library formed the nucleus of what is today the American Antiquarian Society in Worcester, the world's largest collection of printed American material from the nation's colonial beginnings through the 1870's.

Judge Jedediah Foster of Bathsheba Spooner's hometown is arguably, along with women's rights activist Lucy Stone, the most significant personage to hail from the Brookfields. During Brookfield's bicentennial in 1886, Lyman Whiting, with just enough hyperbole to suit the occasion, observed of Foster that "no man has ever dwelt among us, who held so many local trusts—lived in such intimate sympathy with the people, cared for and served them so abundantly and excellently—and yet so far excelled them in station and character."[15] Eight months following the executions, Foster helped to draft the Massachusetts constitution at Cambridge, a document that would have a major impact upon the US constitution. It was the most lasting legacy of a man recommended to George Washington at the Provincial Congress back in 1775 in Philadelphia as one of the "Massachusetts men on whom he could especially rely in the great struggle before the colonies...one to whom the Commander-in-Chief could confide his counsels, and from whom he could expect unwavering fidelity as a patriot."[16]

The other key presiding justice, William Cushing, as Chief Justice of the Supreme Judicial Court during the Spooner case, would maintain that position until the start of the Washington administration, when he was appointed to the US Supreme Court, a position he held until his death in 1810.

Dr. John Green, Bathsheba Spooner's brother-in-law who served as midwife at her second exam, became one of the county's most prominent physicians, assembling what would become in its time New England's largest medical library, now housed at the University of Massachusetts Medical School in Worcester. His wife, Mary (Ruggles) Green, who had suffered so much following her sister's execution, provided John with ten children, in addition to the sole surviving child from her first marriage. She outlived John by fifteen years, and was buried alongside him and his first wife, also Mary, on Worcester Common.

Robert Treat Paine, the prosecutor, continued on as Massachusetts attorney general until 1790. During his tenure, he served briefly on the governor's council, and the same year was named a delegate to the state constitutional convention. He ended his career as a justice on the state supreme court, holding that position from 1790 to 1804. Despite his distinguished record at the state level, his only time spent on the national stage was prior to the Spooner trial, when he served with the Continental Congress in Philadelphia, from 1774-76. It was there that he achieved his greatest fame, signing the Declaration of Independence as a member of the Massachusetts delegation, his signature appearing rather prominently below the diminutive signature of rival John Adams.

Paine's counterpart at the trial, Levi Lincoln, achieved even higher prominence. For three years prior to the Spooner trial, and continuing for another three years (the entire span of the Revolution), Lincoln served as a probate judge, during which time his chief function was to prosecute claims against Loyalists. It is highly likely that he handled the case against the estate of Bathsheba's exiled father, Timothy Ruggles. Very little money was ever realized from the seizure of those estates.

In 1781, three cases which Lincoln brought before the state supreme court helped to abolish slavery in Massachusetts. A delegate to the state constitutional convention in 1789, Lincoln helped to draft the final document, and went on to serve in both the Massachusetts house and senate. In 1800, Lincoln found himself beneficiary of the intimate world of early American politics, when he was named to the US House of Representatives, filling the seat vacated by Spooner diarist and man of letters, Dwight Foster, who had moved on to the US Senate. In 1801, Thomas Jefferson chose Lincoln as his attorney general, a position bestowed upon him in recognition of his support for the Republican cause against that of the Federalists. Although in the post-colonial era the attorney general's position was only part-time, Lincoln became a close friend of the president. For a two-month period, he even served as secretary-of-state.

In 1805, Lincoln resigned as attorney general, and was eventually elected lieutenant governor, then governor, an office his son would also hold. President Madison asked that he serve on the US Supreme Court, but Lincoln, now suffering from poor eyesight, refused the honor. In his final years, Lincoln's sight recovered, just enough to indulge long-neglected passions for gardening and classical study.

Following the murder of Joshua Spooner, no one came to know his widow more intimately than Rev. Thaddeus Maccarty, her spiritual counsel. As one contemporary described him, "Living in 'troublous times', he had his full share of trials; but under them all he honored the ministry, and his ministry honored him. In seasons of peril, he was calm and steadfast; and though darkness was above and around him, he was looking with the patience of hope for light."[17] Maccarty, who in concert with Dr. John Green became one of the earliest pioneers in smallpox inoculation, was laid to rest on Worcester Common six years after the executions. His epitaph reads "Under a slow and painful decline he discover'd an ardent love to his Master by a chearful attention to his service, and at the approval of death he patiently submitted, in the full hope of a glorious Resurrection from the grave."[18]

In some ways, the miserable marriage of Joshua and Bathsheba was both anticipated by, and reflected in the marriage of Bathsheba's parents, Gen. Timothy and Bathsheba Ruggles. When Timothy was exiled in 1774 as one of the state's most infamous Loyalists, Bathsheba's mother chose to stay behind on the family estate in Hardwick. The estate, with its many varieties of fruit trees, prize-bred livestock and deer park, had become perhaps the grandest in Worcester County. Twenty months later, in January of 1776, most of Timothy Ruggles' holdings were auctioned off, including "three of the best pews in the Meeting House at

Hardwick."[19] Bathsheba Ruggles and son were allowed to keep the home and a small portion of the land. In 1779, the remainder of Ruggles' property in Hardwick and Princeton was confiscated and sold. The sale netted the Patriot cause nearly 32,000 pounds, a princely sum. Caleb Mirick, the Princeton innkeeper who hosted the sale, billed the government forty-five pounds for the entertainment and refreshments he provided.

Years later King George III, who had earlier rewarded Ruggles by granting him the huge parcel of land in Princeton, reimbursed the general for the loss of that same land, a generous gesture by the Crown enjoyed by few others; in fact, the reimbursement may have been the most generous ever bestowed upon a Loyalist.

Ruggles, like many Tories, passed most of the war years in New York, joining the British troops on Staten Island. The last British contingent remained there until finally capitulating in 1784 per terms of the Treaty of Paris. There is no indication that the New York newspapers printed any information about the Spooner case, nor do we have any surviving letters from the general to his daughter, letters which even if they had existed would have been likely seized before they were ever mailed.

Out of a white population of about two million (enslaved African-Americans numbered another half million), nearly five percent, or 100,000 Loyalists were banished from the colonies, half of whom served in combat. Although some fled to England, the majority made their way to Canada's maritime provinces. Timothy Ruggles resettled in Nova Scotia, thanks to the king's largesse, who granted him ten thousand acres for his lifetime loyalty to the Crown. It remains unclear precisely when Ruggles left Staten Island—the earliest reference to his presence in Canada is not until 1783.

In 1755, at the outbreak of the French and Indian War, on the pretense that they had not sworn to the Crown, between six and seven thousand French Canadians were expelled by the victorious British to the American colonies, some to France, and others to Louisiana, their homes in Nova Scotia burned. Now, ironically, nearly thirty years later, Ruggles, already exiled from his native Massachusetts, would be cast off again, this time to Nova Scotia, from which so many French Canadians had been expelled, one result of the war in which he had been a prominent player.

The ten thousand acres granted Ruggles were in the village of Wilmot, Nova Scotia, in the county of Annapolis, a few miles inland from the north central coast along the Bay of Fundy. Ruggles' immense tract of land, several times larger than his total property in Massachusetts, was heavily wooded. Most of his land in Wilmot, a tiny rural outpost even today, was part of what was once called Ruggles Mountain, today Phinney Mountain, covered by birch and coniferous trees, with logging trails leading to the bay.

Much of what was cleared from the mountain was done by Ruggles himself (now in his seventies), with the aid of hired men who, after removing the ancient forest, dug a cellar hole nine feet deep, dressed in granite from a quarry in Quincy, Massachusetts. Ruggles was joined in Wilmot by two of his sons, John aged forty-one, and Richard, two years younger, both of whom were also Loyalists.

Following the seizure of his lands and goods in America, Ruggles petitioned the Crown for losses of nearly twenty thousand pounds, and was compensated for a quarter of that amount, meanwhile receiving an annual pension of one-hundred-and-fifty pounds until his death, which guaranteed him a comfortable retirement.

Always a man of action, in Wilmot Ruggles created what would become one of the country's most enviable estates, beautifying his land with a variety of exotic plants, shrubbery and trees not yet seen in Nova Scotia, including the first apple trees in Annapolis County, the seeds coming from his orchard in Hardwick, Massachusetts. Those seeds became the forebears of Nova Scotia's apple industry, second only to Ontario.

Meanwhile, four years after his arrival, Worcester Magazine published the death notice of his estranged wife, Bathsheba, in March of 1787. Bathsheba had lived on what remained of the family's Hardwick estate. The property had been tended by their eldest son, also Timothy, who now had a family of his own; the year following the execution of his sister, he named his first child Bathsheba.

Why, following the seizure and auction of the Ruggles estate, would Worcester County's most radical citizens permit Ruggles' eldest son and his mother to continue residing there? It is true that, following the war, some Tories had been welcomed back to their communities, however reluctantly. But to allow the wife of the infamous Timothy Ruggles to remain during and after the war seems unimaginable. We know, however, that in 1771, Timothy Jr. had been named captain of the town's newly formed militia. It is safe to assume that any militia formed in the year after the Boston Massacre would be one dedicated wholeheartedly to the American cause. As a Patriot, Timothy Jr. may have been invited to stay. Although there is no clear evidence, it is at least a possibility that his mother was suffering from mental illness, which may have induced even the most fervently patriotic townspeople to permit her to stay in the only home she had known for the past thirty years. Her own political sympathies remain a mystery.

Within a few years, the estate whose elaborate dinner parties once surpassed those of any in central Massachusetts fell to disuse. In the mid-1800's, what remained of the manse was demolished, and today, on the road leading east to Gilbertville, only the fieldstone foundation and one of the outbuildings remain. Each year, many hundreds flock to the Hardwick Agricultural Fair, America's oldest, founded by General Ruggles in 1762, partly as a way to showcase his horticultural wonders and prize-winning livestock.

Eight years following the death of his estranged wife, Timothy Ruggles passed away, on August 4, 1795, at the age of eighty-three. His obituary in the Royal Gazette (Nova Scotia) read in part

> The district of country in which he lived will long feel the benefit resulting from the liberal exertions he made to advance new agricultural interests of the province. It may not be without use to remark for much the greater part of his life he ate no animal food nor drank any spirituous or fermented liquors, small [weak] beer excepted, and that he enjoyed health to his advanced age.[20]

A biography of Ruggles written by a descendant nearly a century later noted "The sad events in the life of [daughter Bathsheba], whose insanity and tragic death had darkened the closing years of her exiled father, [events which] need not be dwelt upon here..."[21]

General Ruggles was laid to rest in the churchyard of Pine Grove Church, Wilmot, in an unmarked grave. The neighboring town of Middleton erected a memorial in his name. His eldest son, Richard, continued to live on the Wilmot estate until his own death four decades later.

Joshua Spooner's gravesite, tucked just inside the gate of the old Brookfield cemetery, still receives the occasional visitor. Many years ago, Harvey Bennett, the cemetery's caretaker, added further mystery to his death. "Funny thing about the stone—we've never been able to grow grass near it. I don't know why. I tell people it's because it's been trampled on so they won't think there's something about it."[22]

What of the final resting place of Bathsheba and her unborn son? Following the autopsy, it is believed that Bathsheba's sister, Mary Green, claimed the bodies. Assuming that all necessary details had been handled expeditiously, the bodies could have been placed in the cart while it was still late afternoon, to begin the nearly mile-long trek. Given the pressing crowds, military escort, and humid conditions, the procession may have taken a couple of hours.

Once the cortege had arrived at the Green mansion, burial would have been immediate. The mansion, the original part of which dated from the 1750's, by the late 1770's consisted of perhaps ten rooms. A century later, it had expanded nearly sixfold; in 1957 it was demolished by the city, a victim of expensive upkeep and encroaching vandalism. As the home grew, so had the estate, from a couple dozen acres to about five hundred by the 1880's.

One of the city's most enduring mysteries is where Bathsheba and her unborn child may have been buried. Over the centuries, many theories have been offered: near the home, under it, under a prominent boulder, by a stone silo a quarter mile distant (now long gone), etc. Mary Green herself was laid to rest in the old burial ground on Worcester Common decades later, which would indicate that there had never been a family plot at Green Hill. The few acres which had surrounded the mansion have been pored over for many decades in hopes of finding evidence of Bathsheba's grave, to no avail. It is believed that her gravesite, like her father's in Nova Scotia, was unmarked, to discourage visitors.

New York City's crown jewel, Central Park, owes its existence to alderman Andrew Haswell Green, who may have gained inspiration for the grand park while a boy on his vast Worcester estate; it was largely due to Green's influence that Olmstead and Vaux were chosen as the park's designers. Green was instrumental in unifying metropolitan New York's many boroughs and the city of Brooklyn into one metropolis, as well as in the founding of the New York Public Library, the American Natural History Museum, and the Metropolitan Museum of Art. "The city itself," said early twentieth-century New York Mayor Seth Low, "in some of its most beautiful and enduring features, is the monument of his love."[23] At the age of eighty-three, while entering his apartment building, he was shot dead by a jealous husband mistaking him for his wife's lover. Few New Yorkers have ever heard of him; today, he is remembered with an island bearing his name in the Niagara River, a bench in Central Park, and a two-acre park on Manhattan's East Side.

Following Andrew Green's death, the estate was transferred to three nephews and two nieces, who promptly offered the five-hundred acre expanse to the city for the assessed value of $104,000. The new owners contributed $50,000 toward the purchase price, on condition that the estate become a city park bearing the name Green Hill. For many years before this, the family had informally opened the grounds to visitors, early on establishing the site as a welcome haven from the increasingly industrialized city.

That same year, another member of the Green family purchased a house lot a few miles to the west, on the southwest corner of Moore and Pleasant Streets, soon the site of a handsome Dutch colonial home which became the new residence of Lucy and Mary Pomeroy Green, who had vacated the Green estate. Mysteriously, the sisters hired a crew of workers to hoist a massive boulder which had rested among a row of several near the mansion onto a horse-drawn cart, which plodded its way across town to their new home. Hundreds turned out to view the odd procession, inspired by rumors that the stone had in fact marked the spot of Bathsheba's burial.

In the late 1970's, the new home's later owner, familiar with the legend, hired a backhoe to dig up his Pleasant Street lawn to discover if the boulder might be hiding something beneath (the event, complete with photograph, was given ample coverage by the Worcester Telegram).[24] Nothing was found—it's perplexing to consider what the Green sisters would have brought along with the rock from their estate, a century-and-a-quarter after Bathsheba's death.

Barely a Halloween goes by without at least one Worcester County newspaper publishing an article about Bathsheba Spooner. A fanciful portrait of Bathsheba was painted for the lobby of the former Worcester County Courthouse (now converted to apartments), roughly on the site of the original courthouse where she was indicted (the building was moved to a location about a half-mile northwest). The portrait shows Bathsheba more in the style of the seventeenth century, standing by a tree from which hangs a noose, complete with a glaring black cat.

In nearby West Boylston, in the Bigelow Tavern (which dates from the same decade as the hangings), a series of drawings, discovered only in the 1980's, were etched into the attic walls, apparently depicting the Spooner hangings. The drawings include that of a man in profile (either Ezra Ross or Thaddeus Maccarty) next to what is certainly a representation of Mrs. Spooner, wearing her hat complete with ostrich plume. In the second drawing, a trio of women (next to a few stick-figured men?) observe the hangings below the scaffold, from which two bodies are suspended; a figure to their right stands near the top of a long (rope?) ladder; he may be cutting the bodies loose. What appears as "Lucy Gervis" is written prominently on one wall. This Lucy may be Ross' partner who visited him during his last days, and who possibly stayed at the tavern since the time of the trial (a series of notches seems to count back to the days before the indictment), or it could be Ezra Ross' sister, as speculated by West Boylston Historical Society member Frank A. Brown.[25]

In 1938, Esther Forbes' 'The General's Lady', a novel very loosely based on the Spooner saga, was published. It has been suggested that Forbes, a distinguished historian ('Paul Revere and the World He Lived In' won the Pulitzer Prize in history two years later; her novel Johnny Tremain became a Disney film) chose not to write an actual history of the Spooner case so as not to offend descendants of the Green and Ruggles families, even one-hundred-and-sixty years later. At a publication party, Forbes commented "Only one person in Worcester today knows exactly where Bathsheba is buried...and that person isn't telling."[26] Eighty years later, the mystery grows only more obscure.

NOTES

Chapter One The Baron of Hardwick

1 R. Lamb, Original and Authentic Journal of Occurrences During the Late American War (Dublin: Wilkinson & Courtney, 1809), 66.

2 Henry Stoddard Ruggles, General Timothy Ruggles, 1711-1795 (privately pub., 1897), 19.

3 reprint (n.d.), n.a., The New York Genealogical and Biographical Record (Oct., 1894), 4.

4 Ruggles, 5.

5 Charles M. Ellis, The History of Roxbury Town (Boston: Samuel J. Drake, 1847), 6.

6 Franklin Ladd Bailey, The Genealogy of Thomas Ruggles of Roxbury, 1637 to Thomas Ruggles of Pomfret, Connecticut and Rutland, Vermont, etc. (privately pub., 1896), 18, also Ellis, 129.

7 Francis S. Drake, The Town of Roxbury (privately pub., 1878), 365.

8 same, 18.

9 same, 15.

10 Chris Beneke and Christopher S. Grenda, The First Prejudice-Religious Tolerance and Intolerance in Early America (Philadelphia: University of Pennsylvania Press, 2010), 229.

11 Owen Stanwood, The Empire Reformed: English America in the Age of the Glorious Revolution (Philadelphia: University of Pennsylvania Press, 2011), 100.

12 Drake, 108, 365.

13 Ellis, 145.

14 R.A. Lovell, Jr. Sandwich: A Cape Cod Town (pub. Town of Sandwich, MA, n.d.), 137.

15 same, 140.

16 Ray Bearse, ed. Massachusetts: A Guide to the Pilgrim State (Boston: Houghton Mifflin, 1971), 323-4.

17 Lovell, 60, 120, 140.

18 Ruggles, 9.

19 Lovell, 155 ff.

20 same, 155-6.

21 Frederick Freeman, The History of Cape Cod: The Annals of the Thirteen Towns of Barnstable County (Boston: L. Rand & Abery, 1862), v.I, 100.

22-24 Lovell, 158.

25 Ellis, 145, also William T. Davis, "Hardwick" in History of Worcester County. With a Genealogical Register (compiled by D. Hamilton Hurd, n.d., n.p.), 1122, 1133.

26 Lucius R. Paige, History of Hardwick, Massachusetts with a Genealogical Register (Boston: Houghton Mifflin, 1883), 22-3, 25.

27 Lovell, 158-9.

28 Ruggles, 135. also Lovell, 159.

29 Richard B. Morris, Fair Trial: Fourteen Who Stood Accused from Anne Hutchinson to Alger Hiss (New York: Knopf, 1952), 99.

30 Samuel Swett Green, Incidental Remarks at American Antiquarian Society, October 22, 1888 (Worcester: AAS, 1889), 80, ft. 2.

31 Paige, 79.

32 Thomas Woody, A History of Women's Education in the United States (New York: Octagon Books, 1966), v. I, 132.

33 Louis B. Wright, The Cultural Life of the American Colonies, 1607-1763 (New York: Harper, 1957), 104-5.

34 Woody, 130-31.

Chapter Two Who Can Find a Virtuous Woman?

1 Freeman, 99.

2-3 Lovell, 160.

4 Davis (in Hurd), 1133, also Jim Dautrich, A Brief History of the Units that Took Part in the Raid on St. Francis in 1759, 7. (www.rogersrangers.com/pdf/senior/locked/Jim_Dautrich_lockedpdf)

5 Ellis, 11.

6 Lovell, 159.

7 William Lincoln, History of Worcester (Worcester: Charles Hersey, 1836), 58, ft. 1. Francis Everett Blake, History of Princeton, Massachusetts (Princeton, by town, 1915), v. I, 55, 42.

8 Navas, Murdered By his Wife (Amherst: University of Massachusetts Press, 1999), 30.

9 Ellen K. Rothman, Hands and Hearts: A History of Courtship in America (New York: Basic Books, 1984), 30.

10 same, 36, 66-7.

11 Alice Morse Earle, Customs and fashions in Old New England (New York: Charles Scribner's & Sons, 1894), 37.

12 Laurel Thatcher Ulrich, Good Wives: Image and Reality in the Lives of Women in Northern New England, 1650-1750 (New York: Vintage Books, 1991), 14.

13 same, 11.

14 Fairfax Downey, Our Lusty Forefathers, Being Diverse Chronicles of the Fervors, Frolics, Fights, Festivities and Failings of Our American Ancestors (New York: Charles Scribner's & Sons, 1947), 35-6.

15 Marilyn Salmon, Women and the Law of Poverty (Chapel Hill, UNC Press, 1986), 59.

16 David T. Courtwright, "New England Families in Historical Perspective, Families and Children" The Dublin Seminar for New England Folklife: Annual Proceedings June 29 and 30, 1985, ed.

Peter Benes, 20-1.

17 same, 20-1.

18 Rothman, 45.

19 Downey, 166.

20 John Adams Diary 6, 2 December 1760-3 March 1761. Adams Electronic Archives. www.masshistorg/digitaladams/aea/cfm/doc.cfm/doc.cfm?idD6

21 Louis E. Roy, M.D., Quaboag Plantation Alias Brookfield—a Seventeenth Century Massachusetts Town (Worcester: Heffernan Press, 1965), 95.

22 Timothy Ruggles in Boston Post Boy and Advertiser, May 5, 1766.

23 John Adams Diary 1, Thursday, January 16, 1766 (Massachusetts Historical Society).

24 Papers of John Adams, v.2, February 6, 1775 (Massachusetts Historical Society) "To the Inhabitants of Massachusetts Bay".

Chapter Three And Lady Which I Much Admired

1 David Freeman Hawke, Everyday life in Early America (New York: Perennial Library, 1989), 88-9.

2 Susan Geib, "Changing Works: Agriculture and Society in Brookfield, Massachusetts, 1785-1820", v.1 (unpublished dissertation) 1981, 157-8.

3 Rothman, 77-8.

4 R. Turner Wilcox, Five Centuries of American Costume (New York: Scribner's, 1963), 126.

5 Rothman, 78.

6 same, 79.

7 Oscar and Lilian Handlin, A Restless People: Americans in Rebellion 1770-1787 (New York: Anchor Press, 1982), 11-13, 96, 148.

8 Worcester County Registry of Deeds, Joshua Spooner as purchaser, acreage bought from 1765 Joshua White 100 + 7 1767 Thomas Dodge, Silas Walker, Solomon Walker, Zebulon Walker 406 1768 Experience Rich 500 1769 unknown ("Brookfield Commission") 25 1770 Zebulon Walker 64 1770 Gideon Walker 92 1771 Jonathan King 11 1771 Zebulon Walker 92 (same as 1767?) 1771 John Rich (acreage unknown) 1772 Timothy Ruggles 550 1775 Joshua Upham 90 1777 Ephraim Walker 60 1777 John Gilbert 80.

9 J.H. Temple, History of North Brookfield (Town of North Brookfield, 1887), book II, Wilbur, n.p.

10 Worcester County Registry of Deeds, 1731-1839 grantors, 158.

11 Joseph I. Foot, A Historical Discourse Delivered at Brookfield, Massachusetts, November 27, 1828, the Day of the Annual Thanksgiving (Brookfield, E. & G. Merriam, 1829), 4-5.

12 Lyman Whiting, A Bicentennial Oration Made in West Brookfield, July 4, 1860 At the Celebration of the Two Hundredth Anniversary of the Town of Brookfield (West Brookfield, Thomas Morey, 1869), 4-5.

13-14 Dennis A.Connole, The Indians of the Nipmuc Country in Southern New England, 1630-1750 (Jefferson, NC, McFarland & Co., 2001), 168.

15 Letters and Diary of John Rowe, Boston Merchant 1759-1762, 1764-1779, ed. Anne Rowe Cunningham (Boston: W.B. Clarke Co., 1903), 96.

16 Geib, 162-4.

17 see Ulrich, 15 ff.

18 Handlin, 97.

19 Alice Marie Earle, Home Life in Colonial Days (Macmillan reprint, New York: Corner House, 1975), 375.

20 same, 374-5.

21 Ulrich, 127-29.

22 same.

23 George Henry Moore, Notes on the History of Slavery in Massachusetts (New York: Appleton, 1866), 124.

24 Chandler A. Chase, "Worcester" in A History of Worcester County (Boston: C.F. Jewett, 1879), V. II, 577.

24 Samuel G. Drake, History and Antiquities of Boston (Boston: Luther Strauss, 1856), 730.

26 Lincoln, 19.

27 Esther Forbes, Paul Revere and the World He Lived In (New York: Mariner, 1999), 306.

28 Ellis, 12.

Chapter Four Jarring Strifes Between the Parties

1 James H. Stark, The Loyalists of Massachusetts and the Other Side of the American Revolution (Boston: pub. by author, 1910), 329.

2 Worcester County Registry of Deeds, grantors 1731-1839, p. 350, 1772, Timothy Ruggles to Joshua Spooner, book 69, p. 32.

3 Jeremiah Lyford Hanaford, History of Princeton, Massachusetts (Worcester: C. Buckingham Webb, 1852), 26-7.

4 Wallace Brown, The King's Friends (Brown University, Providence, 1965), 34.

5 John to Abigail Adams, Adams Family Papers, Falmouth, July 7, 1774, p. 2.

6 Davis, in Hurd, 525.

7 Temple, 225.

8 Lamb, 243.

9 Davis, in Hurd, 525.

10 Albert Alonzo Lovell, Worcester in the War of the Revolution: Embracing the Acts of the Town from 1765 to 1783 Included (Worcester, Tyler & Seagrave, 1876), 22-23.

11 Ellis, 14.

12 same, 15.

13 Lamb, 245.

14 Dwight Foster, in letter to Mr. J. Clarke, Northampton, March 5, 1778, AAS, Foster papers, box 6, folder 6.

15 Rev. E. Smalley, D.D., The Worcester Pulpit (Boston: Phillips, Sampson & Co., 1851), 97.16 John Pearl Spears, Old Landmarks and Historic Spots of Worcester, Massachusetts (Worcester: Commonwealth Press, 1931), 99-100.5 Lincoln, 74.

16 John Pearl Sears, Old Landmarks and Historical Spots of Worcester, Massachusetts (Worcester: Commonwealth Press, 1931), 99-100.

17 Lincoln, 74.

18 Lovell, 27-28.

19 same, 28-29.

20 same, 38.

21 Ray Raphael, The First American Revolution, Before Lexington and Concord (New York: New Press, 2002), chap. 4, ft. 90.

22 Lincoln, 92-93.

23 Lincoln, same.

24 Stark, 227.

Chapter Five These Rebellious Wretches

1-3 Thomas Gage, General Gage's Instructions of February 22, 1775 to Captain Brown and Ensign D'Berniere, etc. (Boston: J. Gill, 1779), 8.

4 same, 3.

5 same, 8-9.

6 same, 9.

7 same.

8 same.

9 same.

10 Forbes, 241-44.

11 Lyman Whiting, A Bicentennial Oration, July 4, 1860 (West Brookfield: Thomas Morey, 1869), 44.

12 Ruggles, 35.

13 Samuel Adams Wells, The Life and Public Services of Samuel Adams (Freeport, NY: 1969 reprint, 1865 ed.), II, 296-97.

14 History of Worcester County (n.a.), I, 584.

15 D. Hamilton Hurd, History of Essex County, Massachusetts (Ipswich, MA: John W. Lewis, 1888), I, 576.

15 same, 569.

16 from journals of Rev. John Cleaveland, pastor of a Chebacco parish, and chaplain of Bagley's regiment, January 24, 1775 in Thomas Franklin Waters, Ipswich in the Massachusetts Bay Colony, 1700- 1917 (Ipswich: Ipswich Historical Society, 1917), 316-17.

17 same.

18 (n.a.), Salem Gazette, September 18, 1860, in The Historical Collections of the Topsfield Historical Society, XX, 1915, 16-17.

19 William Bentley, The Diary of William Bentley, D.D., IV, January 1811-December 1819, (Salem, MA: Essex Institute, 1914), October 30, 1811, 61.

20 same, 60.

21 Albert Bushnell Hart, American History Told By Contemporaries, II: Building of the Republic (New York: MacMillan, 1899), 483.

22 Waters, 325-26.

23 Peleg W. Chandler, American Criminal Trials, II: trial of Mrs. Spooner and Others (Boston: T.H. Carter, 1844), 44.

24 Hurd, History of Essex County, 609.

25 (n.a.), Massachusetts Soldiers and Sailors of the Revolutionary War (Boston: n.p., 1905), XIII REA-SEY, 583.

26 Brown, 31.

27 Stark, 252-3.

Chapter Six An Invitation to Defile Her Marriage Bed

1 The Massachusetts Spy, July 27, 1776.

2 Abigail Adams to John Adams, September 29, 1776 (Massachusetts Historical Society), 2.

3 Brown, 55-6.

4 Charles Knowles Bolton, The Private Soldier Under Washington (Port Washington, NY: Kennicut, 1964), reprint 1902, 77.

5 same, 84.

6 same, 94.

7 same, 99.

8 Henry Belcher, The First American Civil War: First Period, 1775-1778, in 2 v. (London: MacMillan, 1911), II, 85.

9 Bolton, 178.

10 Elijah Fisher's Journal While in the War for Independence (Augusta, ME: Badger & Manley, 1888), 5.

11 A. Philips Wilson, A Treatise on Febrile Diseases, in 2 v. (Hartford: Olive D, Cooke, 1809), I: 45.

12 same, 52-3.

13 same, 53.

14 same, 93, 97.

15 Bolton, 181.

16 petition of Jabez and Joanna Ross, Ipswich, May 26, 1778, (Massachusetts Archives).

17 Chandler, 1-2, ft. 1.

18-19 Massachusetts Soldiers, XIII, 583.

20 same.

21 Tim Holmes and Libby Smith-Holmes, Saratoga: America's Battlefield (Charleston: The History Press, 2012), 114.

22 Ross petition, 1.

23 Worcester County Registry of Deeds, 1731-1839 grantors, 152.

24 testimony, Susanna Wills.

51 testimony, Sarah Stratton.

25 Chandler, 10, ft. 1.

26 Massachusetts Soldiers, XIII, 583.

27 diary of Ebenezer Parkman, September 1777-October 1778, Parkman Family Papers, American Antiquarian Society, entry June 25, 1778.

28 testimony, Sarah Stratton.

29 Handlin, 180.

30 Nelson Manfred Blake, The Road to Reno (New York: MacMillan, 1962), 36.

31 Peter Charles Hoffer, Law and People in Colonial America (Baltimore: Johns Hopkins, 1992), 77.

32 Salman, 58, 60, 68.

33 same, 66.

34 Earle, Home Life in Colonial Days, 138.

Chapter Seven To Take Him Off By Poison

1 Donald Barr Chidsey, The War in the North (New York: Crown, 1967), 194.

2 n.a., "Col. Henry Vassall", in Cambridge Historical Society Publications (Cambridge, MA., 1917), X, 51-2.

3 Hurd, History of Worcester County, ii, Rutland, 1292-3.

4 Mary I. Gozzaldi, Elizabeth Ellery Dana, David T. Pottinger, The Vassall House, in Cambridge Historical Society Publications (Cambridge, MA, 1930), xxi, 29.

5 Samuel F. Batchelder, Burgoyne and His Officers in Cambridge (in same), xiii, 30.

6 same, 23.

7 Stark, 85.

8 Lamb, 222-3.

9-11 same, 222.

12-13 journal of Elisha Fisher, in Bolton, 185.

14 same, 187.

15 letter from Worcester Committee of Correspondence and Safety, March 8?, 1778, US Revolution Collection American Antiquarian Society, Box 2, Folder 7, 1.

16 Roger Lamb, Memoir of His Own Life (Dublin: J. Jones, 1811), 242-3.

17 Alice Morse Earle, Two Centuries of Costume in America, 2 v (New York: MacMillan, 1903), I, 694.

18 Chidsey, 195.

19-20 broadside, July 2, 1778, The Lives, Last Words, and Dying Speech of Ezra Ross James Buchanan and William Brooks, etc. (confession, Worcester: Isaiah Thomas), 1.

21 diary of Ebenezer Parkman, September 1777-October, 1778, Parkman Family Papers, entry April 24, 1778 American Antiquarian Society.

22-23 testimony, Alexander Cummings.

24 confession, 1.

25 Donald Lamar Jones, The Transformation of the Law of Poverty in Eighteenth Century Massachusetts, 173, in Daniel

Coquillette, ed. Law in Colonial Massachusetts 1630-1800 (Boston: Colonial Society of Massachusetts, 1984).

26-7 confession, 1.

28 Worcester County Registry of Deeds, Joshua Spooner to William Spooner, November 1, 1777.

29 Dwight Foster to Mr. J. Clarke, Northampton, March 5, 1778, American Antiquarian Society.

30 see testimony, Loved Lincoln.

31 Foster.

Chapter Eight Having No Fear of God Before Our Eyes

1 confession, 1-2.

2 testimony, Loved Lincoln.

3 confession, 2.

4 testimony, Jesse Parker.

5 testimony, Lincoln.

6-7 testimony, Alexander Cummings.

8-9 testimony, Reuben Olds.

10 confession, 3.

11-13 testimony, Olds.

14 confession, 2.

15 Cotton Mather in W.J. Rorabaugh, The Alcoholic Republic (Oxford University Press, 1979), 30.

16 diary of John Adams, May 29, 1760, Massachusetts Historical Society, reel 1.

17 same.

18 George Washington in Rorabaugh, 6.

19 George Ticknor in same, 6.

20 Benjamin Rush in same, 6.

21-22 confession, 3.

23 letter from Worcester Committee, March 8?, 1778.

24 confession, 3.

25-30 same, 4.

31-32 same, 5.

33 testimony, Mary Walker and Prudence.

34 Massachusetts Spy, Dec. 11, 1776, American Antiquarian Society.

35 confession, 5.

36 testimony, Walker.

37 confession, 5.

38-39 testimony, Prudence.

40 testimony, Walker and Prudence.

41 same.

42 testimony, Prudence.

43-44 testimony, Walker.

45 testimony, Walker.

Chapter Nine Such Vile Purposes

1 all preceding dialogue refashioned from confession, 5.

2 The Massachusetts Spy, August 16, 1775.

3 same.

4-5 testimony, Mary Walker.

6-7 Deloraine Pendre Corey, The History of Malden, Massachusetts (Malden: by author, 1899), 474, ft. 14.

8 testimony, Prudence.

9 The Massachusetts Spy, June 25, 1778, American Antiquarian Society.

10 testimony, Charles.

11 testimony, Alexander Cummings.

12 Chandler, 44.

13 Hurd, History of Essex County, 620.

14 confession, 5.

15 Downey, 53.

16 testimony, Alexander Cummings.

17-18 confession, 6.

19 testimony, Ephraim Cooley.

20 testimony, Jonathan King.

21 testimony, Sarah Stratton.

22-3 confession, 6.

24 from "The Examination of Brooks, Before the Justices", The Massachusetts Spy, June 25, 1778, (American Antiquarian Society).

25 indictment, April 21, 1778.

26-27 confession. 6.

28 testimony, Sara Stratton.

29-30 confession, 6.

31 same, 6-7.

32-34 testimony, Alexander Cummings.

35 testimony, Sarah Stratton.

36 confession, 7.

37 testimony, Sarah Stratton.

38 confession, 7.

39 testimony, Mary Walker and Prudence.

40 testimony, Mary Walker.

41 testimony, Prudence.

42 testimony, Mary Walker.

43 confession, 7.

44 testimony, Mary Walker.

45 confession, 7.

Chapter Ten Poor Little Man

1 testimony, Alexander Cummings.

2-5 testimony, Ephraim Cooley.

6 Milton Halpern and Bernard Knight, Autopsy (New York: St. Martin's, 1977), 7-8.

7 same, 81.

8 testimony, Jonathan King.

9 Halpern and Knight, 189.

10 same, 187-8.

11 testimony, Mary Walker.

12 confession, 7.

13-14 testimony, Joshua Whitney.

15 testimony, Loved Lincoln.

16 US Revolutionary Collection, Worcester Committee, March 8? 1778 (American Antiquarian Society).

17 Boston Independent Chronicle, March 12, 1778.

18-19 Foster Family Papers, Box 6, Folder 6, Dwight Foster's letter to J. Clarke, March 5, 1778.

20-21 inquest, March 2, 1778 (see Chandler, 4).

22 testimony, Asa Bigelow.

23-25 testimony, Obadiah Rice.

26 The Massachusetts Spy, August 8, 1799 (American Antiquarian Society).

27 testimony, Obadiah Rice and Elisha Hamilton.

28 testimony, Samuel Bridge.

29 testimony, Elisha Hamilton.

30-31 US Revolutionary Collection, Worcester Committee, March 8, 1778, (American Antiquarian Society).

Chapter Eleven A Most Horrid Piece of Villainy

1 letter from Samuel Barrett to Samuel Salisbury, March 6, 1778, Salisbury Papers, box 3, folder 6 (American Antiquarian Society).

2 diary of Ebenezer Parkman, March 4, 1778.

3 letter from Samuel P. Savage to his wife, Saturday?, 1778, Samuel P Savage papers II 1763-1783 (American Antiquarian Society).

4 R.A. Lovell, 237.

5 Dwight Foster to Mr. J. Clarke, March 5, 1778.

6 diary, Dwight Foster, March 15, 1778.

7 Boston Gazette and Country Journal, March 9, 1778.

8 letter from Brookfield Committee of Safety and Correspondence to Worcester Committee, March 5, 1778, US Revolutionary Collection, box 2, folder 7 (American Antiquarian Society).

9 Journals of the House of Representatives of Massachusetts 1777-1778 (Boston: MHS, 1988), 201.

10 The Boston Gazette, March 12, 1778.

11 Rev. E. Smalley, D.D., The Worcester Pulpit (Boston: Sampson, 1851), 57.

12 same, 52.

13 William Lincoln, 151.

Chapter Twelve A Complicated Scene of Wickedness

1 Waters, 62-3.

2 diary, Dwight Foster, March 15, 1778.

3-6 Nathan Fiske, A.M., A Sermon Preached at Brookfield, etc. (Boston: Thomas & John Fleet, 1778), 6.

7 William Blackstone, Commentaries on the Laws of England (Chicago: Chicago University, 1979, reprint, Oxford University, 1765-69), IV, 349-50.

8 Richard B. Morris, "Legalism versus Revolutionary Doctrine in New England" (reprint, New England Quarterly, IV, 1931, 195-215) in Essays on the History of Early American Law, ed. David H. Flaherty (Chapel Hill: University of North Carolina, 1969), 421.

9 same.

10 Andrew Roth and Jonathan Roth, Devil's Advocates: the Unnatural History of Lawyers (Berkeley, CA: Nolo Press, 1989), 74.

11 same.

12 Marian C. McKenna, Tapping Reeve and the Litchfield Law School (New York: Oceana Publications, 1986), 11.

13 same, 14.

14 same.

15 n.a., History of the Town of Hingham, Massachusetts, 3 v. (Cambridge, MA: 1893), I, 333.

Chapter Thirteen A Matter of Surprise and Amazement to All

1 indictment, April 21, 1778.

2, 3 same.

4 Diary, April 20, 1778, Robert Treat Paine Papers, 24 April 1775-2 April 1785, reel 10, case 18, (Massachusetts Historical Society).

5 Diary of Ebenezer Parkman, Parkman Family Papers, April, 1778.

6 arraignment, April term, 1778.

7 John C.K. Knowlton and Clarendon Wheelock, Carl's Tour in Main Street (Worcester: Sanford & Davis Press, 1889), 4th ed., 43.

8 Whitney, 52.

9 n.a., Inscriptions from the Old Burial Grounds in Worcester, Massachusetts from 1727 to 1859, (Worcester: Worcester Society of Antiquity, 1878), 46.

10 An Historical Discourse Delivered at West Brookfield on the Occasion of the 150th Anniversary of the First Church in Brookfield, October 16, 1867 by Samuel Dunham, pastor (Springfield, MA: Bowles & Co., 1867), 6.

11 Chase, 556.

12 diary, John Adams, December 3 or 4, 1758, 14.

13 same.

14 John Hostettler, Fighting for Justice: The History and Origins of Adversary Trial (Winchester, England: Waterside Press, 2006), 27.

15 Tom Keymer, Richardson's 'Clarissa' and the Eighteenth-Century Reader (Cambridge, England: University of Cambridge, 1992), 239.

16 Readings in American Legal History, compiled and ed. By Mark de Wolfe Howe (Washington: Beard Books, 2001, reprint Harvard University, 1949), 147.

17 Foster Papers, Box 6, Folder 6.

18 Parkman Family Papers, Octavo 7.

19 testimony, Ephraim Cooley.

20 testimony, Joshua Whitney.

21 testimony, Reuben Olds.

22 testimony, Alexander Cummings.

23 testimony, Asa Bigelow.

24 testimony, Elisha Hamilton.

25 testimony, William Young.

26 indictment, April 21, 1778.

27 confession, 6.

28 same.

29 Lincoln Family Papers, Octavo 4, #24.

30-32 same, #9.

33 Frank T. Lindman and Donald M. McIntyre, Jr., ed., The Mentally Disabled and the Law (Chicago: University of Chicago, 1961), 8.

34 see Christa Grossinger, Picturing Women in Late Medieval and Renaissance Art (Manchester/NewYork: Manchester University Press, 1997), chapter three, 94-138.

35 diary, Ebenezer Parkman, Parkman Family Papers, April 25, 1778.

36 diary, Dwight Foster, Foster Family Papers, May 15, 1778.

37 Massachusetts Spy, May 7, 1778.

38 Foster Family Papers, May 6, 1778.

Chapter Fourteen A Lewd, Artful Woman

1-4 petition, Jabez and Johana Ross, May 26, 1778.

5-6 petition, John Buchanan, William Brooks, Ezra Ross, Bathsheba Spooner, May 20, 1778.

7 Lamb, 244.

8 John Hostettler, A History of Criminal Justice in England and Wales (Winchester, England: Waterside Press, 2009), 45.

9 George L. Craik, ed., English Causes Celebres: or Reports of Remarkable Trials (London: Charles Knight & Co., 1890), 252.

10 petition, Bathsheba Spooner, May 20, 1778.

11 Morris, 113.

12 reprieve, May 28, 1778.

13 writ de ventre inspiciendo, May 28, 1778.

14 diary, Ebenezer Parkman, Parkman Family Papers.

15 Abigail Adams to John Quincy Adams, June 16, 1778 (Massachusetts Historical Society).

16 Return of the Sheriff, June 11, 1778.

17 Morris, 111.

18 petition, Bathsheba Spooner.

19 testimony, Sarah Stratton.

20 testimony, Prudence.

21 testimony, Mary Walker.

22 Thaddeus Maccarty, addendum to second Spooner petition.

23 Navas, 92-3.

24 Charles Martin, The Life of Artemus Ward (New York: Artemus Ward?, 1921), 91.

25 Nathan Goold, History of Colonel Jonathan Mitchell's Cumberland County Regiment (Portland, ME: Thurston, 1899), 26.

26 Opinion of Midwives to Board of Councillors, June 27, 1778.

27 same.

28 Massachusetts Spy, June 25, 1778.

29 Elizabeth A. Fenn, Pox Americana: The Great Smallpox Epidemic of 1775-82 (New York: Hill & Wang, 2001), 9.

30 diary, Ebenezer Parkman, Parkman Family Papers, June 25, 1778.

31-34 same.

Chapter Fifteen A Necklace of Gold or Diamonds

1 M.V.B. Perley, Lesslie, James of Topsfield, Mass., and Some of His Descendants, Essex Historical Institute—Historical Collections, LI, 1915, 244.

2 Joseph B. Felt, History of Ipswich, Essex, and Hamilton, Massachusetts (Cambridge, MA: Charles Folsom, 1834), 117.

3 diary, Breck Parkman, Parkman Family Papers, July 2, 1778.

4-10 Thaddeus Maccarty, A.M., The Guilt of Innocent Blood: A Sermon Preached at Worcester, July 2, 1778, etc., (Norwich, CT: Isaiah Thomas & Co.), 1778.

11-12 appendix to sermon.

13 Massachusetts Spy, July 2, 1778.

14 John Lawrence, A History of Capital Punishment (New York: Citadel Press), 1960.

15-16 Lawrence, 4.

17 Maccarty.

18-19 Lamb, 244-45.

20 Massachusetts Spy, July 3, 1778.

21-23 Massachusetts Spy, August 6, 1778.

24 Robert Treat Paine, 2 July 1778 (Massachusetts Historical Society).

25 from diary kept by Lt. Amos Farnesworth of Groton, Massachusetts, April 1775-May 1779, notes and introduction by Samuel A. Green (Cambridge, MA: John Wilson & Son, 1898), 26.

Chapter Sixteen Multiple Acts of Unfaithfulness

1 diary, Ebenezer Parkman, Parkman Family Papers, July 2, 1778.

2 Felt, 117.

3 Maccarty (appendix).

4 diary, Breck Parkman, Parkman Family Papers, July 2, 1778.

5 diary, Ebenezer Parkman, Parkman Family Papers, July 3-4, 1778.

6 sermons, Ebenezer Parkman, 2-5.

7 same, 6-10.

8 Green, 6.

9 Paige, 482.

10 J.H. Balfour Browne, The Medical Jurisprudence of Insanity, 2nd ed. (San Francisco: Sumner Whitney & Co., 1875), 324-25.

11 same, 322.

12 Michael L. Peplin, The Jurisprudence of the Insanity Defense (Chapel Hill, N.C.: Carolina Academic Press, 1994), 133.

13 Herbert M. Sawyer, History of the Department Of Police Service of Worcester, Massachusetts from 1674 to 1900 (Worcester: Worcester Police Relief Association, 1900), 28-9.

14 Elizabeth Cady Stanton, letter to the editor, New York World, 1899, ed. n.a.

15 Whiting, 52.

16 same, 53.

17 n.a., Proceedings of the Worcester Society of Antiquity, March 6, 1877 (Worcester: pub. by the Society, 1877), 48.

18 William Sumner Barton, Inscriptions from the Old Burial Grounds in Worcester, Massachusetts from 1727 to 1859 (Worcester: Worcester Society for Antiquity, 1878), 48.

19 Stark, 252.

20 Ellis, 23.

21 Stoddard, 21.

22 n.a., "Epitaph Belies Passion of Sentimental Crime", Springfield, MA: Springfield Daily News, Feb. 13, 1989.

23 Samuel Swett Green, "Andrew Haswell Green—A Sketch of His Ancestry, Life and Work", Proceedings of the American Antiquarian Society (Worcester: pub. by the Society), XVI, #2, Oct. 1904, 200.

24 David Bushnell, "Mystery of Bathsheba Lies Deeper than Six Feet Under", Worcester, MA: Worcester Telegram, August 13, 1979.

25 see Frank A. Brown, "A Dreadful Scene" (booklet) (West Boylston (MA) Historical Society, 1997).

26 Ivan Sandrof, "The Hanging of Bathsheba Spooner", Worcester, MA: Worcester Telegram, Oct. 10, 1947.

Made in United States
North Haven, CT
23 September 2023